LORD JAKOBOVITS

LORD JAKOBOVITS

*The Authorized Biography
of the Chief Rabbi*

CHAIM BERMANT

WEIDENFELD AND NICOLSON

LONDON

To my dearest Binty,
without whose love and support
this book could not have
been completed

First published in Great Britain by George Weidenfeld & Nicolson
Limited 91 Clapham High Street, London SW4 7TA

ISBN 0 297 81142 8

Printed by Butler & Tanner Ltd, Frome and London

Contents

Illustrations

Julius Jakobovits's and Paula Wreschner's engagement photo, 1919 (*courtesy of Joseph Jacobs*)

Immanuel, Lotti, George and Joseph, 1929 (*courtesy of Joseph Jacobs*)

Julius Jakobovits on holiday with Immanuel and Lotti (*courtesy of Joseph Jacobs*)

Lotti (*courtesy of Joseph Jacobs*)

Rabbi Jakobovits at the Wailing Wall, Jerusalem, 1947

Immanuel and Amelie's wedding day, Paris, 1949

Chief Rabbi of Ireland with mother, wife and four children

Chief Rabbi of Great Britain (*photo: Clive Barda*)

With Elie Wiesel (*photo: Sidney Harris*)

Relaxing on a foot-plate

With David Ben Gurion and Duncan Sandys, 1964 (*photo: Sidney Harris*)

With Menachem Begin and James Callaghan (*photo: Sidney Harris*)

With Mr and Mrs Thatcher (*photo: Sidney Harris*)

On holiday in Caesarea, 1989

Greeting Her Majesty The Queen (*photo: Sidney Harris*)

With the late Moshe Davis en route to Moscow, 1975

The Jakobovits children assembled for their father's introduction to the House of Lords, 9 February 1988

About to take his seat in the House of Lords (*photo: Universal Pictorial Press & Agency*)

Apart from the photographs from Dr Joseph Jacobs, all the pictures are from the Chief Rabbi's private collection and are reproduced with his kind permission.

Acknowledgements

The idea for this book came from Lady Jakobovits and there must have been moments when both she and her husband may have regretted her rashness. However, they were never less than helpful and I am grateful to them both for the patience with which they answered my questions, tolerated my intrusions and coped with my importunities.

I am indebted to Simon Cohen, until recently the head of the Chief Rabbi's office, and to Norma Pearlman, the Chief Rabbi's secretary, for supplying me with his papers.

Stanley Kalms, Fay Kornbluth and Fred Worms read parts of this manuscript, and Norman Cohen read it all, and they were kind enough to save me from numerous errors of judgement and fact. They are in no way to blame for any which may persist.

I am also grateful to my editor Linda Osband, who, not for the first time, checked an irresistible urge to repeat myself and helped me reduce this book to manageable size and readable form.

And finally, while this is an authorized biography, it does not necessarily mean that either Lord or Lady Jakobovits always agrees with my sentiments or conclusions.

CHAIM BERMANT
Hampstead Garden Suburb
London
February 1990

Good Lord

*T*HE 1988 New Year's Honours list carried the usual array of famous and worthy names — actors, writers, scientists, captains of industry and commerce, sportsmen, soldiers, sailors and, of course, civil servants — but only one name among them excited international attention and almost universal acclaim: Chief Rabbi Immanuel Jakobovits.

The Times wrote: 'It is good that the Chief Rabbi, Sir Immanuel Jakobovits, has been made a peer. He is not a cleric who could be accused of wrapping his religious message in a packaging calculated to win him secular popularity.'

The *Financial Times*:

On a battlefield fixed points and strong positions are enviable possessions. If it is true that there is a general search for a moral universe within which to locate our fragmented lives then those who are discovered to be occupying firm rocks already — preferably rocks of ages — will benefit. Sir Immanuel Jakobovits, Chief Rabbi of the British Commonwealth, ennobled in the New Year's Honours list, and the first rabbi to have been so, stands on such a rock.

The *Daily Mail*:

Courage is honoured — as it should be. And talent. And long service to the state. But there is one name in the New Year's list which creates a splendid precedent by defying the predictable. A peerage is bestowed on Sir Immanuel Jakobovits.... He is the one religious leader in Britain whose views are as clear as cold spring water, and as bracing. He believes in personal responsibility and effort; in moral standards and retribution.

The *Evening Standard*: Mrs Thatcher 'is known to respect the Chief Rabbi enormously and is in contact with him regularly. Unlike the meddlesome bishops of the Church of England, Jakobovits talks about God rather than spending cuts, and emphasizes the eternal Jewish virtue of self-help to solve problems.'

1

The *Observer*: 'He is the one prelate whose preaching did not, in the view of Mrs Thatcher, give God a bad name.'

And so it continued day after day, in the national papers and the local ones, and in overseas papers as diverse as the *New York Times*, the *West Australian*, the *Jerusalem Post*, the *International Herald Tribune*, *Die Welt* and the *South China Morning Post*.

In the Chief Rabbi's ornate St John's Wood home, the phone never stopped. Messengers came and went laden with flowers and greetings, while Lady Jakobovits set up a kosher canteen for a constant succession of camera crews and the place was bathed in arc-lights from morning till night.

The Chief Rabbi gave considerable thought to his territorial title. The most obvious one would have been Baron Jakobovits of St John's Wood, but the conjunction of Rabbi and Saint would have sounded awkward. He toyed with the possibility of Maida Vale, but opted finally for the verdant associations of Regent's Park.

He took his seat on 9 February, the day after his sixty-seventh birthday, and went through the ceremonies almost in a daze. The House, with its majestic proportions, vaulted ceilings, book-lined corridors and busy rush of black-clad attendants, was intimidating in itself.

He was greeted by one white-haired, gold-chained figure, who passed him on to another, who led him into a panelled chamber dominated by a huge painting of Moses holding the tablets of the law, as if it was placed there for his benefit. It was the vestry, which was generally known as the Moses Room because of the painting. Both Houses of Parliament, he was to discover, abounded in biblical associations so that there was almost a touch of the inevitable to his own apotheosis, as if he were filling a pre-ordained role.

A little later he was at the bar of the House, a tall, stately figure in his scarlet and ermine, flanked by one Tory peer (Lord Young of Graffham) and one Labour (Lord Mishcon). After doffing his hat – under which he wore a small, black skullcap – three times and swearing allegiance to the Queen, he sat down on the cross-benches.

Even his choice of sponsors was the result of careful deliberation, for if some of his ideas were close to those of the Prime Minister, others were close to those of the Labour Party and he liked to think that he represented a body of beliefs which were above party politics.

To Lady Jakobovits, surrounded by children and grandchildren in the Distinguished Strangers' Gallery, it was 'like a Bible story – something out of the Book of Esther'.

Rabbi Jakobovits, a modest man, was as gratified by the honour as he was overwhelmed by the attention. 'What', he kept asking, 'have I done to deserve it?'

Different commentators gave different answers, but all agreed on one point: that the Prime Minister found in the Chief Rabbi a forthrightness, consistency and moral certainty that she missed in her bishops and that, in a sense, he had become her father confessor. She also had an almost mystical belief in Jewish talent. While Jews formed less than one per cent of the population, they, at one time, formed twenty-five per cent of her Cabinet, and she saw in the Chief Rabbi many of the qualities she admired in the Jew.

They first met in 1971 when she was Minister of Education. He had always regarded schools as the first line of a nation's defences and teachers as the shock-troops of society, and he had said to her, 'You are really the Minister of Defence.'

She was taken both with the metaphor and the man. They met again when she was Leader of the Opposition, and when she became Prime Minister she invited him to Downing Street; he, in turn, entertained her in St John's Wood.

Like many daughters of self-made provincial households she was brought up on the Bible and she found in his conversation distant echoes of almost forgotten precepts: self-reliance and self-help, constancy and fidelity, love of family and love of land, reward and retribution. Where others spoke of rights, he spoke of duties; where others voiced doubts, he offered convictions. He brought the past to bear upon the present. Her own prelates tried to burden her with guilt; he, in a way, offered absolution.

The Prime Minister has never been immune to external attractions, and with his tall bearing, small beard, silvery hair, handsome profile and blue eyes, Lord Jakobovits looks like a well-kempt prophet, the benign representative of a benign deity, who brought her in touch with the very roots of her own beliefs.

Her attitudes were neatly summed up by Peregrine Worsthorne in the *Sunday Telegraph*:

Mrs Thatcher, the first non-conformist ever to head the Conservative Party, has chosen to revive what might be called the strict parts of the Christian message. But the strict parts of the Christian message are essentially those which stem from the Hebrew tradition. It is the mode of commandments and, if those commandments are not fulfilled, of punishments. There is no room in it for excuses for failure based on Marxist or Freudian arguments that undermine individual responsibility. The Judaic lesson of the Old Testament seems to be that we live in a harsh world where only our own efforts and a trust in God and obedience to His commandments will carry us through. In dealing with the British people, who have never realized how precarious their own position in the world is, or woken up to the fact that the world does not owe them a living, this is a far more appropriate religious note than the Sermon on the Mount.

The Chief Rabbi was an important influence in the crystalization of her ideas and he became one of her principal allies in the assertion of Victorian values.

Victorian values are not, in fact, native to Britain. They were introduced to this country by the Prince Consort, Albert of Saxe-Coburg and Gotha, a man of almost insufferable rectitude and impeccable virtue, and they remained intact in the Jewish communities of Germany long after they had atrophied elsewhere.

They were certainly intact in the small East Prussian Jewish community of Königsberg into which Immanuel Jakobovits was born on 8 February 1921. They implied high-mindedness, hard work, probity, piety, clean-living, a concern for the less fortunate, sobriety and thrift, all of them qualities extolled in both the Bible and the Talmud; and if the experience of German Jews — even before the rise of Hitler — was not always happy, they nevertheless found a new Jerusalem in Prussia's green and pleasant land.

Jakobovits was thus not a convert to Victorian values, but a natural Victorian himself, which does not mean that he sees himself in such terms, for he believes that the views he expounds, if not always fashionable, transcend time and place. He also feels that the Victorians were too smug and complacent, that they lacked compassion and rarely lived up to their ideals, yet anyone who spends a few hours in his company can come away with the feeling that not only the old queen but the Hohenzollerns are still on the throne.

He has developed in many respects, but has never changed his basic attitudes. What he preached when he became a minister of the Brondesbury Synagogue in 1941 — and what his father had preached before him — was substantially what he preached in 1990. He may have revamped his language, but not his ideas, and although he believes that Jewish teaching has universal application, he has been surprised at the extent to which his words have been followed in the general press.

One reason is that they are worth following. He speaks with authority, conviction, and a forthrightness and vigour uncommon among clergymen, so that he is nearly always good copy. The other lies in his readiness to call a spade a spade. The churches, which have always hesitated to condemn sinners, have reached the point where they are reluctant even to condemn sin and tend to explain it away in terms of social deprivation, with the result that censure and reproof have all but vanished from their vocabulary. They are, however, still extant in the language of the synagogue and Rabbi Jakobovits has never hesitated to use them. He is the nearest thing Britain has to a

Savonarola, and there are a number of issues on which he is regarded as the High Priest of the new Right.

Yet he first came to prominence as the voice of Jewish liberalism, when he expressed his unhappiness at the plight of Palestinian refugees and the continued occupation of the West Bank and Gaza. Other Jews had spoken out before, mostly in private, but he was the first Orthodox rabbi of any eminence to voice his reservations in public. He seemed to combine conservatism at home with liberalism abroad, but he would deny that there were any contradictions in his attitudes, and he could quote a dozen passages from both Scripture and the Talmud to support them.

To which one must add that neither Scripture nor the Talmud speak with one voice, and one can find passages to support almost any given attitude. A liberal will draw on liberal teaching, a conservative on conservative teaching, and Jakobovits would answer any charge of inconsistency with the claim that he is consistently reasonable with a consistent distaste for extremism and extremists. He is as anxious to temper the excesses of liberalism in England as to limit the excesses of conservatism in Israel.

For a Jew he is oddly apolitical and has never joined any of the Zionist parties with which the Jewish community abounds. His conservatism is the product both of his faith and his experience. He has lived by the letter of the Mosaic Law, which is a good deal more demanding than any other body of laws, and he likes to think that the disciplines which have sustained the Jewish people for so long, and which have brought him and his family so much happiness, could do the same for mankind.

The family is central both to his creed and to Jewish life and he tends to regard it as basic to all civilized life. He thus thinks of the Seventh Commandment – 'Thou shalt not commit adultery' – as a precondition of civilized living and the permissive society as a symptom of national decline. He would not suggest that everything was all right in Victorian England or, for that matter, in Wilhelmine Germany, but he would argue that while in the past men did not always live up to the standards set by society, today they are not even aware that they have gone wrong.

He is thus, for example, appalled by the ready acceptance of sodomy, which, given its associations with Sodom, is seen in Jewish lore as almost the symbol of human depravity. Scripture denounced it as an abomination. Jakobovits also regards it as a threat to family life and even to the continuity of the human race, and he has suggested that AIDS is an obvious consequence of thoughtless self-indulgence. (He has, incidentally, said nothing about lesbianism, but then neither has Scripture.)

He has never insisted that AIDS or other plagues were a divine punishment for human misconduct, but he has argued that people are, in the last resort, responsible for their own actions and occasionally even for their own misfortunes. It is not a view which recommends itself readily to the liberal press.

Nor do his views on the Church of England's report, *Faith in the Cities*.

Jakobovits is a deeply compassionate man and added to his own natural feelings are the exhortations of Scripture: 'For the poor shall never cease out of the land: therefore I command thee, saying, thou shalt open thy hand wide unto thy brother, to thy poor, and to the needy in thy land.' He claims that he is nearer to the thinking of the Labour Party than to Mrs Thatcher on many welfare issues, and for all his conservatism he denies vehemently that he is a Conservative.

He has every sympathy with inner-city families condemned to a stultifying cycle of poverty and despair, and he agrees that everything possible should be done to help them. Where he differed from the report was in its tendency to blame the Government for their problems and to look only to the Government for a solution. He did not deny that the Government had a role to play in the matter, or that it was to an extent culpable for some of the ills described, but he could not accept that every pauper was the helpless victim of external forces and could do nothing to help himself, and he suggested that the very tendency to blame external forces and to look for outside help was in itself a cause of poverty.

It was not so long since the Jews were the inhabitants of the inner city – he was, for a time, one himself. They had no Race Relations Act to protect them, no Race Relations Board to help them, no free medical services, no unemployment benefits and no social security. Some jobs were closed to them because of their religious observances and they were excluded from others by prejudice. They were often hungry and ragged and lived ten to a room, but they did not riot to draw attention to their plight and treated every handicap as a challenge. The sick, the lame, the helpless, the hapless and the feckless were helped not by faceless public agencies but by family, neighbours and friends. Every synagogue was not only a house of prayer but a mutual aid society, and within a generation or two the Jews were moving out of the ghettos and into the suburbs. They helped themselves by their exertions, and Jakobovits felt that they could help others by their example.

Hard work is forgivable in England provided one does not appear to be industrious, but Jakobovits comes near to glorifying it as a virtue in its own right. He likes to quote a famous passage from a talmudical compilation called *Ethics of the Fathers*: 'The day is short, and the work is great, and the labourers are sluggish, and the master is demanding. It is not thy duty to complete the work, but neither art thou free to desist from it.'

The same compilation also contains the passage: 'Beware of the ruling powers, for they draw no man near to them except for their own interests.' But then there are ruling powers and ruling powers, and Jakobovits tends to find in the policies of the Prime Minister many of the attitudes he has preached, while she finds in his preaching the moral support denied her by the established church. He not only, in general terms, shares her philosophy, but has sanctioned it and made her feel that she has God on her side.

He also enjoys a certain popular acclaim because he speaks in plain terms and with transparent sincerity. His robust defence of old-fashioned virtues can evoke sympathy even among people who rarely conform to them, if only as a change from the apologetic tones adopted by other prelates. His elevation to the peerage has enhanced his appeal, for a lord enjoys an exalted place in the popular imagination, and this is especially true of the Lords spiritual (though formally the Chief Rabbi is a Lord temporal), who are, so to speak, presumed to enjoy rank both in this world and the next. His ideas may seem archaic, but archaisms also have their appeal. In an age where conservation is all the rage, he has emerged as prime conservator of the impalpable. Here too he has not jumped on the bandwagon; the bandwagon has trundled round to him.

Not everything he says is greeted with applause and he used to be startled by the controversy he provoked, for he thought that he was uttering no more than self-evident truths. He has since discovered that there is nothing more controversial than the truth, which does not mean that he is content to keep his counsel to himself.

He often tells the story of Jonah, the reluctant prophet, who tried to evade his own destiny. He does not regard himself as a prophet, but he does take his duties as a rabbi seriously and has applied himself consistently to the transmission of Jewish teachings even where – especially where – they are in conflict with the dominant mores of his age.

He recently suffered a heart attack, but after a major operation he has been restored to good, even rude, health and is approaching his eighth decade with the restless energies which have characterized his whole career; but more than that, he feels he has been spared for new tasks and wider responsibilities, for much as he loves study, he has an even greater love of action.

In keeping with the articles of his engagement he will have to retire when he becomes seventy on 8 February 1991 (though he has been asked to remain in office for a further six months to enable his successor to attend a study course in Israel). Retirement is an un-Jewish concept, and one of his predecessors was fond of saying that 'Chief Rabbis never retire and only rarely die'; it was only because that predecessor became so impossible towards the end of his life that the retirement rule was introduced. After his retirement, it is unlikely that Lord Jakobovits will fade into oblivion. He has impressed himself too deeply on the public imagination for that. He is also a man with many interests and passionate feelings, and his seat in the Lords will offer a ready platform for his ideas.

He often contemplates with disbelief how far he has gone in the fifty-five years since he left Königsberg and likes to think that a destiny which has showered him with so many welcome surprises in the past may still have a surprise or two in store, and that in some respects his best years may be still ahead.

Genesis

KÖNIGSBERG, or Kaliningrad as it is now known (it was annexed by Russia with the rest of East Prussia in 1945), was an ancient university city which in more recent years also served as a naval base. Its situation on the borders of Poland made it a transit point for East European Jews fleeing from Tsarist oppression. The newcomers, Yiddish-speaking, outlandish in manners and dress, did not quite know what to make of their German-speaking co-religionists, with their ornate, church-like synagogues and their German ways. Each tended to look askance at the other. Each was made uneasy by the other and the latter, while always ready with material assistance, were more inclined to help the newcomers move on than move in. The Königsberg Jewish community, which by the 1920s numbered some 4,000 souls out of a population of about 300,000, was fairly homogeneous in character: prosperous, cultured, proud of its Jewish and Germanic heritage, and not insecure.

To say that it was homogeneous, however, is not to say that it was united — very few Jewish communities are. Most of the Jews in the city belonged to the Reform movement, but a sizable minority was Orthodox. Moreover, as German Jews were among the first to receive the benefits of emancipation, the scions of many a family who had suffered martyrdom for their faith became Christian the moment they were free to live as Jews.

The attractions of German culture were overwhelming, and Jews were drawn to the philosophy of Kant and Hegel, the music of Bach and Beethoven, the poetry of Goethe, Schiller and Heine (who, though born Jewish, adopted Christianity as 'a ticket to European culture'). Jewish children were told stories from the Brothers Grimm rather than from the Old Testament, and they fell asleep to the sound of German lullabies sung by German nursemaids. Even with the prevalence of anti-Jewish feeling, it was a fairly cosy world and German Jews liked to think that there was nothing in German culture to alienate them from their faith, and little in their faith to estrange them from German culture.

The principal progenitor of this view was the philosopher Moses Mendelssohn, who was short, deformed, with a head out of all proportion to his body, penetrating eyes, great charm and vast erudition. Born in Dessau in 1729, he received a traditional Jewish education, but at fourteen he moved to Berlin and to his knowledge of German and Hebrew he added Latin, Greek, French, English and Italian, so that he was at home in almost every major European culture. He also acquired mathematical skills, yet he remained an obscure figure working as a book-keeper by day and writing by night until the philosopher Gotthold Lessing helped him to publish his works on meta-physics and aesthetics. These quickly brought him to the forefront of German cultural life and he was recognized as one of the most original minds of his age. It was only in 1763, however, that he was granted formal residential rights in Berlin, and when elected to the Prussian Royal Academy, his election was vetoed by Frederick II.

He did not let personal setbacks affect his hopes of Jewish advancement, which he felt must come with the spread of enlightenment, but argued that Jews in turn must themselves become more enlightened. He saw no conflict in Judaism between faith and reason, for to him the God of Israel was the God of reason, and he pleaded for the preservation of Jewish usage, again on rational grounds, as an expression of Jewish uniqueness. He was himself in practice a deeply Orthodox Jew.

The same cannot be said of his disciples, who founded the German Reform movement. They embraced his rationalism but eschewed his particularism and jettisoned the dietary laws, abandoned fasts, curtailed feasts, limited the stress on Sabbath observance, conducted their services mainly in German rather than in Hebrew, introduced church-style organ music, and deleted any reference to the Temple, Temple sacrifices and the return to Zion from their prayers. They had found their Zion in Germany and tended to think of themselves as Germans of the Mosaic persuasion rather than as Jews.

They were also influenced by the ideas of Mendelssohn's contemporary, the sage of Königsberg, Immanuel Kant (1724–1804). The two were at one in probing the heavens, but while the former deified reason, or rather rationalized God, the latter pointed to the limits of reason and argued that the existence of God cannot be proved except as an empirical necessity to moral advance-ment. He thus saw religion as basically a system of ethics, in which respect he found Judaism, with its stress on statutes and laws, inferior to Christianity. However, he was embraced eagerly by the Reform movement, which began to place ethics at the centre of its creed. Yet, at the same time, Orthodox Jews saw in Kant's relegation of reason a vindication of their creed. He came to be regarded in some ways as the kosher philosopher, and when Dr Julius Jakobovits, the rabbi of the Königsberg Orthodox synagogue, had a son in 1921, he named him Immanuel in tribute to his memory, though the name itself is Jewish in origin and consists of two Hebrew words, *Immanu El*, meaning God is with us. In the event, it proved to be entirely appropriate.

Julius himself was born in 1886, the eldest of a rabbi's nine children, in the small town of Lackenbach in what was then Hungary and is now Austria. The area as a whole, known in Hebrew as the *Sheva Kehillot* (the Seven Communities), was a fief of the Esterhazy family, who were favourably disposed to the Jews and allowed them a degree of local autonomy. In towns like Lackenbach Jews were in the majority and a Sabbath or festival could be felt in the very serenity which settled on the streets.

Those were the golden years of Habsburg Jewry. There may have been distant stirrings of anti-Semitism, and even the occasional blood libel, but God was in His heavens, Franz Josef was on the throne, and the Jews felt secure both in their situation and in their faith. Although they still referred to themselves as exiles in their prayers, in practical terms they were at home.

The outside world had its attractions, but they were unequal to the warmth and tranquillity of Jewish small-town life, where the rabbi functioned not only as communal leader but as teacher, counsellor and guide, and where almost every action was governed by ancient usage. Thus, while Reform Judaism made rapid headway elsewhere in the Habsburg Empire, the Seven Communities formed a citadel of Orthodoxy, drawing their inspiration from the philosophy and teaching of Moses Schreiber, better known as the Chatam Sofer, who died in 1839 but whose ideas were kept alive by a dynasty of sons, sons-in-law and grandsons, to say nothing of countless disciples.

Where Reform Jews sought a confluence of Jewish and secular culture, Schreiber insisted that everything worth knowing was to be found in the Torah and the Talmud and he tolerated secular knowledge only to the extent necessary to earn a livelihood. He set his face against all change and argued that anything novel, being novel, was in itself forbidden. He even discouraged the struggle for emancipation because it threatened the separateness of the Jewish people and he preached what might today be called a voluntary apartheid of a sort which is again becoming fashionable in Jewish life.

He established a yeshiva (talmudical college) in Pressburg, which became one of the principal centres of rabbinic learning in Europe and which formed the fountainhead of modern Orthodoxy. It was, however, modern only in the sense that its students wore mufti, spoke German and were familiar with German culture, but they adhered to every precept of traditional Judaism, or at least tried to.

Schreiber, in common with Reform Judaism, laid stress on ethics, but argued that ethics were best observed through the meticulous observance of the divine law as given by Moses on Sinai, and that the Jew, at least, could only become a perfect citizen through becoming a perfect Jew.

Julius Jakobovits left home at eleven to study first in the small local yeshiva near Lackenbach and then at the Schreibers' Pressburg yeshiva, but he could not have subscribed entirely to its ethos for he then went on to study at the Hildesheimer rabbinical seminary in Berlin.

The idea of a rabbinical seminary was in itself regarded as vaguely heretical by many Orthodox rabbis. When it was established in 1873, it aroused a great deal of opposition, for with its scientific approach and its study of philosophy and theology it, so to speak, suggested a readiness to look God in the teeth.

The founder of the seminary, however, Azriel Hildesheimer (1820–99), who came from the same corner of Hungary as the Jakobovits family and who was for a time a rabbi in the area, believed that Orthodox Judaism was perfectly capable of standing up to scientific scrutiny. He had himself studied at the universities of Halle and Berlin and everything he learned had reinforced his faith.

By entering Hildesheimer's, Julius Jakobovits thus distanced himself slightly from the influence of the Schreibers. He distanced himself further when he entered the University of Berlin and wrote a thesis on a purely secular subject drawing on purely German sources. He emerged a fairly typical product of German, rather than Hungarian, Orthodoxy and obtained his first post in the small community of Randegg, in the Grand Duchy of Baden, in 1913. It gave him a training in pastoral work but did not offer sufficient scope for his talents. Four years later, he moved to Königsberg.

He was rather an impressive figure, tall, slim, handsome, with refined features, large, pensive eyes, and a dress sense which smacked almost of vanity but which owed everything to the stress he attached to the dignity of his office. A rabbi, he believed, should not only dress with care, and talk with care, but even walk with care, a view which did not make for a relaxed life; in fact, he rarely relaxed.

He was an able preacher and his rabbinical diploma and doctorate attested to his learning, but as a rabbi, and especially an Orthodox rabbi, he suffered from one serious deficiency – at thirty-one, he was still single.

The first of all commandments in the Torah is 'be fruitful and multiply', and, as the Talmud argued, a single man was not a complete man and should ideally be married at eighteen. Jewish life presumes a family and a rabbi who was not himself a family man was not fully equipped to cope with the needs of his parish. Julius Jakobovits, however, was rather shy and retiring by nature, more at ease among books than among people. He was also as fastidious in the matter of choosing a wife as in everything else. A rabbi, he felt, could not marry just anyone. She had to be from the right family with the right background, with a proper level of education and intelligence and the right values. The disruptions of war with their restrictions on travel had also limited his choice, so that in a way it was a miracle that he married at all, but marry he did.

In 1920, he was introduced to Paula Wreschner, an attractive young woman, petite, demure, bright-eyed and, like Jakobovits, of a rather retiring nature. Her father was a rabbi in Posen, which, before the war, was in Germany, but which had since been returned to Poland, and she was happy to find herself again in a German milieu. They made an attractive couple and their marriage, until external circumstances intruded, proved to be particularly happy. Their seven children – five sons and two daughters – followed in fairly rapid succession, and Paula was a devoted wife and zealous mother, pious, caring, though a trifle over-protective and a little too eager to please, for she was in awe of her husband and a little afraid that she was not quite up to her duties.

Immanuel, as we have noticed, came first. Lotti was next, followed by George and Joseph, all between 1921 and 1925. There was then a gap of four years before another sister, Shulamith, was born, followed by Solomon and Manfred.

A special relationship developed between the first two, as if they did not quite belong to the same generation as the others, and they tended to act as prefects. Immanuel was not bossy by nature, but he was conscientious and had been imbued at an early age with the duties which fell upon him as eldest brother. No such duties devolved upon his sister, but she was a natural prefect, with a natural tendency to give orders and to organize everybody and everything. However, nobody resented their domination. They were a happy family, close and affectionate, and the fact that Immanuel found all the companionship he needed within his own family circle was to make it difficult for him to form intimate friendships in later years.

There were about 600,000 Jews in Germany in the inter-war years divided into over a thousand communities large and small; each had its own central organization to which all synagogues were affiliated and which had powers in law to levy dues on all its members. Individuals who did not consider themselves Jewish in any religious sense of the term were free to opt out of the community, but more remarkable were the groups who thought that the community was not Jewish enough and kept their distance from it. They resented the domination of the Reform movement in communal life and feared its influence, and in several towns they formed their own small, separate congregations. Dr Jakobovits was rabbi of one such group.

He was, of course, deeply opposed to almost everything that the Reform movement stood for, but unlike many of his Orthodox colleagues he was not afraid of it. He did not believe in separatism, looked for common ground where he could find it, and tried to create it where it did not exist, and after a few years in Königsberg he was able to persuade his congregants to rejoin the general community. His success in this field made a lasting impact on his eldest son, who sought to follow his example in very different circumstances and with very different results.

His work in Königsberg did not pass unnoticed and, in 1928, he was invited to act as Dayan (ecclesiastical judge) to the Jewish community of Berlin.

There were about 200,000 Jews in Berlin at the time (forming about five per cent of the city's population), with sixteen synagogues, seven of them Orthodox, and a host of cultural and welfare institutions including primary schools, grammar schools (or gymnasia, as they were called in Germany), centres of higher learning, a hospital, an orphanage and youth clubs, all under the aegis of the central community. It was as an employee of the central community − and not the separatist Adath community − that Dr Jakobovits came to Berlin, though his children all went to the Adath school.

As a Dayan he was concerned mainly with the supervision of kosher meat and poultry. Though he never underestimated the importance of Jewish dietary law, he was not particularly excited by it and he was soon appointed communal rabbi, which provided not only a higher status and salary, but more absorbing work.

There were thirty rabbis employed by the Berlin community, most of them Reform, and Jakobovits found no difficulty in working with them. He was always happier in the mainstream of a community than in any narrow section of it and relished the challenge of conflicting ideologies without ever compromising his own. He was on particularly amicable terms with the saintly Leo Baeck, the doyen of the Reform rabbinate who came to be regarded as the spiritual leader of German Jewry, and he counted several Reform colleagues among his personal friends. 'A hundred friends are too few,' he would say, 'but one enemy is too many.'

Life for the Jakobovits family in Berlin, certainly before the rise of Hitler, was not unpleasant. Communal salaries were based on the number of children so that they enjoyed a modest prosperity, lived in a spacious apartment and had the benefit of domestic help. In the summer they went on holiday to the Tatra mountains in Czechoslovakia or to other resorts, or among the wind-swept sand-dunes of the Baltic coast.

But holidays, even when the children were small, were never entirely carefree. There was schoolwork to complete, or some passage from Scripture or the Talmud to contemplate, and their father was always around, stern but not unkind, questioning, testing and disposed to offer instruction. There were also, of course, the thrice daily assemblies for prayer.

Torah study, as they were frequently reminded, was the highest good and there was never a holiday from the demands of their faith. The household represented a confluence of two cultures, both earnest, both demanding, and neither of them with much patience for the childishness of children.

Dr Jakobovits was never quite at ease even on holiday. The duties of a rabbi are almost in direct proportion to his orthodoxy, for it is not only that Orthodox services are more lengthy and frequent, and observances more numerous, but that Orthodox worshippers are more demanding. In Germany, at least, parishioners tended to regard their rabbi as a sort of oracle with insights denied to lesser men, and they would call at his door with their problems at all hours of the day and most hours of the night, and the cares of his office often weighed heavily upon him.

There is no presumption of death in Jewish law. Where a husband vanishes, or leaves without giving his wife a divorce, she remains, to use the Hebrew expression, an *agunah*, or 'chained', which is to say that she is never free to remarry. The upheavals of the post-war years had brought a great influx of East European Jews, amongst whom were many wives who had been abandoned by their husbands, or had otherwise lost contact with them and were unable to trace them. Dr Jakobovits combined Jewish compassion with German rigour. Where the law allowed him a loophole he made every effort to help them, but he never took liberties with the law itself and the heartbreak which ensued haunted him to the end of his days.

In March 1947, he suffered a severe heart attack and, though very feeble, could not sleep. When his eldest son asked what was troubling him, he said, 'The *agunoth*, I can't get them out of my mind and they give me no peace.' These were among his last words, yet — and in this respect he was like his son — he never questioned the wisdom of the law itself and felt helpless to amend it.

He was not an easy man to have as a father, for demanding much of himself he expected much of his children. A poor school report could earn stern rebuke and his eldest son, who was not a brilliant pupil, does not recall his school-days as the happiest days of his life. But they were active days. Immanuel was a born organizer and at fourteen he already found himself forming youth societies and addressing youth services like a rabbi in embryo, though the tendency may have owed as much to youthful exuberance and exhibitionism as to missionary zeal. His ambitions at that stage were still undefined. In any case, the whole foundation of German Jewry was by then under threat, though

15

no one could anticipate the scale of the calamity to follow.

Most German Jews had infinite faith in Germany. The country had suffered a prolonged war, a humiliating defeat, a punitive peace treaty, revolution, turmoil and ruinous inflation, but had somehow managed to surmount them all. There were still occasional riots in the street, with demonstrations and marches and counter-marches. Where there had been threats from the red-shirts, there were now threats from the brown-shirts, and Jews were singled out for particular attack. They caused natural anxiety, but Jews had faith in German good sense; and to their belief in Germany Orthodox Jews added a belief in a God who had seen them through earlier difficulties and would no doubt see them through these ones.

There was, moreover, the comforting effect of prayer, such as Psalm 91, intoned every night by children in Orthodox households: 'I will say of the Lord, He is my refuge and my fortress. . . . He shall deliver thee from the snare of the fowler . . .', and the refrain: 'In the name of the Lord, the God of Israel, may Michael be at my right hand; Gabriel at my left; before me Uriel; behind me Raphael; and above me the Divine Presence.'

The Jews lived comparatively secluded lives, attending Jewish primary schools, Jewish secondary schools and Jewish youth clubs; and if, as they matured, business brought them into the outside world, they hurried home to a Jewish one. Their whole existence revolved round the synagogue and the home, with the one an extension of the other. Their contact with the wider society, or even with non-Orthodox Jewish society, was limited, and they were thus among the last to become aware of what was actually happening to Germany and the perils which they were about to face them-selves.

But one by one external events made their painful intrusions. Already in 1923 there were attacks on Jews in the Grenadierstrasse and Dragonerstrasse, major centres of Jewish population, and on 12 September 1931, on the eve of the Jewish new year, Rosh Hashanah, Jews returning from synagogue were attacked in the Kurfürstendam. Each attack brought horrified reactions, yet each was dismissed as an isolated incident. Jews kept assuring themselves that they were, after all, in Germany and that if things got no worse they would be all right.

But, of course, they did get worse. 'Sometimes walking with my father,' Lord Jakobovits recalls, 'rowdies came behind and hurled insults, and we walked faster. A little later they began hurling stones, and we walked faster still. Sometimes we broke into a trot, which my father hated because it was so undignified. It was unpleasant, frightening, but it became so normal that we eventually got used to it.'

Jewish students were assaulted in the universities, Jewish children were set upon in the street, Jewish property was attacked and synagogues were vandalized, but one got used to that too. Every small outrage inured one to large ones, until the large seemed small. Worse things had happened in the past, and were still happening in Poland. Germany, with all its problems, was, after all, Germany and not some benighted corner of Eastern Europe.

Then, in 1933, Hitler came to power. One of his first acts was to order a boycott of Jewish shops, which was followed by legislation to exclude Jews from the professions. Jews were also excluded from public schools. All of this brought a revival in Jewish life: existing Jewish schools were expanded, new ones were opened, and a new stress was given to Jewish studies.

No Jewish community had prospered as rapidly as the German one and none had strayed so far from its roots. Although this was not Dr Jakobovits's view, many of his Orthodox colleagues tended to regard Hitler as an instrument of divine displeasure to whip straying Jews back into the fold, and they liked to think that they would in time emerge chastened and strengthened from their ordeal. However, it soon became clear that even this was too optimistic a view, and the more far-sighted Jews, for all their faith in Germans and Germany and their love of German culture, began to pull up their roots and leave.

It was not easy for Dr Jakobovits to follow their example. There were his duties to his community and to his family. He was nearly fifty, without a knowledge of English or even Yiddish; even if he had known both, there was no shortage of rabbis or ecclesiastical judges in the outside world, and he did not feel equipped to be anything else. He had no relatives or friends in America or Britain who could help him, and he had seven children, most of them in their infancy and one a babe in arms.

There was, he felt, nothing for it but to remain in place and weather the storm. In the meantime, however, he decided to send Immanuel to start a new life in England, so that he could, if necessary, throw a lifeline to the rest of the family.

It was not an easy decision. An Orthodox upbringing not only ties one to usage but breeds an aversion to all change. The boy, moreover, had had a sheltered upbringing, had not yet finished school and did not seem ready to face the world on his own, but after prolonged family debate they felt that there was no alternative.

Immanuel went reluctantly. They were a close family. His siblings were his most immediate friends and he had a particularly happy relationship with his sister Lotti, but he did not question his father's wishes.

Relatives and friends assembled to see him off. It was a sombre occasion, with little jollification and many tears, more a wake than a party, for he was not sure when, if ever, they would meet again. On 15 November 1936, he left Germany never to return. He was fifteen.

Exodus

LONDON in November was cold, bleak, foggy and uninviting, Lord Jakobovits recalls. There were still rowdies in the streets, but there was nothing sinister about their cries, and he could walk home in the evening without feeling threatened by the sound of footsteps behind him. It was only after settling in London that he realized how insecure he had felt in Berlin.

At first it was all bewildering. He had never been abroad before, except on family holidays, and those were always in German-speaking lands. A non-German country, in his imagination, was almost beyond civilization. He did not know England or speak the language or understand its ways. Several Anglo-Jewish Committees had been formed to offer emergency aid to German refugees, and he had been brought over by one such committee headed by an energetic, buccaneering rabbi called Solomon Schonfeld, who was shortly to become the son-in-law of Chief Rabbi J. H. Hertz.

Schonfeld had an acute sense of urgency and a limited sense of discipline, and once set on a course he never let lack of funds or authority stop him. He travelled back and forth between London and Germany trying to snatch out whomever he could, and Jakobovits was one of the hundreds, perhaps even thousands, of young people he saved. Jakobovits and Schonfeld were later to have their differences (Schonfeld had his differences with everybody), but, as Jakobovits has acknowledged more than once, 'If I am alive today, it is entirely due to the efforts of that man, and the same can be said for countless others.'

His initial experience of London was daunting. It was a city of mists and fogs and confusion. He was placed in a crumbling edifice in Stamford Hill, which had been quickly converted into a hostel. Nobody seemed to know what was happening. There were beds everywhere, and suitcases, and a whirl of volunteers, and urgent voices, and plaintive cries, and conflicting orders in a variety of tongues, and confounded youngsters wandering around as if in their sleep.

Jakobovits was assured food, clothing and shelter, but he was a stranger

19

among strangers, without his brothers or sisters, and without the guidance of his father or the attention of his mother. But it was as if the very lack of attention and the prevailing chaos offered a new stimulus.

He had been one of the less brilliant pupils of the Adath gymnasium in Berlin. His school reports were often the despair of his parents, and he was never allowed to forget the burden of expectations he carried as the eldest son. Now, possibly because he was free of parental anxiety and pressure, he found aptitudes in London he had lacked in Berlin.

He went to a Jewish school in Stamford Hill, which had been established some years earlier by Rabbi Schonfeld's father and which was being consolidated by Schonfeld himself. It lacked the discipline and order he had known in Berlin. Many of the pupils, and not a few of the staff, were recent arrivals and he sometimes heard more German than English, but he still managed to acquire a working knowledge of the language within a matter of weeks. Nine months later he passed his matriculation certificate (the pre-war equivalent of today's GCSE) and he eventually obtained a place at Queen Mary's College in East London to read science.

He had turned to science because he had never shown any particular skill in the humanities and because he thought it offered better scope for a livelihood. He had also read many scientific works and was interested in the mysteries of creation – though they never impinged upon his basic beliefs. His father, however, was unhappy with his choice and persuaded him to enter the rabbinate.

Jakobovits admits that he took up his father's suggestion less out of a sense of vocation than of duty, for he could not ignore parental wishes or the pressures of family history. He stemmed from a long line of rabbis on both sides of his family. As the eldest son he felt more than a passing obligation to follow in their footsteps, and after just one week at Queen's Mary's, he enrolled in Jews' College and Etz Chaim Yeshiva.

The term yeshiva is sometimes translated as rabbinical college, but whereas the latter is specifically designed to produce clergy, the former seeks to produce scholars, who may then go on to become rabbis. Yeshiva literally means sitting: it is a place where men – and only men – sit and learn the Torah, or more specifically the Talmud, for its own sake as the highest good.

Jews' College, housed on the second storey of Woburn House, a drab building in Bloomsbury, was to Britain and the British Empire what the Hildesheimer seminary had been to Germany. The level of Jewish education it offered was perhaps less profound, and its regime was less rigorous, but then British Jews expected less of their clergy than their German brethren.

The British rabbinate had been largely an immigrant's occupation and, in

1855, the elders of the community felt that it was time that Britain and the Empire had English-speaking, English-trained clergy. Jews' College added to such traditional subjects as the Talmud, Scripture, Hebrew and ecclesiastical law, a knowledge of history, homiletics, Latin and Greek. It also sought to inculcate a certain style, or rather tone, which was modelled largely on that of the Church of England. Graduates were accorded the title of Revd rather than Rabbi (though in later years they could, after further study, obtain a rabbinical diploma), and were as likely to quote Shakespeare or Milton as Rabbis Akiva or Gamaliel. They wore canonicals in synagogue and dark suits and dog collars outside, so that in appearance there was little to distinguish them from their Anglican colleagues, and when preaching the very cadences they assumed gave them an Anglican tone. This may explain why Jakobovits joined Etz Chaim Yeshiva. He had also acquired an appetite for the Talmud which Jews' College could not satisfy, but which Etz Chaim did.

Etz Chaim, compared to the famous talmudic seats of learning which had enriched Jewish life in Eastern and Central Europe, was a rather homely affair. Housed in a small, tumbledown building with creaking floorboards and damp walls in the East End of London, it only had a handful of full-time students, plus perhaps a score of youngsters who dropped in for the occasional hour of study after school. It was, however, led by two exceptional figures.

One was the principal, Rabbi Eliyahu Lopian, a renowned authority on *musar*, the ethical teachings of Judaism, on which he would expound for hours with many insights into both Jewish law and Jewish lore. The other was Rabbi N. S. Greenspan, a small, unassuming figure who combined deep piety with vast erudition and was one of the greatest talmudic scholars to have lived in England, though a little surprisingly he combined his knowledge of the ancient codes with considerable secular learning. Both lacked the polish and hauteur of the rabbis Jakobovits used to meet in his father's circle, but exuded a warmth he had not known before. They, for their part, must initially have found him a trifle precious, but he soon established a rapport with both and each functioned partially *in loco parentis*, shaping his outlook and directing his ways. With the exception of his own father, no one had a greater influence on his subsequent career. They were in many respects his role-models. He recalls them with affection and gratitude and continues to quote them to this day.

Jakobovits was eighteen by then and had moved all his life among Hungarian, Austrian and German Jews. The Jews he encountered in the Yeshiva were a step — if that — from Lithuania and Poland, and instruction was given in Yiddish, a language whose use was discouraged in Germany; he had never even heard it before coming to London and it initially grated on his ear, but he soon picked it up and became more adept in Yiddish than in his native German.

In moving between Jews' College and the Yeshiva, between Bloomsbury and East London, Jakobovits moved between two worlds, both of them Jewish, both Orthodox, both dedicated to the preservation of Jewish tradition and the Jewish ethos, but both of them different.

In the former, there were formal lectures measured by the hour with students in silent rows taking notes. There were essays to write, tutorials to attend, regular hours and written exams at the end of each term. In the latter, students assembled for prayer at dawn and then applied themselves to their studies for the rest of the day, and often late into the night, largely on one subject, the Talmud, which, its devotees argued, includes every subject.

There would be the daily lesson on one tractate or another given by the principal, and others given by Rabbi Greenspan, but for the rest the students were expected to learn from one another. They would sit in pairs swaying backwards and forwards as they pored over the massive folios, with the older instructing the younger, the more informed, the less informed, in loud sing-song voices and with much weaving of thumbs.

Rabbi Dr Isidore Epstein, the principal of Jews' College, a short figure with a confident walk and a neat little beard tucked into his wing collar, was a profound scholar, wide-ranging in his interests and penetrating in his insights. He also had considerable literary gifts and was the author of what is still the most popular English book on Judaism, but he was rather dry, too self-consciously modern and did not have the same lasting effect on Jakobovits as his colleagues at Etz Chaim. Nor did Jews' College.

There was no rivalry between the two institutions, for they lived in different worlds and catered for different needs, but the Yeshiva tended to regard Jews' College as slightly non-kosher, while the College tended to regard the Yeshiva as more than slightly outlandish, and the fact that Jakobovits belonged to both was to involve him in some controversy.

Given his German upbringing, the Yeshiva should have been more alien to him than the College, but he found it more congenial. There was a carefree attitude among the students of Jews' College which, to someone hailing from Germany, verged on the frivolous and which made him feel foreign, while in the Yeshiva he was a foreigner among foreigners, or at least among people who had not entirely assimilated into English ways.

Jews' College had close links with London University and some of its courses were taken at University College, and for the first time in his life Jakobovits came into day-to-day contact with non-Jews, with *goyim*.

In Eastern Europe the Jew lived in one world and the gentile in another, not always in the happiest proximity. Each was ignorant of the ways of the other and what little he knew he disliked. It was otherwise in the German-speaking lands of Central Europe, where Jews were largely assimilated and where – before the rise of Hitler – even the Orthodox acknowledged that there was much in the German way of life worthy not only of admiration but of emulation. Yet while the Jakobovits family had not estranged themselves from German society, the children had occupied an insulated corridor within it, along which they rushed to and from synagogue and their Jewish day schools so that *goyim* were an unknown quantity, sometimes benign, sometimes hostile, but never quite predictable and always different.

Jakobovits's first contact with gentiles was reassuring. He was surprised to discover how genial, friendly and accommodating they were, but he could never adopt their relaxed attitudes and carefree ways, or acquire their appetite for pleasure. They seemed young for their age, while he, with his strenuous programme of studies at two different establishments, in two different languages, and his earnest sense of duty, was old for his, and he never felt entirely at ease in their company, which was another reason why he was happier at the Yeshiva. Etz Chaim thus became his true spiritual home. It carried the authentic echoes, the sounds and even the smells of traditional Jewish life. When he finally qualified, he took a BA degree of London University through Jews' College, but he was to receive his rabbinical diploma from Etz Chaim.

It was all rather symbolic, for Jakobovits has always been torn between the wider appeal of the university and the particular appeal of the yeshiva, between the secular and the religious, between this world and the next, and the conflict has not yet been entirely resolved.

If German Jewry was predominantly Reform, Anglo-Jewry was, nominally at least, predominantly Orthodox. Jews' College was largely financed by the United Synagogue, which represented the mainstream of Anglo-Jewish Orthodoxy and which included all the larger synagogues in and around London. As a result, it naturally took its clergy from among the graduates of the College. New graduates, however, tended to start in the provinces from where, if they had ability, they would eventually be transferred to London. Jakobovits was spared such preliminaries. Before he had even taken his degree he, somewhat to his own surprise and not a little to his dismay, found himself ministering to one of the principal congregations in the capital, and at the centre of a rather unpleasant controversy.

Britain was at war by then and many leading rabbis were serving as chaplains to the forces. As a result, the members of Brondesbury Synagogue found themselves without a minister and Jakobovits came to their attention. Though young, cadaverous and clean-shaven, his very earnestness gave a suggestion of years. He also had something of his father's dignified bearing and had shown himself to be an intelligent student, with great application, piousness, helpfulness and sincerity. His accent was rather foreign and, when he got excited, his voice became grating and high-pitched, but, for a newcomer, he had a remarkable facility for words and pronounced oratorical skills. He had impressed the tutor and his peers, and, when asked to address the synagogue, he impressed the congregation. He was invited to become their minister at a salary of £200 a year.

Brondesbury, consecrated in 1905, was a plum post, a large and fashionable congregation in a fashionable part of town, and his appointment, perhaps not surprisingly, caused an immediate outcry. The first salvo came from someone signing himself A. J. C. – which suggested a disgruntled Associate of Jews' College – in the *Jewish Chronicle*:

Your readers must have read – as I did – with incredulity of the appointment which those responsible ... have thought fit to make at Brondesbury Park. A youth, barely twenty, of German nationality, who only came to this country as a refugee five years ago, is appointed to the ministry of a Synagogue, by no means the least important in the metropolis. There is not even the excuse that he is a Rabbi famed for his learning and now exiled from a position of dignity and importance abroad, as so many are. The inference, of course, is clear, that there is no one among the recent graduates of Jews' College of English birth, no one holding a ministerial position in a less important London Synagogue or provincial congregation, who is worthy enough or fit to be translated to the important Brondesbury Synagogue. When one recalls the continuing complaints that are made as to the standing and quality of the majority of the Anglo-Jewish clergy, one can fully realize why the community cannot obtain the best men.... What encouragement is there for a young man to enter the clergy when he sees posts filled in this way? However eminent this young gentleman may be, even his best friends could not pretend that he is the only person who could lay claim to an appointment of this importance. The Anglo-Jewish community is at the moment in a state of flux. It has before it problems of the most difficult kind. It requires for its guidance men of experience, not only of these problems, but with a background that would make them understand not only their own co-religionists, but their English fellow citizens of other creeds. However brilliant this young man may be ... he possesses no background as far as English life is concerned – he was, until comparatively recently, living in a country which will be, quite properly, abhorrent to all right-thinking people for generations to come; and I repeat, twenty years of age, an age when, it seems to me, with the incessant and crying need for man-power, he might have considered interrupting his career for some more active contribution to the war effort.

Jakobovits had his admirers even then and several rushed to his defence, for as a matter of simple fact it was a temporary job, a stop-gap, and he had been selected because, for all his youth and inexperience, he stood head and shoulders above the other available candidates.

The office of minister, for someone not particularly conscientious, can be a sinecure. He is required to give the occasional sermon – the more occasional, in some instances, the better – attend the statutory services and officiate at rites of passage, which between them need not, on average, occupy more than the equivalent of a working day. A conscientious man, however, can be kept busy day and night, and Jakobovits was nothing if not conscientious, but as the months passed it became fairly clear that he was not quite the man for the job.

Anglo-Jewish Orthodoxy was not German Orthodoxy. People often drove to synagogue on the Sabbath and, even if they walked, they usually carried their personal possessions, which is also against Jewish law. Few homes were strictly kosher so that Jakobovits could not easily accept hospitality. In Germany, a rabbi stood a little above his community, while in England he was expected to be part of the crowd. Though not unsociable, Jakobovits was not gregarious and preferred the company of his books. Moreover, he was still a little awkward and shy and found himself painfully isolated on the Sabbath and holidays.

The controversy surrounding his appointment had singled him out for critical scrutiny and he was made constantly aware that he was being weighed and measured. At that age he was, as anyone would be, sensitive to every breath of criticism.

He was also a little too earnest and too conscientious. English rabbis like to enliven their sermons with some light-hearted anecdote or amusing aside. He was to change in later years, but at the time he did not feel that a synagogue was a place for laughter, and his sermons were excessively weighty and doom-laden. Nor was he afraid to utter the occasional word of rebuke, and middle-aged, middle-class people were not readily disposed to accept admonitions from a young man, who, no matter how pious or learned, was hardly more than a schoolboy, and a foreign schoolboy at that.

Finally, he was still continuing his studies at Jews' College and Etz Chaim and he had to cross London to get there. This left him exhausted at the end of the day, especially as the Blitz often made such journeys drawn out and hazardous.

His whole family had moved to London shortly before the war and his younger sister Lotti, with whom he had always been on the closest terms, kept house for him and made his stay bearable. However, she could see that the experience was wearing him down and suggested that not only was he not cut out for Brondesbury, but that Brondesbury was not cut out for him. That, indeed, was his own view of the situation, but it represented a challenge, and he hoped that with sufficient application and goodwill they might yet warm to each other. It was all to no avail. The harder he tried, the worse he fared. After struggling on for two unhappy years, he moved to New Cross in south-east London.

New Cross, once a major congregation, had been decimated by the Blitz and was now so small that it could not afford a full-time minister. The office was combined with that of synagogue secretary, but it was that much less demanding and left Jakobovits with more time for study. By 1946, however, he had completed his courses both at the College and the Yeshiva and had applied for a vacancy at the Queen's Park Synagogue, Glasgow, the largest congregation in the city and one of the leading congregations in the provinces.

He spoke twice, the first time on Saturday morning, and the second, unusually, on Sunday afternoon, but if he pleased some parts of the congregation, he displeased others.

The king-makers in most provincial Jewish communities in the post-war years were usually small businessmen who had arrived from Lithuania or Poland some forty or fifty years before. Though traditional in outlook, they were not always meticulous in their observances and still spoke a broken English, but they wanted their ministers not only to be more Orthodox then them, but more English, and expected them to have a good command of the language.

Barnett Janner, a popular Jewish politician, once asked a large Jewish gathering whether he should address them in Yiddish or English. 'English,' they answered in unison. 'Yiddish we can speak ourselves.' To British Jewry at that time, the Englishness was everything, even in Scotland.

Jakobovits's English was by then perfect, but he still had a slight accent and was not only foreign but, worse, sounded foreign. He was also measured against his predecessor, Rabbi Kopul Rosen, one of the foremost orators of his day, and found wanting. Finally he was, at twenty-five, still single, which was a major deficiency in an Orthodox rabbi, and, as if that were not enough, he was said to be 'too froom', or too Orthodox (a charge which was to be raised again twenty years later).

Congregants were perfectly aware that they themselves were not 'froom' enough, that they were lax in their observances and lackadaisical in their attitudes, and their clergy, in a sense, were expected to compensate for their deficiencies, but Jakobovits, it was rumoured, was inclined to overdo it and applied himself to his creed with a rigour that was – well – Germanic, rather than Lithuanian. He did not get the job and returned a little crestfallen to his small community in New Cross.

He was to have a similar experience about a year later when he applied for a vacancy at the Prestwich Synagogue, Manchester, and was again rebuffed for much the same reason. He often comforts younger colleagues with the thought that while he has had six different jobs in his life, he has never been given a position he has sought – and never sought the positions he has been given. Seek not and ye shall be found.

Jakobovits, as we have noted, came to London in 1936. A little later he was joined by his younger brother George, but the rest of the family remained in Berlin. However, their situation worsened in November 1938 after a German diplomat Ernest von Rath, had been killed in Paris by a young German Jew whose parents had been deported to Poland. The Nazis immediately retaliated by attacking Jewish property and by arresting thousands of Jews. On the night of 9–10 November, *Kristallnacht*, nearly two hundred synagogues were set ablaze and seventy-six were completely destroyed, including the famous Fasanenstrasse Synagogue in Berlin and the vast, 2,500-seat synagogue in Neukoln, which Dr Jakobovits served.

There were, even then, severe restrictions on immigration to Britain, but Rabbi Schonfeld had received permission to bring in a number of German rabbis. With German Jewry doomed, Dr Jakobovits dropped all hesitation about leaving and finally moved to London with the rest of his family.

They were given furnished rooms and charity hand-outs, but it was a period of intense hardship, made harder by the fact that the head of the family, who had held an important position in Berlin, now had to work at all. He could always occupy himself in study and give the occasional lecture to other exiles, but he had not only ceased to be a spiritual leader and guide, he had ceased to be even the breadwinner. As a result, he aged visibly under the strain.

Things eased a little when Joseph, then fifteen, found work in a factory and brought in eleven shillings a week. George found casual employment and brought in the occasional shilling, and Immanuel himself small sums which he earned from private tuition. Three of the children, however, were still at school and had to be fed and clothed. Mothers and daughters busied themselves with needle and thread to adapt old garments to new use, but there was a minor crisis whenever a child needed a new pair of shoes. They were sometimes saved from going hungry on the Sabbath by the arrival of a well-wisher with a boiled chicken, a plate of fish or a tray of potato *kugel*.

Dr Jakobovits had often preached on the importance of charity, but nothing had prepared him for the fact that he might one day be in need of it himself. For a man of his pride, the indignity was more painful than the hardship, and he comforted himself with the thought that things could only get better.

In the meantime, they got worse. In June 1940, shortly after the fall of France, both the father and the eldest son were rounded up with thousands of other German refugees and interned on the Isle of Man as 'enemy aliens'. They were not treated harshly and their billets were not uncomfortable, but they had been separated from their families, and the sudden appearance of uniformed figures and the peremptory orders to pack were at once alarming and bewildering and brought unpleasant echoes of Nazi Germany. They were also appalled by the sheer absurdity of the situation. Yet their experience, if painful and confusing, was short-lived and they were released three months later.

Things then began to improve. The son was offered the job at Brondesbury while the father found work, first as rabbi to a community of Jewish evacuees which had been formed in Bedford, and then as rabbi of the small Jewish community in Windsor and Slough. (Some twenty years later, when Jakobovits was guest of the Queen at Windsor Castle, he took some pleasure in recounting these events and told Her Majesty that his father had been the Royal Family's only rabbi.) The job was temporary and poorly paid, but he was no longer dependent on charity. In 1945, he was invited to become a Dayan of the London Beth Din (rabbinical court), a post in some ways analogous to the one he had held in Berlin.

His fortunes were restored. He now had a good salary and a comfortable room and he once again enjoyed recognition and standing. His children were nearly all grown up and advancing in business or the professions, but the anxieties, the humiliation and the privation of the recent past had sapped his health. Early in 1947 he collapsed with a heart attack and died a few days later. He was sixty-one.

Immanuel had not only been very close to his father, but had almost worshipped him and sought to emulate his attitudes, his manner, his dress and even his small idiosyncrasies. He was startlingly like him in appearance and had the same tone of voice; in later years, many an individual who met the son thought, for a moment, that he was speaking to the father. He was almost a doppelgänger. He had looked to his father as a mentor and guide, and even after he became a minister in his own right, they frequently studied together. He would consult him over any major address he had to give or any appointment he was offered, and his father's untimely death was a blow from which he was slow to recover.

To this day, whenever he is faced with a serious problem he tries to reflect on how his father would have approached it, and there are few important occasions at which he does not invoke his memory.

Traditional Jews are urged to walk in the ways of their fathers, but although Jakobovits is almost something of a reincarnation, he did differ from his father in certain respects. The father found public speaking an ordeal; the son rather enjoys it. The former approached his duties with anxiety, as if afraid that he might be unable to fulfil them; the latter is rather more self-assured and less nervous of criticism. He is also even more Orthodox, for coupled with the Germanic attitudes he inherited from his father are the East European attitudes he acquired from the Yeshiva. Both had their own qualities to commend them. If German Orthodoxy was rigorous and consistent, it was, or tried to be, this-worldly. If East European Orthodoxy shunned this world and was less rational, it was also less rigorous and took more account of human frailties. Jakobovits acquired the most exacting qualities in both, and by the time his father passed away the man we now know was in all important essentials fully formed.

A few months after his bereavement he received his rabbinical diploma from Rabbis Lopian and Greenspan at Etz Chaim Yeshiva. As a result, he was once again caught up in controversy.

In theory, any qualified rabbi could bestow rabbinical authority on any student who had reached a requisite standard of knowledge. The examination was oral and the standards were never strictly defined, or, if defined, they were not always strictly applied, with the result that the Jewish world teemed with individuals brandishing rabbinical diplomas of doubtful authenticity and dubious value.

To limit the abuses which had thus arisen, Chief Rabbi Hertz set up a Central Examining Board on which Jews' College, the London Beth Din and the Etz Chaim Yeshiva were represented, which would assure that anyone seeking a rabbinical diploma, whether from Jews' College or the Yeshiva, had the necessary qualifications. These too were not strictly defined, but Dr Israel Brodie, who succeeded Hertz as Chief Rabbi in 1947, argued that they should include not only Jewish learning but wide general culture. Immanuel Jakobovits, as a graduate of Jews' College and Etz Chaim, in fact combined both, but by accepting his diploma from the Yeshiva without submitting himself to the Central Examining Board, he was, in a sense, undermining the Chief Rabbi's authority.

However, there was more to it than that. It was a clash between the discipline and order which the Anglo-Jewish establishment was trying to instil and the chaos associated with East European Jewish institutions. Jakobovits, whose very instincts placed him on the side of order, had acted in all innocence and could not understand what the fuss was about.

The *Jewish Chronicle* cast no blame on Jakobovits himself but felt that the action of the Yeshiva was reprehensible, to which Rabbis Greenspan and Lopian retorted that they knew nothing about the agreement to set up a Central Examining Board and were never a party to it.

The controversy raged for some weeks, but it was soon forgotten, and presumably forgiven, because a few months later Jakobovits was appointed minister of the Great Synagogue. As if in keeping with the dignity of his new station, he acquired a beard.

The Great Synagogue, in Duke's Place on the borders of the City and the East End, was, as its name implied, the premier synagogue in London, and the cathedral synagogue, so to speak, of the British Isles. Built in 1722 and enlarged and remodelled in 1790, it could accommodate nearly two thousand worshippers and was for over a century the seat of the Chief Rabbi. Lord Rothschild had a pew in the front row and would attend services on Yom Kippur. However, the synagogue had been destroyed in the Blitz in May 1941 and most of its congregants were scattered by the war. By 1947, it was housed in a Nissen hut set among the ruins, but it was still the Great Synagogue in name and still reverberated with echoes from the past, and a certain amount of status still attached to its officer-holders both lay and clerical.

To Jakobovits, Duke's Place represented the nearest thing he had in England to home ground. Etz Chaim Yeshiva was just a few streets away, and his father had worked as a Dayan in nearby Adler House and had lived in Mulberry Court, a United Synagogue property which was still occupied by his mother and younger brothers. He was therefore able to move in with them.

Before the war the East End had been the main centre of Jewish life, but whole streets had been obliterated in the Blitz and the few erect buildings stood out amidst the devastation like surviving teeth in an aged mouth. It was now basically an accommodation address, for while most Jewish institutions were still located in the area, the Jews themselves were moving out. Jakobovits described the place as 'a shambles', but he regarded the very difficulties he faced as something of a challenge.

He made youth his first priority. He had established a thriving youth club in New Cross and now sought to do the same in Duke's Place. The East End was not short of Jewish youth clubs, but they were Jewish only in name and were devoted mainly to social and sporting activities. Jakobovits wanted a Jewish club with Jewish content and, to this end, he established the Carmel Youth Society, which had discussions, debates and the occasional lecture and which attracted a considerable number of young people. As with almost all Jewish societies, it was also an opportunity for boy to meet girl and, perhaps to make sure that the occasion was not abused, Jakobovits offered a course on marriage education. Thus emerged one of his major interests: chastity and stability in family life.

To those who found him too puritanical, he retorted, with a ponderousness which some of his listeners may have found amusing but which was then characteristic of his style: 'The complex human intellect and emotions –

differentiating man from the brute — are such that only a certain amount of religiously regulated continence and self-control can vouchsafe the success of intimate human relations,' by which he meant that lust must be tempered by responsibility.

With his slight stoop (which he has since straightened out), forbidding attitudes and shrill, piping voice, he must have sounded an insufferable young prig. One or two of his former congregants still recall him as such, but he was in earnest. A model of propriety himself, when a national Jewish Marriage Guidance Council was formed he, though still a bachelor, became its moving spirit.

He had no dreams of restoring the Great Synagogue to its former glories, but he rescued it from dereliction and its congregation began to show signs of animation. He showed that there was still life among the ashes. He was accessible to young and old, and where they did not call on him, he called on them. He was endlessly industrious and persevering. His sermons, rich in content and forceful in presentation, if a little too sententious and wordy, attracted attention and comment, for even where people did not agree with his views, they were impressed by his sincerity and conviction. He began to contribute fairly regularly to the Jewish press. He was emerging from the grey mists of anonymity to which young clergymen are generally condemned in the first years of their career. He was often invited as a visiting speaker by other synagogues and Jewish cultural societies. He was becoming a name and, only eighteen months after taking up his appointment at Duke's Place, he was — a little to his surprise — invited to become Chief Rabbi of Ireland. He was twenty-seven.

Dubliners

IRISH Jewry was always socially and culturally part of British Jewry and was subject to the authority of the Chief Rabbi, but when southern Ireland became independent in 1921 Isaac Herzog, the principal rabbi of Dublin, assumed the title of Chief Rabbi, a role he filled with distinction until he left in 1936 to become Chief Rabbi of Palestine. Thirteen years passed before a successor was appointed.

There were then over 5,000 Jews in the Irish Republic, with tiny communities in Limerick and Waterford, which were by now almost extinct, and another in Cork, which was on the way to extinction, so that Irish Jewry was substantially based in Dublin. And the Dublin community, though not large, consisted of no less than seven different Orthodox congregations, some of them small, but all of them fiercely independent, which may partly explain why the country had been without a Chief Rabbi for so long. It says something for the reputation which Jakobovits enjoyed and the impression which he made that they were able to agree on his appointment. (There was also a small Progressive or Liberal congregation, which had been formed in 1946 and which was not under his authority.)

Ireland had, with the repeal of the External Relations Act, lately pulled out of the British Commonwealth. The strong links between British and Irish Jewry, however, remained and, on 13 February 1949, Jakobovits was inducted into office by Dr Israel Brodie, whose formal title was 'Chief Rabbi of the United Hebrew Congregations of the British Commonwealth and Empire'. At the dinner which followed, the Prime Minister of the Republic, John Costello, was guest of honour.

In strictly pastoral terms, the job of Chief Rabbi of Ireland was no more demanding than that of the rabbi of any sizable provincial community. The 1937 Irish constitution, however, gave formal recognition to Judaism as a minority faith so that the Chief Rabbi had an ambassadorial function and was expected to represent the community at state occasions. Jakobovits, therefore, became involved in an endless round of receptions with government ministers, mayors, cardinals, archbishops, bishops and visiting dignitaries. He had by then lost much of his shyness and all of his awkwardness. He nearly always had the apt word for the occasion and carried himself with self-assurance and dignity, yet photographs of the period often show him gazing disconsolately into the camera and looking a trifle lost.

He was still unmarried, which, if a deficiency in any rabbi, was a major deficiency in a Chief Rabbi. It was particularly striking in his case for he frequently preached on the centrality of the Jewish family to the Jewish faith and had helped to found the Jewish Marriage Guidance Council (which is still in being in much enlarged form as the Jewish Marriage Council). It was a little like Solomon preaching on the benefits of celibacy.

His widowed mother had looked after him while he was a rabbi in the Great Synagogue in London and she now came over to Dublin to see that his domestic arrangements were in order. However, his social circumstances were fairly desolate, and the fact that he had to attend so many occasions, formal and informal, on his own made them more tedious than they need have been. This soon changed when he met a vivacious young Parisienne called Amelie Munk.

Their backgrounds were oddly similar. Like him, she was the eldest of seven children, except that where his family included five sons and two daughters, hers included five daughters and two sons. Her father, like his, was a graduate of the Hildesheimer seminary and served a minor German congregation before moving on to a major post at the Communauté Israélite de la Stricte Observance in Paris, the French equivalent of the German Adath.

Jakobovits had arranged to stop over in Paris en route to Switzerland in the winter of 1948. While there, he attended morning service at Rabbi Munk's synagogue, a charmless edifice in the Rue Cadet, and the Rabbi brought him home to breakfast.

Most Orthodox rabbis keep open house, especially during the Sabbath and festivals, so that Amelie was used to the descent of strangers, but not on a bleak weekday morning in December. She had to be roused from her bed to greet him.

The meeting had been instigated by Eli Munk, a London rabbi and a cousin of her father's, who spoke of Jakobovits in the highest terms.

'With my father it was love at first sight,' she says. Her own reactions were rather less enthusiastic, for apart from anything else she had many friends and admirers and was in no need of introductions. She was ebullient, even shrill; he was earnest, pale-faced, studious, subdued, and young without being youthful. She spoke no English, he spoke no French. They conversed in a halting German and, in so far as she could make out his remarks, they sounded like a sermon. They spent three hours together which seemed like three days. 'I couldn't put him back on the train fast enough,' she recalls.

But he persevered and wrote to her frequently and at length in English. 'My father, who knew a little English, helped me, and we went through his letters with a dictionary. They weren't very personal but they were very interesting and he said the nicest things in the nicest way.'

They met again at the wedding of a mutual friend in Manchester and she gradually warmed to him. 'Mano' — as she calls him — 'was so refined and so learned and so good and everybody spoke so highly of him, and I didn't have any education at all. At first I wondered what people saw in him; now I began to wonder what he saw in me.'

Some of his relatives asked the same question. She was of good pedigree — her father, a rabbi in Paris and the author of a celebrated work on prayer, stemmed from a dynasty of saints and scholars, her mother, the daughter of a prosperous German merchant, was likewise of good stock — but she herself seemed to be a bit too lively and unrestrained for the wife of a rabbi, and especially a Chief Rabbi. She showed her feelings. If gloomy, she looked glum; if upset, she could be tearful; and if happy or amused — as she often was — she could be convulsed, and would convulse others, with laughter. When she talked, she spoke rapidly and with great animation. She not only lacked *gravitas*, but her whole manner verged — as it still does — on the coquettish.

'She'll never make a lady,' her prospective mother-in-law observed.

Jakobovits was willing to take the chance. They married in Paris on 5 July 1949, and, as he has often said, it was the best thing that happened to him.

In earlier years there was something about his appearance which suggested that the world was about to come to an end, and that it mightn't be a bad thing if it did. He quickly lost his lean and hungry look, his eyes became brighter and less soulful, and his face more rounded. Where he used to tarry in synagogue after services, he now rushed home. He was delighted to discover that everything he had preached about the joys of Jewish marriage was borne out by his own experience, and his subsequent career was to be shaped in more ways than one by his remarkable wife.

She, for her part, was not particularly happy. She missed her parents, her siblings and her many friends, and Dublin was not Paris.

They had a large, comfortable but rather gloomy house, the former home of Chief Rabbi Herzog, in Bloomfield Terrace, with a chatelaine in the person of her mother-in-law, who was disinclined to abdicate her responsibilities.

The elder Mrs Jakobovits was a traditional, stern German *hausfrau*, made sterner by heartache and hardship and by the fact that she was the daughter

34

of one rabbi, the widow of another and the mother of a third (she was shortly to become the mother-in-law of a fourth). A quiet, rather subdued woman, she had suffered more than her share of tragedy. Her entire existence — as in most Orthodox homes — had revolved round her husband and, when he died, she felt for a time as if her life had lost direction and meaning. And then, as she began to recover, her youngest son was struck down with polio. A few years later she lost a beloved daughter. Her faith never wavered, but she found it difficult to adapt to her new environment, to put down roots and to lead a life of her own. She therefore flitted from child to child, a small, shadowy figure, drawing her joy from theirs. She was aware of the happiness which Amelie had brought to her son, but felt that her daughter-in-law, though charming, lively and attractive, was perhaps a trifle too light-hearted, too effusive and too free with her words for the wife of a rabbi. However, they soon became close and she lived to see the fond hopes she had for her son abundantly fulfilled.

'She was very good and very helpful,' Amelie recalls. 'There was nothing she wouldn't do for me, but only wished that I was different, and I find it difficult to be the person I'm not. I suppose I also expected someone like my mother, who was very Parisienne and very gay, but we quickly warmed to each other. She stayed with each of her seven children in turn, but I like to think that she was the happiest with us and she died in my arms a few years ago.'

Unlike England, Ireland was a deeply religious society and people showed a friendly, and perhaps even obsessional, interest in the small Jewish community in their midst. Jakobovits's arrival excited considerable attention and his actual induction received press coverage on a scale which would have been undreamt of in England at the time. He was also frequently in demand for press interviews and he began to discover how far, even with the best of goodwill on the part of the reporter, one's views could be misinterpreted. Thus, for example, he was startled to read in the *Dublin Evening Mail* that 'he believed that a religion which was 4,000 years old required some reinterpretation in order to meet the needs of the twentieth century'; in fact, he believed that the ways of the twentieth century should be brought more in line with the demands of religion. He eventually learned how to handle the press, which, however, did not ensure that there would be no misunderstandings in the future.

Shortly after assuming office he was dismayed to learn that a substantial proportion of his parishioners, some of them from the finest families, were, in technical terms at least, bastards.

Under laws passed when Ireland was still part of the United Kingdom, synagogue secretaries, provided they were certified as such by the Board of

Deputies of British Jews, could act as marriage registrars. When Ireland became independent the law was not repealed, but local synagogue secretaries had stopped applying to the Board for certification, so that the marriages they had registered were technically invalid and the issue of such marriages illegitimate. Had a common informer laid the facts before the courts, retroactive legislation might have been necessary, but it was not an issue which kept the Chief Rabbi awake at night, and he did not pass on his discovery to his parishioners.

His chief interest then, as later, was education. In moving from England to Ireland he had moved from an agnostic to a religious society. Irish Christianity helped to keep the Jews Jewish and nearly half of the Jewish children in Dublin attended Jewish day schools, whereas the proportion in England at the time did not even approach fifteen per cent.

In Ireland, one must add, the schools were largely funded by the state, whereas in England they depended mainly on private donors, but they were also sustained by a pride in Jewish culture and an interest in Jewish tradition. The overwhelming mass of the community was, nominally at least, Orthodox, which is to say that they believed in Orthodoxy even if they did not always practise it, and Jakobovits worked hard to convert mere sentiment into actual observance. Some people, as we shall see, felt that he tried a little too hard.

Irish Jewry, possibly because of the nationalist fervour around them, was also strongly Zionist, and social life in the community revolved round the various Zionist organizations and youth groups. People also gave generously to Zionist causes and the migration of Irishmen to America was paralleled by a migration of Irish Jews to Israel. They went with the encouragement and blessings of the Chief Rabbi, but at the same time he noted with concern that he was losing the future leaders of his community to the Jewish state.

John Costello had announced Ireland's de facto recognition of Israel at the dinner to celebrate Jakobovits's induction, and the very timing of the announcement was a gesture of friendship both to the Jewish community and to Israel. It was regarded as a happy augury of things to come, but it was followed by a less pleasant incident.

There had been some agitation in various Catholic countries, including Ireland, about the future of the Holy Places in Israel and especially in Jerusalem. Jakobovits went to see the Primate of Ireland, Archbishop McQuaid, to reassure him on the protection of Catholic rights and property in the Jewish state and to invite his help in preserving the happy relations which had always existed between Catholics and Jews in Ireland. By way of reply, the Archbishop asked him to secure an official declaration on the safety of the Holy Places from the Government of Israel. He wrote:

Such a declaration would greatly assist, too, in preventing unfortunate repercussions such as you stated you fear may arise in Dublin.... It would indeed be a pity if after having traversed a period of worldwide and unexampled crisis, innocent people of your Community should now suffer hurt, by reason of the attitude and actions of irreligious members of Israel whose merely political or commercial aims would never be countenanced by the peaceful members of your Community in Dublin.

The oddly worded letter seemed to suggest that Jews in the Diaspora could be treated as hostages for the policies of the Jewish state. It was almost a threat and showed an extraordinary ignorance both of the situation in Israel and of the sort of influence which the religious head of a small community could bring to bear on the Government of Israel. Most of the Holy Places were in Jordanian hands at the time (a fact which seemed to have escaped the Archbishop), while those in Israel were carefully protected with access guaranteed to everyone, which was not the case in Jordan.

The letter shocked the leaders of the Jewish community. Had it been leaked, it would have caused an international outcry, but the community, which had always lived quietly with its neighbours, had no wish to be at the centre of a *cause célèbre*. Jakobovits liked to think of it as an aberration and he was to experience nothing like it again, but it did leave him with the uneasy feeling that even the most tranquil scene could have its underlying tensions.

When Israel became independent in May 1948, Dublin's main synagogue had adopted the custom of singing the *Hatikvah*, Israel's nation anthem, after the Saturday morning service. When Jakobovits became Chief Rabbi, he ruled that this custom be discontinued. While the synagogue wardens would have hesitated to question his authority on a religious issue, this seemed to be more of a political one and his orders aroused some hostility in what was an intensely Zionistic community. However, he argued that people seemed to have forgotten that Israel was now a fact and that it was no longer necessary to affirm one's patriotism in a regular act of worship. To which one could have answered that Zion was now wide open to anyone who wanted to live there, yet the devout, both within Israel and without, still prayed to be 'returned to Zion, speedily and in our day', as they had done for the past 2,000 years. The Chief Rabbi, however, while regarding ancient usages as inviolate, no matter how irrational they may be, was averse to piling up new ones, and he had his way.

In England, there was a tacit division of powers between the laity and the rabbinate, with the former looking after temporal matters and the latter after spiritual ones. The lay leader of the community, however, Sir Robert Waley-Cohen, managing director of the Shell Transport and Trading Company, a tall, massive figure, who was as formidable in temperament as he was in build, and who ruled the United Synagogue as if it were a subsidiary of Shell, reserved the right to say what was temporal and what was spiritual. Thus Jakobovits's order on the *Hatikvah* was, in a sense, a pre-emptive strike to make sure that the same situation did not develop in Ireland and to assert the authority of his office.

The lay leader of Irish Jewry was Professor Leonard Abrahamson, a former president of the Royal College of Physicians of Ireland, who, while also forceful and determined, was less autocratic. He had great respect for clergymen in general and the young Rabbi in particular. He certainly had no wish to impinge on his authority, but would nevertheless occasionally take him aside to suggest that he was possibly approaching his task with excessive zeal and was asking too much of his congregants, that Ireland was not Germany and that he was expecting a degree of observance which was not practical and perhaps not even desirable.

Abrahamson, for example, readily acknowledged the importance of the dietary laws to Jewish life, and the necessity of supervising the provision of kosher meat, but Jakobovits insisted that wine served at functions supervised by the rabbinate must also be kosher, which, at the time, was unheard of except in ultra-Orthodox circles. The British Chief Rabbinate had made no such demands and there was no feeling that Dublin should be holier than London.

Of rather greater importance was the matter of the *mikvah*, or *taharat hamishpacha* (family purity). Jewish law requires not only abstinence before marriage, but continence within it. Married women are forbidden to have sexual relations during menstruation and for seven days after it, which means that there is a minimum of twelve days' separation within every month, the source of the law being Leviticus 15:19: 'And if a woman have an issue, and her issue in her flesh be blood, she shall be put apart seven days....' At the end of the period, and before she can resume marital relations, the woman must immerse herself in a ritual bath known as a *mikvah*.

Jakobovits had often preached on the importance of this custom. It renewed the natural bond between husband and wife, he said, 'by separating them at periodical intervals, so that the delights of married life would be constantly reborn in the continual cycle of anticipation and fulfilment'.

The practice had more or less lapsed among British Jews. The United Synagogue, for example, which represented the broad stream of Anglo-Jewish Orthodoxy, did not have a single *mikvah* attached to any of its numerous synagogues, but every community of any size had a *mikvah* tucked away somewhere, usually in a lean-to shed abutting on a synagogue, for the benefit of the very Orthodox. In Dublin there was one which was used by perhaps one in a hundred women of child-bearing age. Jakobovits examined it shortly after his arrival and found that it was not only in a derelict and unsanitary state, but that it no longer met the specifications laid down in Jewish law. Professor Abrahamson did not question his opinion, but suggested that as very few women made use of the *mikvah*, its refurbishment was not a matter of particular urgency.

The Chief Rabbi countered that the very state of the *mikvah* deterred women from using it, that Judaism never laid stress on numbers, that if only one woman used the *mikvah* it was still necessary to keep it in good working order, and that it was in some ways more basic to the needs of a community than a synagogue. This more or less ended the argument, though in this instance, as in others, the Professor was more impressed by the strength of the Chief Rabbi's feelings than by the force of his logic.

Despite their occasional conflicts, the relationship between the two was almost invariably cordial and their differences were always amicably resolved, for Abrahamson was impressed with the sincerity, the perseverance and, not least, the achievements of the young man.

In Ireland, as elsewhere, Jakobovits made youth and education his first priorities. He helped to raise the standards of the Jewish primary school and was instrumental in laying the foundations of a new Jewish high school, Stratford College. He also organized classes in his own home and built up a corps of disciples – the Coppermans, the Jacksons, the Yudaikins, the Rifkins, the Kayes, the Segals, the Steinbergs, the Jasons, the Woolfsons and others – who added much to the religious life of Irish Jewry, though most of them eventually moved to Israel.

In the 1920s, an international scheme was broached to establish a world calendar, which would have rearranged the year into 364 days, with a blank day as the 365th. It was never taken up then, but it was launched anew in the 1950s and this time the reform lobby seemed to carry everything before it. As the Jewish Sabbath depends on an unbroken succession of six working days followed by the Day of Rest, the reform would have added immensely to the complexities of traditional Jewish life. All elements in the Jewish world, therefore, combined in a united campaign against it. Jakobovits prepared a special booklet on the subject and wrote:

The Jewish people have not only presented the Sabbath to mankind as one of its most priceless treasures, they have also fought and suffered, often alone among the nations of the world, for its survival and triumph. Jews will not now, after so many centuries of heroic loyalty to the Sabbath, agree to condemn their royal companion, 'Queen Sabbath', to the very wanderings in strange surroundings which they themselves have endured for so long.

He was, however, distressed to find that the main-line churches had no firm view on the matter, and he used his ecclesiastical connections in Ireland to intervene with the Vatican. He was not, of course, the only rabbi to be involved in the effort, but he attacked the issue with more than usual fervour and played a considerable part in the eventual success of the anti-reform lobby.

In 1958, towards the end of his stay in Dublin, the Jerusalem municipality announced plans to build a public swimming-pool open to both sexes. At once cries arose on every side against 'the desecration of the Holy City'. When a petition of protest was circulated in Britain, Jakobovits readily added his name to it. Britain's Chief Rabbi kept out of the fray, as did all the other rabbis belonging to the mainstream of British Orthodoxy, and those who had signed – with the exception of Jakobovits – were all from the extreme Right. The petition was couched in harsh, intemperate language and Jakobovits was criticized for lending his name to it, but he was unapologetic. In a long letter to the *Jewish Chronicle* he declared:

[The] moral revulsion against mixed bathing is founded on good Jewish authority. Because of such 'abominations', the Torah warned us: 'that the land vomit not you out also, when ye defile it, as it vomited out the nation that was before you'.

Jerusalem has a higher proportion of strictly Orthodox Jews than any other city in the world. Many of them have chosen to live within its hallowed confines just because they wanted to escape from the mundane and unholy influences found everywhere else. If some Israelis insist on disporting themselves semi-denude in promiscuous bathing, is the Mediterranean not big enough for them? Must they affront the moral feelings of tens of thousands of pious Jews in Jerusalem, and the sentiments of countless other Jews – and Christians – who cherish the supreme sanctity of the holiest city on earth?

The idea that mixed bathing was an 'abomination' which could imperil the very existence of the Jewish state was a bit much even for his most ardent supporters and where his letter was not greeted with derision, it occasioned surprise. There were Orthodox rabbis who held such views, but it was not thought that Jakobovits, with his Western education, reasonable manner, worldly appearance and young wife, was one of them.

His letters to the press tend, on the whole, to be well judged and well phrased. This particular letter was neither, but the episode highlighted a characteristic which was to become more pronounced as the years went on. He never retracts and never apologizes, and in defending an unpopular position is sometimes inclined to go over the top. Looking back now on what he wrote then, he allows that he would have expressed himself differently, but his opinions would have been the same. However, he regards the whole incident as too insignificant to be worth serious examination.

It was insignificant in the sense that the pool was eventually opened and the whole controversy was soon forgotten. It is, however, significant as a vivid and forthright expression of his views, for though he can be fairly liberal in some aspects of Jewish observance, he is an extreme puritan and will make no concessions on matters like modesty and chastity. The thought of half-naked men and women in close proximity to one another fills him not only with horror but alarm, and if asked to enlarge on the greatest evils of our age he would put sexual promiscuity very near the top.

During his years in Ireland issues like contraception and abortion were often in the headlines, but when he was invited to give his views on them he found that, while there was a profusion of Catholic material on medical ethics, there was nothing in the vernacular on the Jewish viewpoint; indeed, the very expression 'Jewish medical ethics' had never been used. He decided to make good the deficiency by writing a book on the subject himself. It began life as a PhD thesis at London University, which he prepared under the supervision of Dr Charles Singer, one of the outstanding authorities on the history of science (and a son of Rabbi Simeon Singer, editor and translator of the standard Anglo-Jewish prayer book).

Though Jakobovits had never shown any interest in becoming a doctor, there were numerous medical men among his antecedents; thus in turning to medical ethics, he was responding to what was almost a confluence of family tradition. If some doctors – like his brother Joseph – are rabbis *manqué*, he was, and is, a doctor *manqué*. He is excited by medico-ethical problems, likes the company of medical men and even enjoys the ambience of medical institutions. His work bears every mark of his enthusiasm. He received his doctorate in 1956 and his slightly abbreviated book, *Jewish Medical Ethics*, was published three years later. Though it has since been followed by other studies, it is still widely quoted and remains something of a classic.

Jakobovits also kept a close eye on events on the other side of the Irish Channel. His reputation as a preacher and lecturer was now well established and he was frequently invited to address seminars and public functions in England. He travelled back and forth by boat. One Thursday evening as he was about to leave Liverpool, the port became fog-bound and the ferry could not leave until the following day. By the time it reached Dun Loghaire, the Sabbath (which begins at dusk on Friday) had descended. He had warned his wife by radio-telephone that this might happen and had asked her to get the opinion of his colleague, Dayan Alony, on how to deal with the situation.

Different rabbis have made different rulings for such contingencies. Alony adopted the strictest of them and ruled that Jakobovits could not disembark on the Sabbath and that his wife could not embark; she therefore waited for him at the quay with bread, wine and other necessities under one arm, and their two-year-old son under the other. The child and the provisions were taken on board, while she, feeling a trifle sorry for herself, returned on foot to Dublin in the gathering darkness, a distance of some four miles. Father and son then remained together in their cabin, while the ship went back and forth across the Irish Sea; they finally disembarked on Sunday morning, a little poorer in pocket and a little the worse for wear.

With his magnum opus on Jewish medical ethics complete, and his academic reputation enhanced, Dr Jakobovits began to formulate his ideas on the main issues facing the Orthodox rabbinate. In November 1957, he presented them at the founding Conference of European Rabbis in Amsterdam.

Such conferences tend by their very nature to be eminently forgettable, and if the 1957 gathering was rather better remembered, it was largely because of his intervention, which provided the main talking point among delegates and which reverberated well beyond the conference hall. Many of the delegates had spoken of the challenge to Orthodoxy posed by the Reform movement, but Jakobovits felt that the main dangers lay in a rampant secularism.

'People these days look to rabbis for sermons and the discharge of purely ecclesiastical functions,' he complained, 'but for the ultimate realization of the Jewish purpose in history they no longer rely on us or on our Jewish teachings; for national leadership they look to politicians and other secularist guides.' He therefore suggested a six-point programme to make rabbis and rabbinical teaching seem more relevant.

The first was 'to restore to our people a sense of divine choice and mission in this world'. Not since biblical days, he said, have Jews witnessed 'such manifestations of Providence as in our times, yet never have our people been less conscious of the Jewish role in universal history than now'. He felt that it was necessary 'to demonstrate the relevance of Judaism to the contemporary world and its problems'. To this end he called on colleagues 'to limit the tendency to indecision in our rabbinic judgements in matters of both belief and practice' and to promote the growth of a religious intelligentsia. Rabbis, he argued, had to be aware of the currents of thought and scholarship around them. We lived in a scientific age, he said, and could not counter its arguments without understanding its language; if we cannot ensure that our scientific scholars will be religious, we must turn our religious scholars into scientists.

Finally he argued that rabbis and scholars tended by their very nature to be shy and retiring, so that the message they hoped to get across was often lost. He urged them to seek the help of professional communicators and to cultivate the art of public relations.

He was to follow through each of these points with greater or lesser success

in his subsequent years, though when it came to public relations he was to discover that his wife, with her warmth, gaiety and charm, as well as her strong convictions, was more adept at the art than many a professional.

There was, however, one point which he saved for the last, in which, as we shall see, he was rather less successful: his efforts to establish a working relationship, or at least a truce, with the Reform movement. Such a truce, he said, would be 'based on their acceptance of our exclusive jurisdiction in all matters affecting marriage and divorce' – even, he added, 'if this meant closing our eyes to their forms of synagogue services and religious education for the time being'. Such an agreement, he felt, 'could pave the way for their eventual return to our fold'.

His idea was based on the sort of pre-war, German *Gross Gemeinde*, which his father had served and in which Orthodox and Reform congregations formed part of the same communal set-up, with such matters as conversion and divorce vested in the hands of the former. It was, on the face of it, an attractive idea and had worked well in Germany, but then in Germany external pressures had made it necessary for Jews of every persuasion to work together. There was little prospect of it working in the rest of Europe, and none at all in England where the growth of Reform Judaism was due in good part to the unbending attitude of Orthodoxy on the very issues over which he sought exclusive jurisdiction.

He brought immense goodwill to all his efforts and he genuinely thought that he was holding out an olive branch to Reform Jews, when in fact he was virtually demanding unconditional surrender in the one area which concerned them most. When a little later a Reform leader called for greater unity between all sections of the Jewish people, he retorted with some heat: 'It appears that the spokesmen of "Progressive" Judaism now seek to become the apostles of Jewish "unity" in much the same way as the Communists have appropriated the plea for "peace" as their watchword.'

He had, possibly as a result of his Irish sojourn, acquired a certain pugnacity, a combativeness of style which did not quite go with his otherwise gentle nature, though his abrasive retort may also have been due to the pains of rejection. He was to adopt a more conciliatory style in later years, but it did not help either.

A Progressive synagogue (allied to the Liberal Jewish movement in the United Kingdom, which was a good deal more reformist than Reform) had been established in Dublin in 1946, and while its members were ready to acknowledge the Chief Rabbi as representing all Jews in Ireland, they were, understandably, pained by the growing hostility he showed towards them. Attempts to reach an understanding proved abortive, but there was no legacy of bitterness, and when he eventually left Dublin, the journal of the Progressive synagogue noted: 'Whatever our differences with Dr Jakobovits may have been, it would be churlish to deny his exceptional intelligence and brilliant academic qualifications, his unselfish interest in Jewish scholarship and the dignity he lent to the community as a whole.'

Lord and Lady Jakobovits tend to look back on their Irish years as among the happiest of their lives. They had a fairly pleasant home in pleasant surroundings among amiable people. They made many friends and were charmed by the beauty of Dublin itself and the Irish countryside. They had two sons and three daughters in rapid succession and, although Jakobovits often preached on the joys of family life, no claims he made for it were as convincing as the sight of his own family.

He had many demands on his time and his wife tried to guard him from the boisterous intrusions of his children, but the intrusions were welcome for they were his main form of relaxation.

Yet happy though he was, Dublin offered insufficient scope for his energies and ambitions. It was, to use his own words, 'off the beaten track', a marginal community removed from the mainstream of Jewish life. Air travel was not as commonplace then as it is now and the sea crossing — to a man who was not a natural sailor — gave an exaggerated impression of distance.

Moreover, his children were growing up, and proud as he was of the two Jewish day schools under his jurisdiction, neither of them offered the level of Jewish education he had received in the Adath schools in Germany. In other words, he wanted a more intense Jewish environment and he had his eyes on London or Manchester, but fate, aided and abetted by his sister Lotti, was to decree otherwise.

There was only a year between him and Lotti and they were almost like twins; as children they had been inseparable, which does not mean that they were alike in temperament. He, in some ways, is retiring; she was almost frantically purposeful and organized everyone and everything. She had married Fabian Schonfeld, a young London schoolmaster. At her behest they moved to New York and, again at her behest, he became a rabbi and a very successful one. She was determined to have her brother over in America with them and set in motion a chain of events which was to end the Irish phase of his career.

First came a lecture tour with an invitation to address the 1957 midwinter conference of the Rabbinical Council of America. Jakobovits had always wanted to see something of America and the classical way for a rabbi, academic or writer to see the country was to speak his way round it. The tour was organized by the Jewish Center Lecture Bureau of New York.

'Dr Jakobovits', it told subscribers, 'is known as an excellent speaker and the topics he deals with are of interest to all cross-sectional Jewish groups.' It expected that his visit would generate a great deal of attention. 'His fee', it added as a final inducement, 'is nominal.'

He was immediately inundated with invitations from all parts of North America. He was not only an overseas rabbi but a Chief Rabbi, and Chief Rabbi of Ireland at that, which gave him an extra cachet, especially in areas like New York with a large Irish population.

He was officially welcomed by Mayor Wagner of New York, by the Irish Ambassador in Washington, and by the American Irish Historical Society. Apart from his lectures to Jewish societies, he was also invited to lecture at New York University and Yale.

In some areas he was regarded with amused curiosity: 'Shure and begorra he came from the Emerald Isle', began a report in the *Toronto Telegram*, 'and despite the fact that his speech has no brogue (and his skullcap isn't even green) the Chief Rabbi of Eire proves himself an excellent ambassador of his country.' In the Savannah, Georgia, *Morning News*, he was referred to in all seriousness as 'Dr Jak O'Bovits': 'Dr O'Bovits', it reported, 'has been Chief Rabbi of Ireland for the past eight years. He is on a seven-weeks tour of this country and plans to leave Saturday for Ireland, to be home for St Patrick's Day, no doubt.' Even the *New York Herald Tribune*, in an otherwise serious interview, felt obliged to add: 'Rabbi Jakobovits confessed that he is no expert on leprechauns, and doesn't even know if they are kosher, but he knows a Jew in Dublin who manufactures figures of leprechauns.'

Jakobovits himself eventually fell in with the spirit of the occasion and would preface some of his lectures with an apology for not having a green beard. He was acquiring the one thing people did not expect of a German-born rabbi, a sense of humour. In the course of one lecture, he said:

An Irish Jew seemed to be regarded as something of a freak, like the fourth leaf of a shamrock, so to prove that there were Irish Jews a former Chief Rabbi of Ireland became Chief Rabbi of Israel. . . . Next, one of our sons, Robert Bricoe, was made Lord Mayor of Dublin, which is like electing a Catholic to be Mayor of Tel Aviv. Yet people still could not believe that there were Jews in Ireland, so they sent me out to convince you. And if that is not conclusive, something else is about to happen which should clinch it. This year St Patrick's Day and Purim are going to fall on the same day.

(Purim, one should perhaps add, is the nearest thing in the Jewish calendar to St Patrick's Day. One is positively encouraged to drink, and even get drunk, and it is an occasion for almost unrestrained merriment.)

He was not dogged by little green men all the way, though the publicity they excited was not unhelpful and he was received by large and appreciative audiences.

His lectures were not controversial. The most popular subject seems to have been Jewish life in Ireland, but he also spoke on medical ethics, religious observance and the challenge to Jewish leadership arising out of the emergence of Israel.

If occasion demanded it, he could speak off-the-cuff, but he always took his audience seriously and his lectures were – as they still are – the results of detailed research and careful preparation. He could still be a trifle portentous and orotund, but his delivery and choice of language had improved during his years in Dublin. He always spoke with authority, but he now also spoke with confidence. With his tall build and dignified bearing, he had an engaging, attractive presence.

Reports of his tour, occasionally in garbled form, appeared in the Irish press and knowing heads wagged knowingly. 'He'll never come back,' they said.

He began in the south and worked his way northwards to New York, where he arrived at the end of February 1957 in the middle of a blizzard and was greeted by an Irish expatriate called Hymie Ross.

Ross knew of a handful of Jews who had recently broken away from the Park East Synagogue on East 73rd Street and were building a new synagogue off Fifth Avenue on 62nd Street, an area of Manhattan which formed the heartland of the American Reform movement and which Orthodox Jews had regarded almost as forbidden territory. As an endeavour it verged on the presumptuous and they wanted a rabbi who was not the usual run-of-the-mill Yeshiva University product and who would make people sit up. Ross, who was aware of Jakobovits's reputation, felt instinctively that he was their man. He therefore introduced him to the leaders of the group, who included the novelist Herman Wouk, Hermann Merkin, a banker, Henry Hirsch, an industrialist, and other leading figures in the American Orthodox community.

They could not invite him to preach for their synagogue was still being built, and in any case they as yet had no congregation, but they questioned him closely on his attitudes. He was, as always, perfectly frank and his standard of Orthodoxy was rather higher than theirs, but that, they felt, was how it should be. They were impressed with the man, his appearance, demeanour, the strength of his convictions and scheme of priorities, and, as one of them put it later, 'he looked like a winner'. They also liked his wife – which is no small consideration in an American synagogue – and offered him the job.

The scope was tremendous and the challenge attractive, even if the salary – for New York – was not particularly high. (Jews tend to be more generous as individuals than they are as a group.) He was invited virtually to build a congregation from scratch. It was an offer he could not refuse. On 14 September 1958, he was installed as founder rabbi of the new synagogue and entered upon what was, in some respects, the most formative phase of his career.

He was thirty-seven.

New Jerusalem

AMERICA in the late 1950s was not perhaps as self-confident as it had been a decade or so earlier, but it was still the greatest of the great powers and New York, with its two million Jews, if not the capital of the world, was certainly the capital of the Jewish world. It hummed with energy and, for Jews at least, the American dream had been translated into something like reality. They had climbed high and were climbing higher, and one could find them everywhere, in banking, commerce, education, the city administration, the arts, publishing and the media. But, as Jakobovits soon discovered, there was little in their way of life to single them out as Jews and New York itself, though lively, colourful and warm, was not a hotbed of Judaism. On the contrary, it seemed to confirm all his warnings about the dangers of secularism. As he noted sadly in a letter to the *New York Times*, this secularism was largely promoted by the Jews:

There is no ethnic or religious community which does more to limit and reduce the sway of religion in this country than the Jews. They have played a major role in the foundation of such religious movements as Ethical Culture and other substitutes for religion. Jewish agitation and influence and financial backing have taken a leading part in driving God, prayer and the Bible – the greatest Jewish contribution to civilization – out of American schools. Jewish leaders and organizations are the most vociferous in objecting to any manifestation of religion in America's public life.

They had, he suggested, driven God into a ghetto.

He had met secular Jews before, but in Germany they had tended to distance themselves from their community by a conscious act of renunciation. In New York, it was a matter of cheerful drift. They had gradually jettisoned so many observances that they had nothing left to renounce. Yet many of them still thought of themselves as Jews and took pride in their Jewishness. Some were active in the Zionist movement and gave large sums of money to Israel or to innumerable Jewish charities, but there was nothing otherwise in their way of life to distinguish them from the non-Jew, and that, in the main, was how they liked it. They were not Americans of the Jewish persuasion, for they had none; they were Americans who happened to be Jews.

In Europe, unless one made a positive effort to maintain one's Jewish identity, one vanished from all Jewish reckoning, but in New York Jews were in a culture which was partly of their own making. They may have only formed a fourth of the city's population, but they provided its dominant tone. One did not have to make a special effort to stay Jewish in New York any more than one had to make an effort to do so in Tel Aviv.

But because the city was so predominantly pagan and secular, one did have to make a particularly strenuous effort to stay Orthodox and, in the late 1950s, comparatively few Jews were inclined to do so; where Jews belonged to a synagogue at all it was likely to be a Reform or Conservative synagogue. Orthodoxy in those days was not in the big league and in the more fashionable areas of Manhattan it hardly existed at all.

It is difficult to compare American institutions to British ones, especially where they bear the same or similar names, for while the American Reform movement is a good deal more reformist than the British one, the Conservative movement is not quite as conservative as its name implies, for though it venerates Jewish tradition it finds some traditions more venerable than others. In Orthodox synagogues, for example, the sexes are segregated, as they were in the Temple, but in Conservative synagogues they sit together. Few Orthodox synagogues in America have a microphone, while no Conservative synagogue is without one. Mixed choirs are now unknown in Orthodox synagogues, but they are commonplace in Conservative ones.

As if to complicate matters, the Conservative movement as a whole is known as the United Synagogues of America, while the United Synagogue in Britain used to be spoken of as the home of 'progressive conservatism'. The movement is, in fact, a loose association of synagogues, some of which would not feel out of place in the Reform movement, while others are almost Orthodox, but it has one thing in common with the Reform movement in that both are regarded as non-kosher by the Orthodox.

Not that the Orthodox themselves are, or were, all of a piece, but Orthodoxy in general was for many years associated with recent immigrants, greenhorns, people who did not know the language of their new homeland or understand its ways. Where they adapted themselves to American life, they usually became less Orthodox; if they did not, their children almost inevitably did. The few people one found in Orthodox synagogues tended to be the elderly, the poor, the broken, the lame, those who somehow had not made it and never would, and the merely eccentric.

In the late 1930s, however, they had been reinforced by an influx of refugees

49

from Germany and Eastern Europe, whose Orthodoxy was of a stern, lasting quality; they, in turn, were joined in the immediate post-war years by an influx of Hassidim, mostly from Hungary, so that by the late 1950s formidable enclaves of Orthodoxy were to be found in and around New York, ranging in character from the ultra-Orthodox to the so-called 'modern Orthodox'.

What distinguished the latter from the former was that its rabbis not only had a degree in secular studies, but respected secular learning. Moreover, while having their eyes on the next world, they did not forsake this one and, indeed, found it a fairly tolerable place. They watched television and sometimes appeared on it, listened to the radio, read the daily press and contributed to it, and kept in touch with events even to the point of knowing baseball scores and league tables. It was a clean-shaven, plain-clothed, self-confident, urbane Orthodoxy, which, in a way, found its apotheosis in the Fifth Avenue Synagogue.

The part of Fifth Avenue flanking the southern stretches of Central Park had long been dominated by the massive basilica of Temple Emanu-El, the cathedral synagogue of the Reform movement, an assertion of its power and influence, and one of the most impressive ecclesiastical edifices in New York. For an Orthodox synagogue, albeit of compact size and modest proportion, to open in its shadow was almost a *chutzpah*.

As we have seen, it began as most synagogues begin, as a breakaway from another synagogue. Its moving spirit was Henry Hirsch, an industrialist who had built up a fortune from the manufacture of domestic ovens and who had for some years been a leading member of the Park East Synagogue off Park Avenue. In 1957, the rabbi of the synagogue allowed women to sit downstairs, not actually beside their menfolk as in Conservative synagogues, but on the same level as them, which to Hirsch was almost a wilful act of desecration. He argued with the rabbi, but did not have his way; as he was used to having his way, the exchange caused him some distress, and finally his wife said: 'Why don't you set up your own synagogue in the neighbourhood? You can afford it.' He did just that. He brought together other like-minded individuals, underwrote the $2 million loan necessary to acquire a site, and the Fifth Avenue Synagogue was in business.

When Jakobovits was first invited to meet its members they consisted of eleven individuals, but he was as impressed by their ambition as they were impressed by his manner. By the time he assumed office, their number had grown to over one hundred. They doubled within a matter of months, and within a year or two Fifth Avenue was regarded as one of the foremost Orthodox synagogues in America.

Rabbi Shulman of the St John's Wood Synagogue, London, who served for a time as rabbi in Fifth Avenue, ascribed this development to Jakobovits. 'He put it on the map,' he said, which is also the view of many of its members.

Jakobovits himself suggests several causes. One was American-Jewish snobbery, which seems to be even more pronounced than the Anglo-Jewish variety. 'The address itself had an appeal,' he said. 'People didn't associate our type of synagogue with the Upper East Side. It made Orthodoxy fashionable.'

The renown of the founding fathers, most of them famous names in industry and commerce, was another factor. It suggested that Orthodoxy not only offered rewards on-high, but had its compensations in the here and now. 'And then,' said Jakobovits, 'there was my curiosity value, not only as a former Chief Rabbi, but as a former Chief Rabbi of Ireland.'

Yet if people came to gape, they remained to pray, and as the years passed Jakobovits enhanced both his own reputation and that of his congregation. One grew with the other. At first, however, his move to New York seemed something of a comedown. Where he had been Chief Rabbi, he was now plain rabbi; and where he had ministered to the needs of over five thousand souls, he now had a congregation of only two hundred families.

New York was also not an ideal place to bring up a young family. He gave up a large, if somewhat dowdy, home on Dublin's South Circular Road for an elegant and spacious flat — in fact, two flats, for they were not knocked into one until after he left New York — on East 62nd Street, but his children did not enjoy the same freedom of movement. There were few children of their age in the neighbourhood. They had no garden to play in, and Central Park, though nearby, was not considered particularly safe even in the late 1950s; on Saturdays and festivals especially, they tended to be immured within their apartment block.

One of the reasons they had left Dublin was that New York offered a better choice of Jewish day schools. However, the boys, as they grew older, had to cross New York to attend a yeshiva high school in Queens, and while the Manhattan Jewish Day School, which the girls attended, was less distant, both were very expensive, especially compared to Dublin where the Jewish schools, being state supported, were virtually free.

Ireland, moreover, had close associations with the highly organized and closely structured Anglo-Jewish community, with its Chief Rabbinate and rabbinical court, its central board of Jewish education, its carefully supervised kosher foods and its synagogal burial societies. In America, such things were generally left to private enterprise, and there was a chaos of competing rabbinical boards, rabbinical courts, rabbinical supervisors and rabbinical odd-job men, some more reliable than others, some downright corrupt, and all offering their services for a fee.

But Dublin too had had its drawbacks. As Chief Rabbi Jakobovits had to function as a sort of arbitrator, peace-maker and court of last resort, so that whenever some synagogue functionary quarrelled with his wardens — a not infrequent occurrence — or even where they quarrelled among themselves, the matter came to him for settlement. Whatever his verdict, he could be assured of the enmity of one party or the other, and sometimes both. There were even times when he was called on to make peace between husband and wife. If he attended the funeral of a close friend, his failure to pay his last respects to anyone else might be construed as an act of enmity, so in the end he went to everyone's funeral and every house of mourning. His presence was also expected at happier occasions such as circumcisions or Barmitzvahs, while there seemed to be a general belief that any Jewish marriage not blessed by the Chief Rabbi in person was not fully consummated.

Jakobovits had no place of worship which was uniquely his own and would visit the six or seven different synagogues in Dublin on different occasions, and he was watched by each like a hawk in case he should appear to favour one congregation above another.

There were fewer such demands on his time or his patience in New York and at first, rather uncharacteristically, he was content to take a back seat, as he wrote in *Journal of a Rabbi*:

I never shared the predilection of the American rabbinate for turning sermons into political commentaries or for aspiring to a press mention on the front page of the *New York Times*. I was attracted neither to holding office in the Rabbinical Council of America, to which I belonged, nor to participating in the high politics of the New York Board of Rabbis, to which I did not belong....

To which one must add that while the former was composed of Orthodox rabbis, the latter also included Reform rabbis. He tended to limit his contacts with Reform Jewry, though he did sometimes participate in adult education programmes organized by Reform congregations. He was also active in the Religious Commission of the Federation of Jewish Philanthropies, which transcended religious divisions and which brought him into frequent contact with non-Orthodox colleagues.

He became a bemused observer of American-Jewish life and was struck by the intense patriotism of the American Jew. When he took his seat by the Ark in his own synagogue, for example, he found himself flanked by both the American and Israeli flags, as if for some lying-in-state, and he put it to his honorary officers that while such flags were all right for special occasions, they had no place in synagogue as a permanent fixture. They were not happy with his opinion and argued that it was a well-established local custom, but

Jakobovits held his ground and had his way, which was no mean achievement among tycoons used to having theirs.

He was amused to receive a new translation of the Passover liturgy by a Conservative rabbi, with a familiar passage calling on the Almighty to 'break the yoke of oppression from off our necks and may He lead us upright into our Land' changed to read 'may He lead the homeless of our people in dignity to our Homeland'. In other words, Israel was for homeless Jews, but not for Americans.

Once while addressing an Orthodox Synagogue convention in the Midwest, he innocently referred to American Jews as 'being in exile'; he was roundly rebuked for doing so. To speak in such terms, he was told, was an affront to American Jewry – and this from people who prayed thrice daily to be returned to Zion.

He could never quite reconcile himself to the fact that Zionism in America meant philanthropy and not personal commitment. In Ireland, for example, many Zionists actually settled in Israel, and even those that didn't felt that they should. Few American Jews were nagged by such feelings, or, as he put it: 'Israel has still not made any difference to the self-identification of American Jews, however traditional their daily discipline of life, and to challenge their philosophy of national complacency was a cause of censure.'

Where other Jews had settled in established societies, American Jews, even if their ancestors were not on the *Mayflower*, had arrived sufficiently early and in sufficient numbers to affect the character of their new homeland. Thus, while Jewish immigrants in England, for example, had to adapt themselves to a new culture, American Jews lived in one which, for better or worse, was partly of their own making. As a result, they took an almost proprietorial pride in its achievements and greatness, yet they seemed to be eternally on guard, as if everything they had attained was under threat. Jakobovits felt that their concern over the separation between church and state amounted almost to an obsession.

Thus, when it was suggested that the Federal Government should support parochial schools, there was an immediate outcry from almost every major Jewish organization in America. An immense amount of Jewish money and effort was spent on countering the measure, which was eventually blocked in the Supreme Court by a campaign mainly financed by Jews.

Jakobovits watched the campaign with bewilderment and dismay. He wrote to the *New York Times*:

Freedom cannot be maintained without religion, just as the brotherhood of man requires the Fatherhood of God. A generation of heathen hedonists, worshipping the idols of happiness and material success, will be unable to evoke the Herculean strength necessary to contain the mighty tide of godlessness in the defence of liberty. Furthermore, even statistics show that only children reared in a wholesome religious atmosphere are likely to develop the maximum immunity to the scourges of juvenile delinquency corroding our society and undermining its security.

'The wall of separation' between state and church must be constructed with ample gateways to prevent the divorce of education from religion if that wall is not to lay siege to our civilization and starve it to death.

A great many Jewish schools had sprung up since the war, some of which were in financial difficulties, and they would, of course, have benefited from state help. Jakobovits was not at all worried by the possibility that the precedent of federal funds for church schools could lead to the Christianization of America, for he believed that the more Christian America became, the more Jewish its Jews would remain. He liked to quote the medieval adage: '*Wie es christelt sich, so judelt's sich*', which, roughly translated, means that devout Christians make for devout Jews. The reverse was also, of course, true, and he felt that a Christian society posed less of a threat to Jewish survival than a godless one. Most Jews, he pointed out, were lost not to Christianity but to paganism, and he added in *Journal of a Rabbi*:

Schools which do not provide religious training are career factories, turning out morally indifferent robots; they fail in their principal task to produce upright, idealistic and consecrated citizens of sturdy moral fibre. 'The beginning of wisdom is fear of the Lord', and the foundation of education is character-training based on religious virtues and convictions.

This, as he said himself, was a minority view, but Jews had always been in the minority and he did not, as a rule, worry about finding himself in a minority among Jews. One even suspects that he sometimes revelled in it, though he did not care for gratuitous involvement in public controversies.

He was aware that on this particular issue, however, his arguments might be dismissed as those of a newcomer who did not understand America, which was perhaps the case, for American Jews, whose fathers and grandfathers had fled from religious persecution in Europe, ascribed their liberties to the division between church and state. He was familiar with these arguments and gave them due weight, but nevertheless felt that in going to such extremes in defending their liberties, American Jews were hazarding their Jewishness. In fact, they were applying the same principles that Orthodoxy has always used in defending tradition.

For all the controversies which sometimes surrounded him, his American years were exceedingly happy. The disadvantage of serving a small congregation is that it can rarely afford to pay a large salary, but that was not a handicap from which Fifth Avenue suffered (which does not mean that he was paid extravagantly, but then he did not have extravagant tastes or expectations). He was able to get to know each and every one of his congregants while they, in turn, came to regard him as a cherished counsellor and friend, even though, in most instances, he was young enough to be their son.

In London and Dublin, his parishioners may have believed in Orthodoxy but, in the main, they did not practise it. In New York, practice was more attuned to belief, if only because those who found Orthodoxy too demanding could always resort to a Conservative synagogue.

The Fifth Avenue Synagogue is situated in one of the most expensive areas of Manhattan and its members did not, as a rule, travel on the Sabbath, so that anyone within walking distance had to be at least reasonably affluent, if not downright rich. By the time people had acquired the means to afford the rents they were usually well into their fifties or sixties, while their rabbi was only in his thirties, yet in a way Jakobovits was never young, for if he has displayed all the energies and zeal of youth even in middle age, he had all the *gravitas* of age even in his youth. It was something his wife noticed at their first encounter. She did not find it entirely pleasing, but it went with his office and added to his authority.

Many of his congregants were used to giving orders and having their way, but they did not throw their weight around in synagogue, for they accepted that in the house of God the rabbi was king. Nor did they attempt to interfere with his extra-mural utterances, even where they disagreed with them.

As the years passed he acquired some of the hard-hitting attitudes of the prophet Amos. He praised some aspects of American-Jewish life, but did not hesitate to castigate others in terms which, if uttered by a gentile, would have had every Jewish organization up in arms, as, for example, when he expressed his shame that American Jews 'provide the most notorious purveyors of smut and pornography vulgarizing the country and demoralizing countless citizens'.

Nor did he hesitate to speak his mind on his numerous lecture tours. His favourite theme was 'the vanishing Jew' and, in particular, vanishing American Jews, and he complained that not only were they lapsing from Jewish life, but that they were even failing to replace themselves. They were disposed to enjoy the pleasures of sex (which he did not berate) without facing up to their corresponding responsibilities. Millions of souls, he repeatedly claimed, were being lost to the Jewish people through a persistently low Jewish birthrate.

American Jews, he felt, were sufficiently secure to face a few home truths, which was perhaps not quite the case, but his own congregation, certainly, was prepared to accept strictures from him which they would not have taken from anyone else.

Amelie Jakobovits had several brothers and sisters living in Brooklyn, where they were eventually joined by her parents, while Jakobovits had two brothers – George and Solomon – in Canada, and his sister Lotti in New York.

She lived in Kew Gardens Hills and was thus not exactly a neighbour, but the fact that she was within easy reach added immensely to the pleasures of his stay, for though he had many friends, he had few intimates – which is still the case – and they were frequently on the phone to one another and met at every opportunity. She had helped them to move, to settle in and to find schools for the children, and, with all the many calls on her time as the wife of an eminent rabbi, she was always on hand to help them cope with the exigencies of American life. She seemed to have time for everyone, to say nothing of every cause. Whenever her friends were faced with a problem, the usual refrain was 'leave it to Lotti'. She was attractive, but formidable, a whirring dynamo of a woman, and her very pace of life, her very hurry to get things done, suggested an instinctive awareness that she did not have much time in which to do them, which was sadly the case. Early in 1959 she was found to be suffering from leukaemia and died a few months later. She was thirty-six.

It was a tragedy from which her brother was slow to recover. In a tribute to her memory, he said:

Words of consolation are meaningless. When I awoke from a dazed bout of slumber on the first morning following her passing, I could not understand how the sun could rise again, how the world around us could look bright and sunny when there was so much darkness within us. But as the brother who was closest to her in age and nearest to her throughout her life ... I know that she would, with all the certainty and enthusiasm of which she was capable, endorse the confident reassurance of Isaiah which the great prophet of comfort expresses: 'Your sun shall no more go down, neither shall your moon withdraw itself, for the Lord shall be your everlasting light and the days of your mourning shall be ended.'

This was no mere rhetoric. He drew genuine reassurance from such utterances and was able to offer reassurance to others when faced with similar tragedies.

He rarely dabbled in theology, but on Yom Kippur 1962 he delivered what was for him a lengthy sermon on the Jewish concept of the after-life, which, given the age of his congregants, must have been of more than academic interest. He did not dwell on the possibilities of bodily resurrection but saw the hereafter as a purely spiritual state, or, as the Talmud described it, a world in which 'there is no eating, no drinking, no trading, no sensual pleasures; but the righteous sit, with their crowns adorning their heads, and enjoy the splendour of the divine presence'.

It was, he agreed, a state which could appeal only to those trained in this world through 'the supreme fascination of religious studies', to be sensitive to purely spiritual delights, which suggested that the hereafter, as traditionally envisaged, was a fairly exclusive place. But he also believed that everyone could aspire to immortality through some act which outlives them – writing a book, composing a song, uttering a thought or endowing a hospital – for if not everyone is endowed with creative instincts, all are capable of charity and of some immortal deed.

Judaism is not an ascetic faith and neither Jakobovits nor his wife is averse to material comforts. His salary, if high by Dublin standards, did not in fact have the same purchasing power, but he was able to supplement his income with lecture tours and they enjoyed something like affluence. Mrs Jakobovits could occasionally indulge her expensive taste in clothing and jewellery, and take her place among the elegant matrons of the Upper East Side, though with a touch of French chic which was entirely her own.

Her husband's tastes were more frugal. He had few pleasures outside his work or his family, but he liked to travel and when he took a holiday he would make for the hills and open country. In 1965, he hired a trailer and, together with his wife and their five children (a sixth was to be born in the following year), toured the western states. He was overwhelmed by the grandeur of the scenery and the natural wonders he found on every side, and the journey provided him with a theme for a cycle of five sermons which he gave during the High Holy Days a few months later.

He noted that although there were some six million Jews in America, they encountered none on the mountain trails and the desert roads which they explored. In his sermon he said:

Jews today are the most urbanized people on earth, and as a result many of us have become divorced from nature and insensitive to its thrills and quiet inspiration. Most Jews somehow seem to prefer the loud clanging of a dance orchestra to the mystic eloquence of a rushing mountain stream or the sweet, soothing music of a humming bird.

It was an improbable theme for a High Holy Day sermon, especially in an Orthodox synagogue, for Orthodoxy is rarely concerned with the aesthetics of nature. If anything it regards the nature lover as something of a pagan, and in this sense, and in this alone, Jakobovits goes against the main trend in Jewish tradition. He used the call of the wild as a plea to return to simpler lives and simple truths, and complained:

We live artificial, stilted lives, with our horizons narrowed and our vision limited by the very walls our civilization has erected. We draw the air we breathe from air-conditioners, the food we eat from cans and jars, the knowledge we possess from newspapers and magazines, the laughter we enjoy from well-rehearsed professionals....

Even if the points he made were sometimes predictable, his approach was not, and his language sometimes rose to the level of poetry.

He gave three of his sermons on Yom Kippur alone, which may seem like an ordeal, but they were all carefully considered, elegantly couched and short, with the final one lasting a mere five minutes. Uncommonly for a clergyman he not only knew how to start, but when to stop.

He found time to condense his thesis on Jewish medical ethics – which had run to over 400 pages – for general publication and it appeared in 1959 to considerable acclaim. The subject, given the pace of medical and surgical innovations, was constantly expanding and he frequently visited medical schools and universities and consulted different authorities to update his knowledge. He even attended an autopsy to familiarize himself at first hand with an operation which has been the subject of innumerable rabbinic responsa.

Some of the issues he touched on, such as birth control, abortion, artificial insemination and transplants, were of fairly universal interest; others, such as the attitude to autopsies or the problems of Sabbath observance, affected only the observant Jew. The saving of life has absolute priority over everything else in Jewish law, but not every issue facing a doctor is a matter of life and death, and he published a practical guide, the *Jewish Hospital Compendium*, which has since gone into many editions. He also lectured frequently on the subject.

He was not particularly easy on the ear. His voice has since mellowed, but in those days it had a harsh, grating edge and, when excited, it could rise to a scream; but as he got excited he could be exciting, and his appeal lay in the fact that he had something to say and said it with conviction, vigour and, occasionally, as when berating secularism or the Reform movement, with an angry vehemence. His stately bearing and impressive appearance also helped and, although he had planned to take a back seat in communal life, he found himself pushed to the fore almost in spite of himself.

He was thus inevitably in demand as a speaker at charity functions, or, as he described them, 'a continual sequence of breakfasts and dinners together with arm-twisting and stomach-filling exercises, usually culminating in the wholesale award of plaques and other honorific gestures'.

He found, as he still does, such occasions slightly demeaning, but unavoidable. The truly generous may be happy to receive their reward in the hereafter, but in America people liked to have their generosity acknowledged in the here and now, loudly, publicly and repeatedly; and, apart from anything else, it was a means of inducing the non-generous to part with the occasional dollar.

There is no Chief Rabbinate or Chief Rabbi in America. Every rabbi is king in his own parish and any eminence he may enjoy above his colleagues derives not from any title or office he may hold, but from his own standing as a teacher, preacher or lecturer and as a man, and, to a lesser extent, from the standing of his congregation.

The Fifth Avenue Synagogue was new and small, but it was full of famous names and, although it is not one of the glories of American architecture — the candle-light theme of its façade and interior is particularly crude — it smacks of expensiveness and is in some respects an exclusive praying club. Anyone can enter therein to pray, but it is easier for a camel to pass through the eye of a needle than for a poor man to become a member. In a sense, Jakobovits had become a sort of chaplain to Wall Street, all of which added to his prestige.

He was also lucky in his timing. In America in the late 1950s, there was a passion for everything English — English clothes, English cars, English personnel. English writers and poets could attract wide audiences in the course of an American tour, and this was true also of English rabbis. Jakobovits may not have seemed or sounded particularly English in England, or even in Ireland, but he was English enough for America, and the fact that he had also been Chief Rabbi of Ireland was certainly no disadvantage, for among those unfamiliar with Irish history, the Irish were but folksy Englishmen.

Every month seemed to yield some new scientific discovery giving doctors new controls on the process of reproduction and even on the continuity of life itself and raising new questions of medical ethics. Jakobovits's pioneering work in this field meant that he was frequently in demand for comments not only in the popular media, but in learned assemblies, all of which added to his standing.

He was fortunate in another and more important respect. After decades of almost unbroken religious decline, American Jewry in the late 1950s and early 1960s witnessed the beginnings of a religious revival, of which the erection of the Fifth Avenue Synagogue was in itself a symptom and which has since continued at an accelerated pace. Terms such as heritage and ethnicity had not yet become the clichés they are now, but one sensed a growing interest in things Jewish even among gentiles. This could, for example, be seen in the extraordinary success of *Fiddler on the Roof*. 'Speak English, think Yiddish' was a slogan of the day, and there was hardly a major publishing house without a major Jewish writer — sometimes a whole school of them — on its list, and they were not merely writers who happened to be Jews. Herman Wouk's *This is My God*, a deeply felt affirmation of Orthodoxy, published in 1959, became a best-seller. Isaac Bashevis Singer, hitherto known only among Yiddishists, began to enjoy national acclaim. Elie Wiesel, who worships regularly in the Fifth Avenue Synagogue, acquired a cult following. Most American Jews had always held membership in a place of worship, if only as part of their commitment to the American way of life, which did not mean that they were regular worshippers. There was a synagogue building boom which became known as 'the edifice complex', but it was now often accompanied by genuine religious commitment.

The growth of colour consciousness, while exacerbating racial tensions in parts of New York, helped to revive Jewish consciousness. The decline in the public (i.e. state) school system compelled many parents, who might not otherwise have been particularly concerned about Jewish education, to dig deeply into their pockets and establish private Jewish schools, so that by 1960 there was hardly a Jewish community of any size in the United States which did not have its own Jewish day school.

And finally, America was enjoying a prosperity undreamt of in earlier generations, and yet it brought no sense of fulfilment. People, and especially young people, found that there was something still missing in their lives. Some turned to drugs, or to Scientology, or to Zen Buddhism; others, in desperation, even returned to Judaism.

Orthodoxy – often ultra-Orthodoxy – was the main beneficiary of these trends. Where it had been associated with poverty and ignorance, it now spread to the informed, the learned, the opulent, which does not mean that it came without effort. Jakobovits and his congregation were not the passive beneficiaries of an inevitable trend; it only began to seem inevitable after they harnessed it. He said:

Our first and foremost task was to be a corporate witness testifying that traditional Judaism is very much alive, and confounding the prophets of doom who forecast long ago that Orthodoxy could no longer survive in America, certainly not amid the affluence, elegance and modernity of an area as fashionable as ours.... No one anywhere will ever again be able to say that strict Orthodoxy is incompatible with modern life, that our unadulterated traditions are only for foreigners and old-fashioned people, that you cannot reach the top of the economic ladder and still remain faithful to all our ancient convictions and practices.

Jakobovits can be carried away by his own rhetoric, as he was in this instance, and he can sometimes sound smug and complacent, but the pride he took in the achievements of his own congregation was not entirely misplaced.

In the new atmosphere the sort of message which he had always preached and which, in the past, had few hearers, now had a readier appeal, and as the years passed he came near to seeing the fulfilment, at least in New York, of a good part of the six-point programme he had laid down at the Amsterdam Conference of European Rabbis in 1957.

Where secularism had been triumphant, it was now beginning to retreat and more attention was being given to traditional Jewish teaching, Jewish teachers and Jewish values.

Jakobovits had called for the emergence of a religious intelligentsia, and he found one not only in his own congregation but in many of the universities and medical schools which he was invited to address, though it was perhaps most striking in the phenomenal growth of the Yeshiva University, an academic establishment of high repute based on Orthodox foundations. In a way it was to America what Hildesheimer's had been to Germany, except that, unlike the latter, it was also involved in secular studies and included not only a women's college but a large medical school.

He had meagre hopes of a rapprochement with the Reform movement for, as he observed on his return from his first American lecture tour: '... it looks as if the fragmentation of Jewish religious life in the New World is approaching the stage when we have to think in terms of different Jewish denominations of the Christian pattern'.

The Orthodox, Conservative and Reform made common cause on matters of common interest, such as anti-Semitism, Israel and social problems; otherwise, they tended to remain apart. However, as Jakobovits discovered, there was fragmentation even within the Orthodox camp. Where the Reform and Conservative movements each had one rabbinical association, Orthodoxy had three, and the modern Orthodoxy which he represented was often regarded by the ultra-Orthodox with the same disapproval as that with which he viewed the Reform.

For the first and, perhaps, the only time in his life he became part of a set. It revolved round the charismatic figure of Rabbi Joseph Dov Soloveitchick, professor of Talmud at the Yeshiva University, and included Emmanuel Rackman, who was to succeed Jakobovits as rabbi of the Fifth Avenue Synagogue and was until recently head of Bar Ilan University, and Norman Lamm, who is now head of the Yeshiva University. They did not quite constitute a school, but they were high-minded and like-minded and were thought of as the principal proponents of modern Orthodoxy. Their Orthodoxy was unquestioned but their modernity was rather less so. They did not doubt the authority of the written or oral law, nor did they strive unduly to adapt them to modern conditions, but unlike their ultra-Orthodox colleagues, they did not believe that the preservation of Judaism called for a withdrawal from this world. On the contrary, they felt that such a withdrawal was an abdication of moral responsibility. They also felt that while Judaism had a lot to teach, it also had something to learn, and there were positive benefits to be had from being part of an open society.

Jakobovits was on particularly close terms with Lamm, six years his junior, a slight, mercurial figure with a sharp but capacious mind, who, to an extent, was his guide to American Jewry. If alike in outlook, they were unalike in temperament. Jakobovits may not believe that he can solve the problems of the world, but he feels compelled to try; Lamm suffers from no such compulsions. The former thinks in terms of grand strategies, while the latter is inclined to approach problems on an ad hoc basis; but both are moved by a sense of mission and an affinity developed between them which Jakobovits was to share with few other colleagues and which is still intact.

There was a lift in the Fifth Avenue Synagogue which the truly Orthodox could not use on the Sabbath and festivals because it involved the use of electric switches. Jakobovits got round the difficulty by working with engineers on the design of a 'Sabbath elevator', whose movements were fixed by a pre-set time switch and which stopped and started automatically at the required floor.

It so happened that a controversy was raging in England at the time about microphones in Orthodox synagogues and the *Jewish Chronicle* suggested that if a lift in a perfectly Orthodox synagogue was permissible on the Sabbath, microphones should also be permitted. What followed may seem trivial to those not familiar with Orthodox Judaism, but, in a sense, it is what Orthodoxy is about. It also has some bearing on Jakobovits's attitude to larger issues. In a reply to the *Jewish Chronicle*, he wrote:

The analogy between the operation of our automatic elevator and the use of a microphone is misleading. The whole point of our specially constructed elevator control system ... is to avoid any human interference with the electric current on the Sabbath. In the case of a microphone, however, the impact of the human voice on the instrument directly affects the current and possibly ignites tiny sparks on the Sabbath. It is mainly because of this latter consideration that most Orthodox rabbis here and everywhere else are opposed to the innovation.

The use of a microphone, he felt, would, apart from the technicalities involved, also infringe the spirit of the law, which wants communication in the synagogue to be natural, avoiding the artificiality of life outside.

The *Jewish Chronicle* was thereupon inundated with letters from electronic engineers pointing out the fallacy of his argument, and Robert Rosenfelder, a consulting engineer and a member of an ultra-Orthodox London congregation, wrote to him privately:

Contrary to what you write ... there *is*, from the technical point of view, an analogy between the elevator control and the p.a. [public address] system. In both cases, the current is directly being changed by the people using it. Loading the elevator car will increase the motor current almost proportionally to the number of people occupying it and, consequently too, the carbon brushes (if any) at the motor or generator will be caused to spark more extensively. The impact of the voice of the speaker will also cause ... tiny electrical changes in the transmitter system – not current but voltage changes – which eventually appear ... as small current variations to be converted again into sound by the loudspeaker.

Also ... modern public address systems cannot cause 'tiny sparks', as generally nowadays, instead of the obsolete carbon microphones, the dynamic transmitters are used....

Whilst therefore the p.a. systems are practically free from sparking, the elevator systems are inherently not!

Faced with such expertise, Jakobovits agreed that

the sparking argument, mentioned as a principal consideration in the earlier rabbinical responsa, could only apply to carbon microphones, now obsolete. This would certainly reduce, but not necessarily eliminate, the objections to using a microphone on the Sabbath. However, my main contention was, and is, that the case of microphones is not analagous to our automatic elevator ... because the former are activated directly by use on the Sabbath, whereas the latter is not.

No open-minded person reading the correspondence – especially if he is unfamiliar with the intricacies of Jewish law and electrical engineering – could feel that the rabbi had got the better of the argument. To which one must add that not many rabbis get involved in such arguments in the press, but as he had said in Amsterdam, rabbis have a duty to make Jewish law intelligible to laymen, even where they may not succeed in making them acceptable.

There are many leading rabbis who will allow neither a microphone nor a lift to be used on the Sabbath. In fact, Jakobovits, while still opposed to microphones, was never entirely happy about Sabbath elevators (even though his model has since been copied by numerous hospitals, hotels and apartment blocks in Israel). He himself has never even used the Sabbath elevator built to his own specifications in his own synagogue, but he finds the device less objectionable than the resort to non-Jewish lift operators, which brings one to a larger problem.

New York's Upper East Side is not an area of town-houses. Jakobovits lived on the first floor of an apartment block so he was all right. However, the overwhelming majority of his congregants lived ten, twenty and thirty storeys up, and they would have been prisoners in their apartments every Sabbath and festival if they did not use lifts. And, of course, they did use them, but with the help of operators. Jakobovits therefore ministers to a congregation which prided itself on its Orthodoxy, but which knowingly and wilfully desecrated the Sabbath, albeit on a rather minor scale. It could even be argued that by encouraging them to come to synagogue, he was a party to their transgressions, to which he might reply, may that be the worst sin they commit.

But another aspect of the microphone issue also comes into play. Few people regard it as a misfortune if they can't hear their rabbi preach on the Sabbath, and some may regard it as a blessing, so that the ban on microphones in synagogues is no great handicap. However, microphones are also used in the home in the form of intercoms. In the more expensive areas of New York, one cannot just drop in on friends. One approaches a porter or security guard, who phones up to one's host and, even on the Sabbath, the host, or his servant, will answer, which means a further desecration, yet Jakobovits has never seriously addressed himself to this problem either. Emmanuel Rackman agrees that he and his colleagues have been rather remiss in this matter, but Jakobovits himself is less apologetic. He does not dismiss any Jewish observance as insignificant, but he does believe that some issues are more urgent than others. No rabbi can confront every problem in Jewish life, and microphones have a low place in his priorities.

He is on the editorial board of *Tradition*, a learned quarterly publication which describes itself as 'a journal of Orthodox Jewish thought', and, while in New York, he contributed a regular column on contemporary Jewish law as interpreted by leading sages of the day.

Every qualified Orthodox rabbi is, in theory, equal to any other and has the same right as any other to interpret the *halacha* (Jewish law), but in practice he will defer on most issues to the opinion of colleagues who have made a lifetime's study of the matter, and they will rarely, if ever, go out on a limb. Any rabbi prepared to venture an opinion which does not fit in with the prevailing consensus needs not only extraordinary scholarship, but more than ordinary confidence and courage, to say nothing of *chutzpah*, and, through his very readiness to go it alone, is likely to be branded as non-kosher.

As Jakobovits was to show, he is not deficient in courage – certainly on major issues – nor is he deficient in scholarship, but even when offering an opinion on medical ethics, a field of study which he has pioneered and on which he is an acknowledged authority, he generally confines himself to analysing the responsa of others rather than coming up with his own. This may partly be due to natural modesty, but he is also a deeply conservative man, who is disposed to support a rabbinical ruling even if – as in the case of microphones – the grounds for the ruling no longer apply, and may not have had much obvious validity even when first made. Also the very fact that there is popular demand for a particular concession inclines some rabbis to dig in their heels against it. But here we have an example where modesty can be a fault and an excuse for inaction.

Jakobovits, like most rabbis, is a peace-loving man, but if need be he is prepared to confront the Reform movement, Zionism, secularism and the entire liberal-humanist establishment, which is very large and very powerful; but these are all to the left of him. He will go to almost any lengths to avoid a confrontation with those to the right. The fact is that to say nothing is also a way of saying something, and his tacit acceptance of right-wing opinion on such issues as lifts and microphones means that, in his view, a meticulously Orthodox Jew cannot live in a high-rise apartment, so that his compliments to his congregation on maintaining a bastion of Orthodoxy in a sea of paganism were possibly too generous. (It may be interesting to add that one eminent New York rabbi did rule that one can use a lift on the Sabbath, provided one lives on the tenth floor or above. He lived on the eleventh.)

Jakobovits may seem moderate because he looks reasonable, sounds plausible, is well educated, dresses smartly and has an amiable manner, and because he has any number of colleagues who are even more conservative. There is, in fact, hardly a rabbi so rigid in his Orthodoxy as not to be outmatched by someone even more rigid, and there were no doubt rabbis who regarded his synagogue lift, for example, as a dangerous innovation which could lead to the infringement of Jewish law. The most telling fact about that lift, however, was his refusal to use it himself, as if there was one law for laymen and another for rabbis. In short, his modern Orthodoxy has never amounted to moderate Orthodoxy.

A rabbi who searches for a lenient interpretation of the law is called a *makil*; the hard-liner is called a *machmir*. Jakobovits tends to be a *machmir* on public issues and a *makil* on private ones where the personal happiness of individuals is at stake, which is to say that he tempers rigidity with compassion. But as, of course, it is the public issues which reach the public eye, he is generally, if perhaps unfairly, known as a *machmir*.

This reputation, well established by the time he left Dublin, was amply confirmed by his years in New York. Thus when Dr Brodie retired as Britain's Chief Rabbi in 1965, few people regarded him as a likely successor if only because it was feared that a man with his outlook could reduce British Jewry, already riven by what came to be known as the Jacobs Affair (of which more later), into warring factions.

He himself was becoming restive. He had built up a congregation from scratch and had brought it to the forefront of American life. He now hoped to use it as a base for a major adult education programme and even found sponsors for the idea, but when it came to the point the promised funds were not forthcoming. 'There's nothing Mano can't do', his wife once observed, 'except raise money.'

When the *Jewish Chronicle* suggested in 1964 that he might be a possible candidate for the Chief Rabbinate, he dismissed the idea out of hand, but that was before he had suffered his setback over adult education. When Sir Isaac Wolfson, president of the United Synagogue, phoned to sound him out two years later, the idea was more attractive, but he still hesitated. He was aware of the bitterness left by the Jacobs Affair and thought he might be greeted with hostility.

'You'll be giving up a bed of feathers for a bed of nails,' a friend warned him, which in itself was no deterrent for he was uncomfortable about being too comfortable. What did make him apprehensive was the thought of facing hostility he had done nothing to incur.

There was also the fact that New York, with all its drawbacks, was largely a Jewish city, while London, with all its attractions, was not, and both his wife and children were against moving. Unlike him they had no sentimental feelings about England, and at first he was inclined to say 'No'. Sir Isaac, however, was never a man to take no for an answer. Having set his sights on Jakobovits as a prospective Chief Rabbi, he called and cabled, cabled and called, with all the doggedness he used to employ in his takeover bids. Finally he won him round.

In March 1967, Jakobovits and his family embarked for England. He was forty-six.

6

A House Divided

WHEN Chief Rabbi Hertz died in 1946 the most obvious successor was Rabbi Alexander Altmann, who, as Communal Rabbi of Manchester, stood to the Chief Rabbi as York stands to Canterbury. He was also a brilliant scholar with great personal dignity, who would have added immensely to the prestige of the office. He had been born in Hungary, educated in Germany, was a rabbi for a time in Berlin (where he was a colleague of the elder Jakobovits) and still spoke with a slight German accent, which did not prevent him from acquiring a growing reputation as a broadcaster on the BBC. It did, however, mark him out as a foreigner and, in 1946, with the great patriotic war only just behind them, British Jews wanted a native product, someone who not only looked English and sounded English, but *was* English; they found one in the person of Rabbi Israel Brodie.

Brodie had ideal qualifications. He was British-born and bred, had lately served as senior chaplain to His Majesty's Forces and had the courtliness and bearing of an officer and a gentleman, with pips on his shoulders and medals on his chest. He was, moreover, a Balliol, Oxford, man, who spoke the King's English with a beautifully chiselled diction, a rich vocabulary and a mellifluous voice. He had also received his rabbinical diploma at Jews' College and not some East European yeshiva, and had served in the Empire as a rabbi in Australia. And finally, he was an amiable man, with a pleasant, easy-going, English temperament, who could be expected to approach the problems of his office in a sensible English way. He as yet lacked a doctorate, a beard and a wife, but quickly acquired all three. In 1948, he was installed as Chief Rabbi in an imposing ceremony at the New Synagogue, Stamford Hill.

His installation marked the last get-together of the Cousinhood — the Rothschilds, Montagus, Cohens and Waley-Cohens — the old Anglo-Jewish families who had ruled the community for generations. They were to appear again at the installation of his successor, but by then they were no longer in power.

One of the main problems which Brodie faced when he took office was the situation of Jews' College, of which he was president and which, in the 1950s, moved from the drab surroundings of Woburn House in Bloomsbury to ornate new premises in Montagu Place, near Marble Arch.

The College celebrated its centenary in 1955, but it had become old without becoming venerable, for the community could not quite make up its mind about it. To the ultra-Orthodox it dabbled too much in subjects such as philosophy and history to be quite kosher. To others, its uncritical view of Scripture and the Talmud made it a little too kosher.

The clergy it produced in the inter-war years were devoted public servants, but they had tended to be mildly Anglican figures – genteel parsons and callow curates – who would not have been out of place in a Trollopian novel, using much the same language and wearing much the same habit (including the dog collar) as their Christian colleagues. The fault was hardly that of the teaching staff, which was foreign almost to a man, but of the lay readers who appointed the rabbis. The Church of England parson was their ideal and Jews' College students tended, whether consciously or not, to conform to it. It still produced outstanding graduates, but not in sufficient numbers to meet the demands of the community, and many pulpits, especially in the provinces, were filled by recent immigrants.

By the end of the war, with the destruction of European Jewry, the community was thrown back on its own resources, but the College was not even remotely equipped to face the new challenge. The move to the West End increased the cost of the establishment but it did not give rise to an improvement either in the quality or size of the intake. The principal of the College, Dr Isidore Epstein, was approaching retirement, and some of the honorary officers suggested a successor who, they believed, would jolt the College into life. His name was Louis Jacobs.

Jacobs, a near contemporary of Jakobovits, was born in Manchester of working-class parents. He left school at fifteen to study in Manchester Yeshiva and emerged seven years later with a rabbinical diploma. He then went on to the very heartland of British ultra-Orthodoxy, the centre for higher talmudic studies in Gateshead, where he was regarded as one of the outstanding young talmudists of his generation.

On completing his studies he was appointed assistant to Rabbi Eli Munk (a kinsman of Mrs Jakobovits) at the Golders Green Bet Hamedrash, which had been founded by German refugees to recreate something of the Adath synagogues they had known in Germany and, as such, stood well to the right of the United Synagogue. (It would in many ways have been an ideal position for Jakobovits, but he had by then moved to Ireland.)

While in London Jacobs took a doctorate at University College and was then invited to become rabbi of the Manchester Central Synagogue, which was somewhat less to the right than his previous congregation, but still very Orthodox.

It was obvious that a man who bestrode the learning of two worlds would not be left to the obscurity of a provincial pulpit and, in 1953, he was appointed minister of the New West End Synagogue, a magnificent building which was then regarded by some as the flagship of the United Synagogue. Six years later he was appointed a lecturer at Jews' College.

The move hardly amounted to promotion either in terms of salary or status, but various members of the College council gave him to understand that he would succeed Epstein as principal. He, however, received no such assurances from the Chief Rabbi, who had the final say in the matter and who, if anything, was reluctant to accept him even as a lecturer. Moreover, Epstein, who was in no hurry to give way to a successor, received him with a measured courtesy amounting almost to hostility.

Brodie had in earlier years taken a high view of Jacobs's abilities and had even broached the possibility of making him a Dayan, which would have been a definite step up, but by 1959 his attitude had changed.

In 1957, Jacobs wrote a book called *We Have Reason To Believe*, which attempted to answer some of the religious issues raised by his congregants over the years. Although it questioned the nature of divine revelation, it was intended as a defence of Orthodoxy rather than as a critique, but whatever its aims it aroused little interest. Epstein, however, read it with great interest and even greater care and brought it to the attention of the Chief Rabbi.

Epstein loved Jews' College. He had been one of its most brilliant students and, with the exception of a short period as a rabbi in a small provincial community, he had served it all his life. He was the author of numerous learned works and his standing as a scholar had added lustre to the place. In time he had come to regard it almost as his private domain, and he looked on the students and graduates as members of his family. The College thus represented not so much his livelihood as his life and he dreaded the thought of retirement.

All this was known to Brodie, who therefore did not attach too much weight to Epstein's representations. However, when Dayan Grunfeld, a member of the Beth Din and one of his closest colleagues, arrived with an annotated copy of Jacobs's book, with every alleged heresy marked in red, he sat up and took notice.

Brodie could not rescind Jacobs's appointment as a lecturer, but made it clear that he would not appoint him principal. Jacobs, finding himself in an impossible position, had no alternative but to resign. This was the first phase of what came to be known as the Jacobs Affair.

It caused a great furore in the community, especially after it was taken up in the national press. The theological implications of the Affair were vague, but there was the wider issue of academic freedom. A man had been victimized for his religious views in an associate college of a university dedicated to the principles of free inquiry.

Worse was to come. In the first phase of the Affair, Jacobs had not been dismissed. He had merely not received the promotion he had been led to expect, and some people felt that it was wholly reasonable to exclude a man – albeit a distinguished one – from the headship of an institution devoted to the training of Orthodox rabbis if he questioned the very foundations of Orthodoxy. In truth, however, there was a larger issue involved, which was never publicly spelt out: Brodie was due to retire in 1965 and there were fears that if safely ensconced as principal of Jews' College, Jacobs would use it as a springboard to the Chief Rabbinate.

Jacobs has denied any such claim, but if he himself lacked ambition, he had friends in high places – bankers, eminent lawyers, City merchants and the editor of the *Jewish Chronicle* – who were ambitious for him and who felt that British Jewry had come of age and could do with a Chief Rabbi with his range of knowledge and breadth of mind.

It was this which gave the Affair its particular virulence. It was one thing to have a less than Orthodox rabbi as head of Jews' College; it was quite another to have him as Chief Rabbi. There was a feeling that the very foundations of traditional Judaism were being threatened and right-wing elements, who had hitherto been indifferent to the whole issue, rallied round Brodie.

Then came the second stage of the Affair. In 1964, the pulpit previously occupied by Jacobs fell vacant again and he was invited to return. Under the United Synagogue constitution the Chief Rabbi has to certify every rabbi as a fit and proper person to hold office in a synagogue. In this instance Brodie was only prepared to do so on condition that Jacobs retracted his statements on divine revelation and promised not to repeat them. Jacobs gave the only reply which any self-respecting scholar could, and the certificate was withheld. Nevertheless, the New West End confirmed his appointment.

It was an act of open defiance, upon which the issue changed character. Hitherto the debate had been whether an Orthodox rabbi could question the nature of divine revelation. Now it was whether an Orthodox congregation could question the authority of the Chief Rabbi.

Anglo-Jewry is not an assembly of theologians. The full implications of

Jacobs's views were barely understood, but the Chief Rabbinate was another matter. It had been built up as the final arbiter on any religious issue affecting the community and has always been recognized as such. It was one thing to question the word of God and another to defy the authority of the Chief Rabbi. The issue had been brought down to earth.

God, it was generally felt, could fight his own battles, but many who had hitherto supported Jacobs and had worked for his reinstatement, now took the side of Brodie; even those who were not concerned about the rights and wrongs of the case were deeply concerned about the amount of attention it was getting.

The *Jewish Chronicle* was, of course, full of it not only because it was intrinsically newsworthy, but because the editor himself, William Frankel, was a central figure in the whole drama. He was a leading member of the New West End and a friend and admirer of Dr Jacobs. He believed – and was not alone in his belief – that he was by far the most talented rabbi in the Orthodox fold and feared that, if no active steps were taken to keep him in England, he would go to America. He had also believed that he would make an ideal principal of Jews' College and gave him every support, but by the time the second phase of the Affair had erupted it had gone well beyond the Jewish press. It featured almost daily in the national press, on radio and on television, and there were murmurings in the community about 'washing dirty linen in public'.

'Would that this was the dirtiest linen we have to wash,' a Jewish commentator observed, for the whole affair arose out of understandable differences on a series of honourable issues. However, British Jews were not so integrated as to feel at ease in the glow of arc-lights. They wanted an end to the situation.

The highest authority of the United Synagogue is the Council, composed of some 300 representatives from the constituent synagogues. A special meeting was summoned with but one item on the agenda: to dismiss the board of management of the New West End and appoint a caretaker committee in its place. It was passed by acclamation, whereupon Jacobs's followers seceded from the United Synagogue and established their own congregation.

The Jacobs Affair was technically over, but a legacy of bitterness remained. The king-makers, who had selected Brodie as a broad-minded leader in tune with the feelings of British Jewry, felt particularly betrayed, but they were in fact no longer in charge.

The United Synagogue had been established by private act of Parliament in 1870 with the Chief Rabbi as spiritual head and – tacitly – the Rothschilds as temporal heads. The Rothschilds, while not being particularly religious themselves, thought that religion was a good thing and the Jewish religion a very good thing, and acted on the principle of noblesse oblige rather than of deep conviction. They were, so to speak, the lions at the base of the Chief Rabbi's throne; they reinforced his authority and brought solvency, probity and order to Jewish life. The Chief Rabbinate could not have become what it was, or, indeed, what it is, without them. They, in turn, handed down their authority to various kinsmen, collectively termed the Cousinhood, all of them rich, worthy and high-minded, of whom the best known and the most formidable was Sir Robert Waley-Cohen, who, more than anyone, had been responsible for the appointment of Rabbi Brodie.

Again they were not particularly religious, but, like the Rothschilds, they enjoyed a sort of absolution through eminence and were regarded with reverence and awe by most Jews, who were content to leave all major decisions in their hands. However, their influence declined in the post-war years.

The last of the line was the Hon. Ewen Montagu, a tall, lean, choleric figure, who was a son of the second Lord Swaythling and a barrister by profession. He had no particular interest in Jewish observance, but had been brought into the United Synagogue by Sir Robert and groomed as a likely successor. He had been a naval commander in the war and tried to bring to synagogue life some of the brisk, no-nonsense attitudes he had picked up on the quarter-deck, but the ranks had already begun to get restive under Sir Robert – who died in 1952 – and, by the time Montagu took charge, they were on the brink of mutiny.

The first phase of the Jacobs Affair had erupted during Montagu's stewardship. He urged the Chief Rabbi both in private and in public not to veto Dr Jacobs's appointment and, when his advice was ignored, he resigned.

Anglo-Jewry was no longer an immigrant community. Many members of the United Synagogue had served five or six years in the armed forces. They had gone through grammar school and the universities, had prospered in business and risen in the profession. They were no longer flattered by the attention of the older families, or content to be patronized by them, and when Montagu resigned they elected Sir Isaac Wolfson in his place.

Sir Isaac was one of them writ large, the son of Russian immigrants who began work as a picture-frame salesman and had, through his own efforts, built up a vast enterprise – Great Universal Stores – with interests in furniture, furnishings, clothing and almost anything money could buy. He was generous therewith and, what was perhaps more to the point, he was unlike any of his predecessors, a practising Orthodox Jew. Anglo-Jewry had shrugged off the rule of the Cousinhood and had begun to rule itself.

Sir Isaac was no theologian, but Orthodoxy is basically the acceptance of one's rabbi's word, especially where he happens to be the Chief Rabbi. He therefore used his considerable influence – many members of the United Synagogue Council were, or hoped to be, among his suppliers – on behalf of Dr Brodie.

External factors also played their part. The Anglican character of the United Synagogue and the dominance of the Cousinhood were, in part, sustained by the adoration of things English, but, by the 1960s, England was no longer its old self. It was not only that the Empire was no more, but that all the characteristics which had singled out the Englishman as the exemplar of civic virtue seemed to be extinct. 'Swinging London' had become the playground of the Western world. A new age of permissiveness had dawned in which everything went and which questioned all the attitudes which had formed the landmarks of civilization. Many British Jews – amongst others – took a hard look at the outside world and recoiled quietly into their own.

Communal leaders may not have been convinced about the truth of divine revelation, but they were convinced that this was not the time to question them. Forced to choose between progressive forces as represented by Rabbi Jacobs, and those of conservatism as represented by Rabbi Brodie, they chose the latter.

At the same time they were troubled by the backwash of bitterness left by the Affair and, when Brodie retired in 1965, they began to look for a successor of such eminence as to transcend local divisions. They alighted on Rabbi Joseph Dov Soloveitchick of Boston, scion of a famous rabbinical dynasty, a scholar and philosopher of the first rank, and spiritual head of American modern Orthodoxy.

He was, however, sixty-two by then. He might normally have been tempted to accept the call, but the Jacobs Affair, and the international attention it had attracted, had made the office of Chief Rabbi too public and too controversial for his tastes, and he preferred to remain in his house of study.

The selection committee then received an unusual proposal from an unusual quarter. It came from Mrs Sarah Herzog, widow of the Chief Rabbi of Israel, who rang up Sir Isaac – an old family friend – to suggest that her son Jacob would make an excellent Chief Rabbi of Britain. Sir Isaac, the chairman of the selectors, who knew Jacob well, immediately pounced on the idea.

It was thought inevitable that the selectors would have to go outside Britain for the right man, but in this instance they were virtually going outside the profession, for Jacob had never actually served as a practising rabbi. Jacob and Jakobovits had been contemporaries at Etz Chaim Yeshiva in the early 1940s. Jacob had, in fact, qualified as a rabbi, but he had then gone on to take a law degree and eventually joined the Israeli Foreign Office. He served for a while on Israel's delegation to the United Nations and as Ambassador to Canada, but his counsel was often needed at home and he became political adviser to successive prime ministers. A scholarly, retiring, pensive man, he somehow found time among his many duties to produce a widely admired translation of and commentary on the *Mishnah*, a summary of the Jewish oral law which forms the basis of the Talmud.

The fact that he had never actually served as a rabbi, had never given a sermon and had no pastoral experience was, perhaps, something of an advantage, for he had uttered no opinion to which one side or another might take exception. His Israeli associations were another advantage, for if there is one factor which links almost all elements in the Jewish community, it is Zionism. Moreover, his father had been a notably successful Chief Rabbi both in Ireland and Israel, and pedigree has always weighed heavily with Jews in the selection of clergy. And finally, he was a professional diplomat, which, if always useful in a Chief Rabbi, was essential at this particular juncture.

A delegation from the selection committee flew to Israel to see him and they were deeply impressed with the man, his manner, his dignity, his powers of self-expression, his moderate ideas and everything they heard about him.

'First-class chap,' said George Gee, treasurer of the United Synagogue and a member of the delegation. 'Right up our street. Couldn't do better.'

Herzog was at the time Director-General of the Prime Minister's office and, as such, was Israel's top civil servant, but he had gone as far as he could in one career and the office of the Chief Rabbi offered the challenging prospect of another. Prime Minister Levi Eshkol, however, was reluctant to release him, while his wife was not happy about the idea of leaving Israel. Sir Isaac had to use his considerable powers of persuasion to the full before he could announce that he had found a new Chief Rabbi.

Jakobovits noted the news with more than passing interest. He had never aspired to the office, nor, as he wrote, had he 'the slightest interest of crossing the Atlantic again on a one-way trip except eventually to Israel'. But he had warm affection both for Britain and Herzog and he was immensely cheered by the appointment.

Mrs Herzog flew to London to look over the official residence in Hamilton Terrace, which she found rather drab and cheerless. She made a list of changes she would require, while the machinery for the installation was set in motion. However, a few weeks later Herzog was taken ill and, on the advice of his doctors, felt compelled to stand down. Cynics inevitably suggested that he had only just got the measure of what he was in for and that his illness was diplomatic. Unfortunately, it was anything but. He was suffering from leukaemia and died a few years later.

Sir Isaac then phoned Norman Lamm and Emmanuel Rackman (it is uncertain whom he approached first), but neither was interested. A London job had no great appeal to anyone well established in New York and, like Soloveitchick, they felt that the office of Chief Rabbi had been made too controversial by the Jacobs Affair.

It began to look as if British Jewry was doomed to remain leaderless, so Sir Isaac set about his task with new determination. 'Don't worry,' he assured his colleagues, 'I'll find you a Chief Rabbi.' A few days later the phones in East 62nd Street began ringing.

Spot the next Chief Rabbi, or the next Chief Rabbi-but-one, is a fairly popular pastime in synagogue circles and Jakobovits's name was raised as early as 1958 in one Manchester Jewish paper. He had only just moved to America and his stay there had improved his chances, if only because of the ingrained Anglo-Jewish belief that any rabbi who was any good would not be found in England in the first place. Moreover, various influential members of the United Synagogue — and especially Sir Isaac — were often on business in America and, when in New York, they often prayed in the Fifth Avenue Synagogue. They had been impressed both with Jakobovits and the obvious esteem with which he was held by his congregants and, indeed, the good name he enjoyed in America. His manner was more self-assured, his delivery more polished, his language less ponderous, his voice less shrill, but nothing he said, and nothing that was said of him, suggested that he had grown more liberal. Indeed, the very synagogue to which he ministered, though unique, was nearer in spirit to the right-wing Union of Orthodox Hebrew Congregations than the United Synagogue, which still thought of itself as the home of 'progressive conservatism'.

Jakobovits was never the man to hide himself in ambiguities and his speeches spoke for themselves. The following extract from a Yom Kippur sermon delivered in 1961 was not untypical.

We have today some large and powerful pseudo-religious movements founded on the premise that not everything in the Torah is divine and eternal. Their theologians arrogate to themselves the right to discriminate between the laws, picking and choosing what appeals to them and rejecting what they dislike. Ethical laws are fine and popular; these they accept as divine. Ritual commandments are not attractive to their minds; these are consigned to the limbo of history as man-made and obsolete.

This readiness to determine what was divine and what was not, the inclination to use one's own judgement, was, to his mind, a form of arrogance which verged on self-worship and idolatory. To him the entire Torah — and that included the oral law — was divinely inspired.

The *Jewish Chronicle* in particular thought that he was far too fastidious, puritanical and rigid for the tastes of the community, that he was authoritarian and would introduce harsh, unyielding Germanic attitudes to the English scene, and that with his appointment the divisions caused by the Jacobs Affair would be widened. It did not go on to spell out the name of an alternative, but it did suggest that Rabbi Dr Louis Rabinowitz might be more acceptable.

Dr Rabinowitz was born in Edinburgh and, after serving as senior army chaplain in the Middle East and Normandy, became Chief Rabbi of South Africa and professor of Hebrew at the University of Witwatersrand. A large, assertive man, he was formidable as a preacher, scholar and personality. Uncommonly for an Orthodox rabbi, he had taken a courageous stand in his opposition to apartheid and, had he not retired to Israel in 1961, he might have been expelled from South Africa.

While Jakobovits had openly sided with Brodie on the Jacobs Affair, Rabinowitz had kept his counsel to himself, though he was said to have more than passing sympathies with Jacobs. He was less fastidious than Jakobovits about the details of Jewish observance, and less puritanical, and his background was, of course, British.

Yet if Jakobovits was illiberal in some respects, he was fairly liberal when it came to Zionism and he was the first Orthodox rabbi to voice concern about the plight of Arab refugees, while Rabinowitz, though comparatively liberal on other issues, was on the extreme right wing of the Zionist movement and an ardent supporter of Menachem Begin.

The Chief Rabbi is actually elected by a special conference composed of representatives from the United Synagogue plus delegates from the major provincial and Commonwealth communities — there are no women on the electoral college, nor any rabbis — but Sir Isaac dominated the proceedings as Sir Robert had done in the election of Dr Brodie, and most of his colleagues were content to abide by his judgement.

They were all fairly successful businessmen and, if none were in Sir Isaac's league, they were aware that he could not have got where he was without being a sound judge of men. However, a feeling began to develop that he was running away with the show, which swung some opinions in favour of Rabinowitz. On the other hand, few British Jews shared Rabinowitz's veneration for Begin and they recalled an incident in 1947 in which he had dramatically torn off his war medals in protest against British policy in Palestine. If this was forgivable at the time, it did not enhance his hopes of election.

There were no such marks against Jakobovits and it was thought that, while he might occasion controversy among Jews, he would go down well with gentiles.

Of the two, Rabinowitz was the better speaker and writer. Words came naturally to him, while they came with effort to Jakobovits. But Jakobovits had a spiritual quality which one missed in Rabinowitz. Rabinowitz was also fifteen years his senior, and it was felt that the post called for the energies of a younger man.

Sir Isaac thought that the matter was finally settled, but then something of a rearguard action developed. One delegate recalled some of Jakobovits's wilder utterances, like his stand against mixed bathing in Jerusalem. Another recalled the rigour with which he had laid down the law in Dublin and argued forcefully that he was not really their sort of man. It was suggested that a further approach be made to Lamm.

Lamm, retorted Sir Isaac, had made it perfectly clear that he was not, and would not be, available, at which a new name was raised, that of Dr Solomon Gaon, the head of the Sephardi community. Gaon was only eight years older than Jakobovits, an amenable and scholarly individual with moderate views, who was widely esteemed and who, it was argued, was just the man to heal the rifts in the community.

It was an interesting idea, but it aroused so little support that it did not even have to be put to the vote. After further discussion Jakobovits was unanimously elected. On 11 September 1966, he was formally invited to become Chief Rabbi.

It was as if the fates had cleared the way for his succession. If the Cousinhood had still been in charge, if there had been no Jacobs Affair, if Dr Herzog had not been taken ill, he would not even have been considered as a candidate, but when the selection committee finally settled on his name he seemed to be the most natural man for the job.

Among the first to congratulate him was Rabinowitz, who added: 'I always knew the better man would lose.' They were soon to have other, less amiable, exchanges.

Primate

*T*HE office of Chief Rabbi is peculiarly English. Rabbis are sometimes thought of as priests, but among Jews this is a term reserved for the descendants of the Temple priesthood. After the fall of Jerusalem in AD 70, however, the synagogue evolved as the focal point of Jewish devotion and the rabbi evolved with it, but the office did not represent a full-time calling. Some of the most famous rabbis were shepherds, or craftsmen, or brewers, or cobblers. One had even been a gladiator. The title indicated their learning rather than their office, and the rabbinate emerged as a professional class only in the Middle Ages. The term Chief Rabbi, however, remained unknown. There was none in Poland and Lithuania, which for many centuries were the main centres of Jewish life, and if any rabbi enjoyed ascendancy over his colleagues it was through his learning and piety rather than his office. There is no Chief Rabbi in the United States or Canada, and while Chief Rabbis did begin to appear in Central and Western Europe as well as in the Holy Land in the course of the nineteenth century, they somehow never acquired the standing or prestige enjoyed by the British Chief Rabbinate.

Yet the office, like most venerable British institutions, came into being almost by accident. The main synagogue in the country was the Great Synagogue in Duke's Place and its incumbent, who was usually a man of considerable stature, came to be regarded as the premier rabbi of the British Isles and was sometimes referred to as 'High Priest of the Jews'. The status, however, was unofficial and his role was not regularized until Nathan Adler was appointed 'Chief Rabbi of the British Empire' in 1845.

The British Empire in those days was large, while the Jewish community was small, numbering only some 60,000 souls. It was only after the mass immigration at the end of the century, by which time Nathan Adler had been succeeded by his son Hermann, that British Jewry grew to anything like its present size, and the office assumed some of its present importance.

Hermann Adler was born in Germany but brought up and educated in

England, and, in common with the lay leaders of the community, he acquired a veneration of all things English, including the Anglican church. 'I have endeavoured to draw my mental nurture', he declared in his installation address, 'from the rich stores of our dear England's learning.' He regarded himself as a sort of kosher Archbishop of Canterbury, even to the point of wearing gaiters. Edward VII spoke of him as 'my Chief Rabbi', as if he were his father confessor, and made him a Companion of the Royal Victorian Order. Adler wore it not only as an indication of rank and a proof of acceptance, but as a sort of talisman. At a garden party in Lambeth Palace, or some other such gathering of prelates, with his black garb, his gaiters and the insignia of the Order on his chest like a pectoral cross, it could be difficult to tell the rabbi from the bishops.

He was a dignified figure, but if he also seemed imperious, it was not so much out of a natural haughtiness as out of a belief that his office called for it. At the same time he was intolerant of any efforts to upstage him and insisted that all the clergy under his jurisdiction style themselves Rev., partly because of his Anglican predilections and partly because, as far as he was concerned, there was but one rabbi in Britain, and he was the Chief. On the advice of his friend the Bishop of Bath and Wells, he called himself the Very Rev., so that his title in full was the Very Rev. the Chief Rabbi Dr Hermann Adler. (When he died one of the candidates for the succession was the Rev. Professor Sir Hermann Gollancz. One daren't think how he would have been styled had he succeeded.)

The elder Adler was a retiring scholar, the younger was not, and the problems of mass immigration left him little time for scholarship.

The massive influx brought with it an upsurge of anti-Semitism the like of which England had not witnessed in modern times, and one London paper described the newcomers as 'the flotsam and jetsam of the Polish ghettos ... worthless wastrels of the Provinces within the Pale'. Other papers, if less vitriolic, were hardly less hostile. Jews, it was reported, were not only bringing in poverty and disease, but crime. The newcomers nearly all settled in and around the East End and any unsolved crimes in the neighbourhood – including even the Jack the Ripper murders – were often ascribed to them. Adler felt compelled to write to the press to explain that whatever the shortcomings of the immigrants, they were addicted neither to violence nor to blood-lust.

The older Jewish families, who had risen in business and the professions and who were only beginning to enjoy acceptance as Englishmen, felt threatened by the outcry. N.S. Joseph, a leading member of the United Synagogue, complained that the newcomers 'were always paupers and useless parasites in their own country'. This was not a view which Adler himself supported, but he did find the newcomers troublesome and once described them as 'uncultivated and uncivilized'.

Many of them shook off the restraints of their faith the moment they left the Pale of Settlement (some had done so before) and became active in the radical wing of the trades union movement. When they began to agitate against sweated labour, Adler retorted that if sweating meant overwork then he too was a victim. By way of reply a large body of Jewish workers, estimated at about 3,000 by the organizers (and 400 by the *Jewish Chronicle*), led by a brass band, marched on the Great Synagogue where he was due to preach. They were met by a phalanx of fifty policemen under the superintendent and chief inspector of the City Police and forced to retreat.

If Adler was harassed by the godless, he did not have it easy with the godly. The newcomers had their own usages and were disinclined to fall in with the ways of the Anglo-Jewish community, or to accept the authority of the Chief Rabbi. But if his writ failed to extend to them, that of the Rothschilds succeeded.

The Chief Rabbi, for example, had statutory authority to regulate Jewish marriage and divorce, which was sometimes circumvented by the newcomers. A letter of reproof from Dr Adler might be ignored, but not if it was reinforced by one from Lord Rothschild.

The newcomers were not happy with the ornate, cathedral-like synagogues they found in London and established their own small, homely bethels, which served as houses of prayer and study and as club-house, and which were eventually formed into the Federation of Synagogues. The Federation, however, offered no challenge to the supremacy of the more English synagogues headed by Adler, and as people prospered and became more assimilated, they tended to graduate from the former to the latter. The Chief Rabbinate was thus, in a way, an agent of anglicization, but all under kosher supervision so that one became English without jettisoning anything essentially Jewish.

The new community was not Adler's only source of worry. He had troubles enough from the old, and in 1890, when the newly opened Hampstead Synagogue appointed the Rev. Morris Joseph as minister, he was faced with an issue which was to be echoed some seventy years later in the Jacobs Affair.

Joseph had sanctioned the use of instrumental music in synagogues on the Sabbath, which was bad enough, but he also had serious reservations about liturgical references to sacrificial rites, which was worse. When he publicly declared that they must make any sensible soul shudder, Adler refused to sanction his appointment.

The unity of the various congregations under the Chief Rabbi's authority is due in good part to the fact that Jews as a people are not given to theological disputations. Had Adler been asked if he believed sincerely in the restoration of such rites, he might have found it difficult to say 'Yes', but he did believe sincerely in keeping his synagogues united and, as Joseph himself recognized, he therefore had no alternative. 'I would not have anyone cast a stone at the kind and learned man who has passed upon me the sentence of minor excommunication,' he said. 'The Chief Rabbi is but the administrator of a system, and so long as the community acquiesces in the existence of that system, it is only the community that is really responsible.'

Adler was in many respects a tolerant man. For example, the Board of Jewish Religious Education, of which he was the head, included among its members Claude Montefiore, one of the founders of the Liberal Synagogue. He was urged to dismiss him, but he admired Montefiore as a scholar and as a man, and he remained in place. Such breadth of mind would have been unthinkable under his successors. He also allowed small modifications in the liturgy, was not too rigorous in his interpretation of Jewish law, and it was during his years that the 'progressive conservatism' of the United Synagogue came into being.

He was, however, intolerant of any challenge to his own authority, not merely out of *amour propre* but because, with mass immigration, he had to guard against the factionalism and chaos endemic in Jewish life. The centralization and conformity which he sought and obtained brought a necessary degree of order and discipline to the community and the Chief Rabbinate as we now know it is largely his legacy.

No man could have been more suited to the ruling elite of Anglo-Jewry, for as a distant kinsman of the Rothschilds, a grandson of Baron de Worms and a first cousin of the first Lord Pirbright, he was a grandee in his own right, and at his happiest in the ornate drawing-rooms of Kensington. He was rather less happy, and less revered, in the East End, and he knew it, and before his death in 1911 he left a will urging that his successor should be acceptable to both the new community and the old.

Joseph Herman Hertz was acceptable, but he was not appointed until 1913; by the time he had settled into office, the First World War had broken out. When peace came, he was faced with a new situation: the new community was no longer that new and the old was not that old. A substantial part of the latter had passed out of the Orthodox fold, or out of Judaism altogether, and their places were taken by recruits from the former who were moving out of the East End and into the suburbs.

Hertz was born in 1872 in what later came to be known as Czechoslovakia and moved to America as a child. He studied at Columbia University and the newly formed Jewish Theological Seminary in New York, of which he was the first graduate (though as the fountainhead of the American Conservative movement it is now regarded as non-kosher). In 1898, he became a rabbi in Johannesburg and was almost at once involved in conflict with the head of the South African Republic, Dr Kruger, who viewed Jews and other uitlanders with deep disfavour. Hertz protested vehemently at the treatment of minorities in the Transvaal, a little too vehemently for the taste of the authorities, and in 1899 he was expelled. He returned to Johannesburg after the Boer War and became friendly with the British High Commissioner, Lord Milner, who much admired his qualities.

The Empire featured hugely in the imagination of British Jewry in those days — and, indeed, for some time after — so that such a friendship had its uses. There were several eminently suitable candidates available at home, but none of them had Hertz's connections and he was largely appointed on the recommendation of Milner.

Hertz had little patience with the routines of his office, preferred the company of his books to that of his colleagues, and produced a scholarly but popular commentary on the Five Books of Moses, which brought him lasting fame and a considerable income.

His years of office were untouched by any serious internal traumas, possibly because they were dominated by external events. After the rise of Hitler he was instrumental in the formation of an emergency committee which sought to bring as many Jews to safety as possible, and one of his beneficiaries was Jakobovits's father. Unlike his predecessor, who had regarded Theodor Herzl's ideas as egregious, Hertz was an active Zionist, too active for some of the honorary officers of the United Synagogue, who tried, without success, to limit his enthusiasm.

In 1945, after the newly elected Labour Government reneged on its promise to open Palestine to Jewish immigration, Hertz sent a telegram to all synagogues under his jurisdiction calling for 'a day of Jewish solidarity with the remnants of European Jewry' and declaring that 'the Jews of England expect the Government to keep faith in regard to Palestine as the only haven of refuge to survivors of Nazi bestiality'. The president of the United Synagogue, Sir Robert Waley-Cohen, was horrified and countered with a warning that the 'last sentence of the Chief Rabbi's telegram to your minister ... may be misinterpreted as advocating introduction of politics into our religious services. . . .'

The telegram in fact did, and was meant to do, just that, but Hertz was never a man to withdraw. It was said of him that he would resort to peaceful means only after all others had failed and he proved to be more than a match even for Sir Robert. Well-meaning go-betweens sought to arrange a reconciliation between them but Hertz died before it could take place.

Sir Robert found it difficult to believe that any reasonable man could seriously disagree with him and ascribed Hertz's attitude to illness and irascible old age (though they were almost contemporaries). Hertz liked to say that Chief Rabbis never retired and rarely died and the United Synagogue promptly passed a law to make sure that they did one or the other, requiring all future incumbents to stand down at seventy.

Lord Jakobovits has described Hertz as 'probably the most dynamic' but 'least creative', except as an author of great distinction, of all Chief Rabbis. He was certainly the most awkward.

Sir Robert's experience with Hertz played a large part in the appointment of Dr Brodie, who seemed as genial and compliant as his predecessor was aggressive and stubborn, but when it came to a crisis he proved to be very much his own man. It was not that he believed that Louis Jacobs was an incorrigible heretic, nor was he a fundamentalist himself – he certainly had no objections to the freedom of expression – but when finally compelled to choose between Jacobs's supporters and his opponents, he felt that the future of British Jewry lay with the latter rather than the former. Once he had made his decision nothing could move him.

Jakobovits has summed up his career neatly:

The only English-born chief Rabbi, he nevertheless emancipated the Anglo-Jewish rabbinate from its insularity and associated, if not integrated, it with the rest of Europe through the Conference of European Rabbis which he founded in 1957.... Though he never studied at a European-type seminary or yeshiva, he did more than anyone else to restore the European pattern of qualified rabbis.... Pacific by nature and mellow by disposition, he yet witnessed and aided a more pronounced swing to the right within the religious community than ever before, and he boldly met the challenge of the most violent religious warfare in Anglo-Jewish history....

But the fact that he had never studied at a European-type seminary or yeshiva made him more than usually beholden to those who had. He was certainly not in a position to challenge their authority, but there is no evidence that, once settled in office, he differed all that radically from their thinking. However, he hated controversy and there is little doubt that had he not been confronted with the implications of Dr Jacobs's philosophy, there might never have been a Jacobs Affair and Jakobovits might still have been in New York.

While progressive Jews to the left of the community, and the ultra-Orthodox to the right, do not accept the religious authority of the Chief Rabbi, and the Sephardi Jews have (or had) their own religious guide in the person of the Haham, the Chief Rabbi has always been regarded by the outside world as the head of British Jewry. The only rabbi to dispute that title was Moses Gaster, the head of the Sephardi community, a man of vast erudition, irascible temperament and boundless *amour propre*.

The Sephardim had at one time formed the aristocracy of Anglo-Jewry and had regarded the Ashkenazim as vagabonds and upstarts, but by the time Gaster became Haham in 1885, they had declined in number and influence and formed only a small part of the community. Gaster, however, was indifferent to numbers. His office was of greater antiquity than that of the Chief Rabbi and his members were of finer pedigree; he was certainly the greater scholar and he yielded in precedence to no one. He tried to establish a rabbinical college of his own to compete with Jews' College, which was a disastrous failure. He had his differences with Adler, with Hertz and with his own congregation and was eventually pensioned off.

All that, however, was long ago. There have been no such difficulties with his successor, Dr Solomon Gaon, but since he retired in 1977 the office of Haham has been more or less in abeyance and overseas Sephardi communities like those of Gibraltar, Singapore and Hong Kong, which used to accept the authority of the Haham, now turn for guidance to the Chief Rabbi.

The Chief Rabbi, as we have seen, was originally styled 'Chief Rabbi of the British Empire', a title which was changed after the Second World War to 'Chief Rabbi of the United Hebrew Congregations of the British Commonwealth'.

Canadian Jews before the First World War tended to turn to England for their rabbis and there was a tacit connection with the Chief Rabbinate, which, however, lapsed with the spread of American influence. Most of the larger Canadian synagogues are now affiliated to the American Conservative movement, and even Orthodox congregations, in so far as they are in need of external guidance, look to America rather than to Britain.

South African Jews used to have a particularly close association with Britain and British Jewry. It was Britain which saved them from the high-handedness of the Boers and, as we have seen, they provided Britain with a Chief Rabbi in the person of Hertz. Many of them either came from Britain or originated from the same parts of Russia as British Jewry, and they share its dominant characteristics. Formal links were sundered when South Africa was expelled from the Commonwealth, but informal links remain and many of its rabbis and all of its Chief Rabbis have hailed from Britain.

Finally there are Australia and New Zealand. Until 1939, Jews, in common with most people in the antipodes, regarded Britain as home. They were nearly all of British origin and tended to look to Britain for their rabbis and to the Chief Rabbi for guidance on major religious issues. To an extent they still do, but after the war there was a large influx of East European Jews who have since moved into positions of influence. In 1971, Rabbi Dr Porush, Chief Minister of the Sydney Great Synagogue, complained that contact with the Chief Rabbi was sporadic and not always meaningful. 'His jurisdiction', he said, 'is a fluid notion. The growth of our community and its increasing independence will probably sooner or later lead to the creation of a local Chief Rabbi....'

The fact is no rabbi, however humble, cares for even the nominal over-lordship of another, however eminent, but air travel has made the world smaller and the connection not only remains, but, as we shall see, has in some ways been enhanced. The title 'Chief Rabbi of the United Hebrew Congregations of the British Commonwealth' is thus not, as yet, either presumptuous or meaningless.

It was only after he took office that Jakobovits discovered both the nature of the traditions to which he was expected to adapt and the range of responsibilities he would have to assume.

As he has often observed, he likes a challenge, but he had little inkling of what he was letting himself in for as he prepared for his installation on a blustery evening in April 1967.

(8)

Defender of the Faith

*A*T about 7 p.m., when the worst of the rush-hour traffic was over, the flow suddenly thickened and policemen controlling the approaches to St John's Wood found themselves faced with a new rush. Movement between Abbey Road and Wellington Road was reduced to a crawl, and in Grove End Road traffic could not move at all.

The new St John's Wood Synagogue, completed in 1964, is one of the largest and most fashionable in Britain and a large society wedding can sometimes cause chaos in the surrounding streets, but nothing this large had been known before. Residents of nearby flats craned their heads out of their windows to get a closer look, and passers-by stopped to gaze. It was mainly the concourse of top-hats which caught the eye. They were the clue to the character of the occasion.

The black topper is the regalia of the *macher*, the Jewish communal office holder, and this was the communal occasion *par excellence*. A new Chief Rabbi was about to be installed.

By half-past seven the vast synagogue with its 1,200 seats was packed. Upstairs in the ladies' gallery (men and women sit apart in an Orthodox synagogue) was a sea of mink and tulle. In the centre of the front row sat Mrs Jakobovits, pale-faced and slightly apprehensive, with Mrs Fanny Brodie, wife of the former Chief Rabbi, on the one side, and Lady Wolfson, wife of Sir Isaac, on the other.

The Jakobovits clan was there in strength, including his mother, whose eyes were aglow at the scene before her, his brothers and sister, his sons and daughters (except for the youngest, who was only a few months old), and his parents-in-law, Rabbi and Mrs Munk, who had flown over specially from Paris.

The congregation was a veritable roll-call of the Who's Who of Anglo-Jewry, and the Who Will Be Who, for youth groups were also represented by youngsters in green caps and red caps and blue neckerchiefs and white shirts. Beyond them, occupying an entire block of pews, were the massed clergy of the United Synagogue, a sanhedrin of rabbis in full canonicals.

The media was also there in force. A television camera scanned the audience for familiar faces and found them in goodly number. There was the Hon. L. H. L. Cohen, president of the Jewish Welfare Board; the Hon. Ewen Montagu; Rabbi Louis Jacobs, a spectator where, but for the grace of God, he might have been leading man; a whole phalanx of knights, including Sir Leon Bagrit, Sir Ben Barnett, Sir Sammy Fisher, Sir Barnett Janner, Sir Seymour Karminski and Sir Frederick Lawrence; two baronets, Sir Bernard Waley-Cohen (son of Sir Robert) and Sir Isaac Wolfson; three peers of the realm, the Lords Cohen, Segal and Swaythling; and neither Hon. nor Sir, neither Baronet nor Baron, but carrying a name which among Jews is a form of nobility in itself, Mr Edmund Leopold de Rothschild.

A choir unseen, but a little too insistently heard, provided background music, while heads turned this way and that to see who there was to be seen. Suddenly the choir stopped, the organ began, and all eyes turned to the door. The choir resumed *fortissimo* with the traditional words of welcome, 'Baruch Haba'; the vast congregation rose as the Chief Rabbi's party entered in a broad, black, slow-moving stream.

The brief installation ceremony was conducted by Dr Brodie. Dr Jakobovits was rather less brief, for he had much ground to cover. He had come to Britain at a time of schisms and he used the ceremony as a feast of unification. The synagogue was crowded with representatives from the entire religious spectrum, from Dr John Rayner of the Liberal Synagogue on the extreme Left, to the late Dayan Weiss of the Manchester Rabbinical Court on the extreme Right, but, as Jakobovits made clear, he could promise no dilution of his own beliefs to accommodate those of others:

I am resolved to preserve the Orthodox traditions of my office and the pre-dominantly traditional character of our community.... I have not become Anglo-Jewry's First Minister in order to preside over the liquidation of British Judaism. I will do my best to serve and unite all sections of the community, but I am not prepared to replace the Torah by an umbrella, either open or closed.... I cannot bend or compromise Jewish law which is not mine to make or unmake, but I can administer it with compassion and despatch.

Instead he appealed to 'those whose faith in the Divine origin of the whole Torah is weak' — meaning Liberal and Reform Jews, and perhaps also Dr Jacobs — 'to rediscover the thrills of traditional Jewish living and the awesome magnificence of our faith; the Divinity of the Torah, the truth of the prophets, the authority of the *halacha*, and the Messianic vision of the future, born of hope and toil.' In other words, he would be happy to embrace the non-Orthodox provided they modified their non-Orthodoxy.

It was an impressive occasion. His speech was forceful and eloquent, but neither the speech nor the occasion was sufficient to repair the divisions he had inherited, and the *Jewish Chronicle* referred to him pointedly as the spiritual leader of only a section of British Jewry. But a few weeks later came a series of events which showed him at his best and which allowed him to emerge as the leader and spokesman of the entire community.

If Britain's Jews are divided by religion, they are united by Zionism. When President Nasser sent Egyptian troops into Sinai and closed the Straits of Tiran to Israeli shipping, war seemed inevitable. The various organizations in the community immediately closed ranks and arranged a solidarity demonstration in the Albert Hall. By the time it was held on 5 June war had broken out and the atmosphere was tense. The Chief Rabbi was the main speaker and he rose magnificently to the occasion:

Nearly thirty years ago my illustrious predecessor, Chief Rabbi Dr J. H. Hertz, addressed a massed assembly in this very hall to arouse the conscience of the world on the catastrophe that lay ahead for European Jewry. Alas, the cry was too weak and too late to avert disaster.

Today we have reached another turning-point in Jewish history, perhaps more fateful than any in our long and chequered past. From the land of our first oppression in biblical days a new oppressor has arisen ... with the avowed and often-proclaimed aim to destroy Israel and to drive its population into the sea....

He called on world Jewry to make sure that 'the hope of two millennia, and the toil and sacrifice of two decades, is not now going to be wiped out in two weeks, in two months'. His appeal went straight to the heart of the vast audience and he sat down to tumultuous applause. His place in the esteem of the entire community was secure, but the honeymoon was short-lived.

First, there was his relationship with Sir Isaac Wolfson, which, though cordial on a personal level, was not without its moments of friction. Sir Isaac was one man in the drawing-room and another in his office.

Jakobovits knew of the difficulties which Hertz and, to an extent, Brodie had had with the president of the United Synagogue, and he had sought, and received, assurances that things would be different. At first they were, but Sir Isaac, though mindful of the Chief Rabbi's prerogatives, could not shake off the habits he had acquired as head of a vast commercial empire. His inclination to refer to the United Synagogue as 'the Great Universal Synagogue' may have been no more than a Freudian slip, but Jakobovits sometimes felt that he was being treated like the manager of a less than profitable subsidiary.

Sir Isaac had given a written undertaking that he would build a Chief Rabbinate Centre, which Jakobovits wanted not only for his staff, but as a sort of educational power-house. It never even got as far as the drawing-board and Jakobovits had to settle for a suite of rooms in the dingy purlieus of Woburn House, Anglo-Jewry's Whitehall.

Jakobovits believes that the first duty of a rabbi is to teach (the word rabbi means teacher) and he hoped to have his own synagogue, with perhaps an assistant to look after routine duties while he himself gave the occasional sermon and a weekly discourse.

Some men are content to learn for themselves, but he likes to share the benefits of his learning. Above all he needs the stimulation of personal contact and he hoped to have around him an immediate congregation who would come under his personal influence and to whom he could look as his disciples. However, the idea proved impractical, not only because there was no available synagogue (or assistant), but because nothing in his experience in Dublin or New York had prepared him for the welter of duties which fell upon him.

He had originally stipulated that he would not be required to attend rabbinical inductions and other such chores, but felt unable to refuse the invitations pressed upon him. There are not all that many synagogues in Britain, and not all that many rabbis, but as rabbis changed jobs with some frequency, inductions were numerous and he found himself criss-crossing the British Isles to conduct the necessary ceremonies. It was in the course of these journeys that he discovered something of the mystique which attaches to his office.

Any rabbi has the authority to install another, but there was a general feeling that if the induction was conducted by a lesser person than the Chief Rabbi, some of the divinity which is meant to surround the ceremony would be lost. This was true even of minor communal gatherings, whether in London, the provinces or the Commonwealth. The Chief Rabbi's presence not only assured a large turnout, but gave a sense of occasion to the most mundane event.

Conversely, however, the Chief Rabbi's absence from an event, which he might reasonably have been expected to attend, could cause the deepest offence. Hell hath no fury like a synagogue scorned and he sometimes felt that for every friend, he made a dozen enemies.

When he took office Sir Isaac had assured him that he would be 'in the driving seat', but he often complained that 'the car has been stalled'.

There was never any major issue at stake, but minor ones kept cropping up on which Jakobovits urged one course of action and the United Synagogue adopted another or, more frequently, none at all. Then some rabbis began murmuring that he was not consulting them often enough, upon which the cantors complained that they were not being consulted at all. 'Shoals of literature go out from the Chief Rabbi's office to ministers-preachers,' their spokesman lamented, 'but we do not receive anything – not even the Chief Rabbi's own sermons and addresses.'

He began to feel victimized, but that was due less to the small differences he had with the United Synagogue and his clergy than with the treatment he was receiving from the Jewish press; which, in Britain, to all intents and purposes, meant the *Jewish Chronicle*.

The *JC*, as it is popularly known, founded in 1841, is by far the oldest and most influential paper in the Jewish world and Jakobovits himself, with all the reservations he had about it, described it as 'probably the world's best Jewish newspaper in the English language'. Jewish papers crop up with every season and expire every season, and where they survive it is usually because they are propped up, or owned by, their local communities. Others, even if solvent, are so dependent on communal advertising that they dare not take an independent line. The *JC* is more fortunate. It is more than a paper, it is a habit – though not everyone would say a healthy one – and is as much part of the Anglo-Jewish Sabbath as candle-light. It may not be bought by every Jew in Britain, and is certainly not loved by every Jew, but it is read by almost every Jew, and as the purchasing power of its readership is considerable, it attracts a good deal of national advertising so that it can afford to take an independent line. All of which does not mean that it has always done so, for given its age it had, in a sense, become part of the establishment itself, and over the years it became predictable, a trifle dull and more than a trifle complacent. In 1957, however, it acquired a new editor in the person of William Frankel and it has not been quite the same since.

Frankel was a barrister by training but with sound journalistic instincts, who wearied of the parochial trivia with which the paper had concerned itself and tried to widen its horizons. He adopted a questing, questioning, irreverent tone, and when the Jacobs Affair erupted three or four years after he took office, he found a cause. As we have seen, he was one of Dr Jacobs's parishioners, a neighbour, a friend and a devotee, and he threw himself into the fray with a partisanship which did not always help the cause he espoused. Jakobovits therefore felt that he had inherited the backwash of the affair. Certainly the editorial on his installation was less than enthusiastic:

Dr Jakobovits ... has all the right visions, visions that will be shared by every Jew of 'the vindication of the age-old Jewish faith in the brotherhood of man'; of the passing of religious hatreds; of 'Zion restored to its old glory'; of a 'forward-looking' Anglo-Jewish community as 'a mighty fortress of our spiritual treasures'.

But there is something sadly unreal about rousing sermons urging the laity to accept current Orthodox formulations of belief and observance. Every minister knows that this is a cloud-cuckoo-land of self-delusion. The laity is, in fact, drifting away from minimal commitment, among them a high proportion of our best minds. To arrest what Rabbi Jakobovits rightly calls 'an emergency of appalling defections', Orthodoxy will have to be reinterpretative now as it was in the past. To ask for the times to be in accordance with Judaism has a fine oratorical ring, but hardly suffices as a practical programme, and is difficult to reconcile with the Chief Rabbi's support for 'the Judaism which is very dynamic and creative'. This, as well as other contradictions in the address, undoubtedly arise from the commendable desire to please everybody. But it frequently results in puzzling and disappointing ambiguity.

To an extent the Chief Rabbi ignored the changes which had overtaken the paper since he had lived in England. In America, the Jewish press rarely reported rabbinical orations and almost never subjected them to critical scrutiny, but what he found more hurtful than the actual criticism was the feeling that his failures were being highlighted and his achievements played down or ignored. He also felt that the editor was trying to belittle his office by referring to him pointedly as head of but a section of Anglo-Jewry, which technically he was, though in fact the overwhelming mass of the community looked to him as their spiritual leader.

Frankel, in fact, had nothing against Jakobovits personally. He knew him well – they had moved in the same circles in their youth – and acknowledged his tenacity, integrity and consistency; he only found fault in his very virtues, for if consistent and tenacious, he found him uncompromising and unbending. Frankel had been brought up in an intensely Orthodox home (his father was an East End synagogue beadle), but it was an Orthodoxy which was combined with tolerance and an understanding of the limits to which observance can be pushed. He had a yearning for what he thought of as the golden years of the United Synagogue, which may not have been all that golden but did embrace certain 'broad-church' attitudes, which he thought would not survive Jakobovits's ministrations. He thus opposed his nomination and, when he failed, sought to limit his influence. The Chief Rabbi's complaints about victimization, if certainly exaggerated, were not wholly unfounded.

A few months after his induction, when still comparatively unknown, Jakobovits was invited to address the annual conference of the Institute of Directors in the Albert Hall, which was newsworthy in itself, for no such invitation had been extended to a Chief Rabbi before. The massed assembly was not sure what to expect and anticipated a sermon. Instead, he stole the show with a cogent address that even had moments of wit. In America, he began, 'the title Chief conjures up visions of befeathered Red Indians; here, at least in our community, Chief is associated with bearded rabbis'. He then quickly warmed to this theme:

Our universities, once so called because of the universality of the knowledge they taught, are now all too often assembly-lines of specialists who cannot see the wood of culture for the trees of departmentalized efficiency.

In religion, the dramatic inter-faith amity and understanding on the highest level has been offset by the recession of religion at the lower levels, creating a moral vacuum filled by a mini-morality and a hippie-culture ... which have turned the pleasure of worship into the worship of pleasure.

After which he turned to an issue he was to develop in later years and which was to make him the High Priest of British Conservatism:

The accent today is on demands not obligations. Everyone thinks of what society owes to him, not what he owes to society. Already our youth are conditioned to ponder on what they can get out of life, and not on what they can put into life ... a society whose catchwords are success instead of service, leisure instead of work, rights instead of duties, must come to grief and disillusionment.

He received a standing ovation, but not a word of it appeared in the *Jewish Chronicle*, which may have been due to the fact that there was nothing particularly Jewish to the occasion or the speech, which had in any case been widely reported in the general press. However, if it had been made by Louis Jacobs, it would undoubtedly have received at least a passing mention in the *JC*.

In December 1971, Jakobovits told a meeting of the Guild of Jewish Journalists, which was, and is, largely composed of *JC* staff, and whose chairman, David Pela, was deputy editor of the paper, that the partisan stance and monopolistic position of the *JC* harmed the creative forces in the community.

Accord was played down, discord played up and it reached the point where Alderman (now Sir) David Hamburger, a leading member of the Manchester Jewish community, who had sided with Jacobs during both phases of the Affair, felt moved to complain of the campaign of 'smear and innuendo' against the Chief Rabbi.

If one goes through the Chief Rabbi's press cuttings for this period one finds not so much smear and innuendo as the feeling that he could not do anything right, but then the press cuttings of almost any public figure would give a similar impression for it is controversy rather than amity which makes headlines. However, the Chief Rabbi in his first years of office did excite numerous controversies, all of them forgotten, but some of them significant and not a few of them newsworthy.

There was, for example, the Clause 43 controversy. The Board of Deputies, the representative body of British Jewry, has a clause in its constitution – Clause 43 – which accepts the guidance of the Chief Rabbi and the Haham on religious issues. Shortly after Jakobovits took office, Reform and Liberal Jews began to demand that their religious leaders be given, if not parity, then at least consultative status and, with the agreement of the Chief Rabbi and the Haham, the Board amended its constitution to that effect. It was not a world-shaking event, but some very Orthodox deputies felt sufficiently shaken to resign from the Board.

Their spokesman, Dr Bernard Homa, a retired physician, complained that the amendment recognized the Reform and Liberal communities 'as legitimate movements within authentic Judaism', and he felt that, as a result, the Board could 'no longer be entrusted with religious affairs'.

As ultra-Orthodox opposition mounted, the Chief Rabbi called on the president of the Board to reopen talks on the disputed amendment. When he was told that this would lead to a Reform and Liberal walk-out, the possibility of phasing out 'some or all of the Board's religious functions' was suggested, which led one commentator to say that it might be best 'to phase out the Chief Rabbinate itself'.

While all this was brewing the Chief Rabbi was to have given the fifth annual Lilly Montagu Memorial Lecture at the London Society of Christians and Jews. Dame Lilly Montagu, a daughter of the first Lord Swaythling, one of the stalwarts of Anglo-Jewish Orthodoxy, would, in a non-Jewish context, have been spoken of as a saint. She was a woman of the deepest personal piety, who had devoted her entire life to public service, but she was not only one of the founders of the Liberal Synagogue, but had functioned as one of its rabbis, and Orthodox eyebrows were understandably raised when it was learned that the Chief Rabbi would give the memorial lecture. In the event he did not, because, as his office explained, he had to travel to Paris for an urgent meeting with the Chief Rabbi of France. He did not, however, offer to deliver his lecture at a later date.

Jakobovits was shaken by the attacks from the Right. They had welcomed his appointment and he felt that, given his track record, they should have been able to reconcile themselves to his policies, or at least mute their misgivings. Thus, when they also turned upon him – and they included members of his own Beth Din – he felt utterly friendless. The cancellation of the Montagu lecture was an act of craven appeasement, which did not, in fact, mollify his critics. It was not his finest hour, but he had not yet acquired the self-confidence to stand his ground.

He had also alienated many moderately Orthodox people by expressing doubts about the policies of the religious parties in Israel, and even questioning the wisdom of having religious parties at all. His reservations – as we shall see in a later chapter – were well founded, but he seemed to be adding to the number of his enemies without acquiring a stable body of friends.

And then came the Melchior Affair. Bent Melchior was a graduate of Jews' College and had preached at several Orthodox synagogues in London during his student days. After he succeeded his father as Chief Rabbi of Denmark, he became a vice-president of the World Council of Synagogues, a loose association founded by the American movement for Conservative Judaism. As a result, he was excluded from the Conference of European Rabbis, which, though of recent origin, was to Orthodox Jewry what the Headmasters' Conference is to the English public school.

Mutterings were also heard about the lenient interpretation which Melchior gave to various Jewish laws, and especially those concerned with conversion, but similar rumours were heard about other rabbis who were members of the Conference. His exclusion was plainly due to his membership of the WCS.

In June 1972, Melchior was invited to preach at the Kenton Synagogue in north-west London, but the Chief Rabbi – who is the final arbiter in such matters – refused to endorse the invitation on the grounds that Melchior was outside the European Orthodox rabbinate. By way of explanation he added that in withholding his endorsement he was merely following a precedent established by Dr Brodie. That may have been the case, but Chief Rabbis are not bound by the actions of their predecessors, and the ban produced a barrage of criticism.

The Chief Rabbi's stringency in this matter is all the more remarkable for the fact that he himself has often been welcomed as a speaker in both Conservative and Reform synagogues in America, but there has never been any reciprocity between those who are looking for the truth and those who think they have found it. Underlying it all was the belief that it is one thing to preach to heathens and another to expose oneself to heathen preachers.

It was not a happy time for the Chief Rabbi – nor, as we shall see later, for his wife – and it was perhaps inevitable that reports began to circulate that he was thinking of giving up his job.

The reports, which originated in Israel, were largely inspired by the fact that Rabbi Isser Unterman, the Ashkenazi Chief Rabbi of Israel, was about to retire and Jakobovits was spoken of as a likely successor. But he had no plans in that direction for, as he told a friend, 'Don't I have enough *tzores* here?' Nor did he ever contemplate the possibility of resigning, although he was often angry and frustrated, for he did not give up that easily. He had too many unfinished plans. Moreover, he was beginning to enjoy England itself.

England lacked the spaciousness of America and it had nothing to match the grandeur of the Rockies or the awesome magnificence of the Grand Canyon, but it had its own charms. In the summer, he liked to hitch a caravan to his Rover and take his family on touring holidays, stopping over for the Sabbath, usually on some remote hillside farm. There his wife would prepare the usual festive fare and the unfamiliar aroma of freshly baked *challa* and simmering *cholent* would drift over the English countryside, and the soft evening air would ring with their hymns and songs of thanksgiving: 'O come, let us exult before the Lord: let us shout for joy to the rock of our salvation.'

If not averse to the exposures of public life, he loved the open country and relished the occasional retreat into complete privacy. Like many a foreigner he was becoming an inveterate Anglophile.

His love of the countryside, one must add, suggested a bucolic streak which represents the one un-Orthodox element in his make-up. Jewish tradition not only insists that study is the greatest good, but regards anything which might divert attention from it as inherently profane and possibly harmful. One famous Babylonian sage even went so far as to claim: 'He who, in walking by the way, breaks off his study to say how lovely is that tree, how pleasant that meadow, is regarded by Scripture as one who has forfeited his life.'

Jakobovits interprets this to mean that one should not interrupt one's studies to contemplate nature. Yet he regards the very beauty of a tree or meadow as proof of divine beneficence and his rural excursions, if anything, reinforce his religious beliefs.

He also found simple relief in informal clothes – in donning a cloth-cap instead of his usual black homburg – and in helping out with domestic chores (though his wife will not let him near the kitchen, not because she feels it is sacred to women, but because he is totally devoid of culinary skills; nor is she happy about trusting him with the shopping because, as she puts it, 'He has no idea what things should cost, and as long as people only ask for money he is happy to pay it').

As the years passed he began to view events in perspective. Britain was not America. In New York, he and his congregation had grown with one another and were virtually tailored to one another. But the experience he had acquired there was almost irrelevant to the challenge he faced in Britain, where he was the spiritual head of a disparate and divided community, which, in most instances, was only nominally Orthodox. In the first, he had preached to the converted; in the second, he often found himself preaching to people who were not only unconverted, but unheeding, and who, if not always Orthodox, were, paradoxically, almost invariably conservative and thus, while demanding changes he could not bring about, were resistant to changes he would have loved to effect.

One almost notes a hint of despair in an address he gave to a gathering of Jewish leaders in March 1973 and his complaint that the community was 'unenterprising, backward-looking, taking pride in past achievements rather than enjoying challenges, innovations and experimentation'. Whenever he proposed any innovations, he said, 'my colleagues are inclined to notice their negative aspects first'.

He had to be all things to all men, of which he was plainly incapable, and it was almost impossible to advocate a course of action, or even an idea, to one group without displeasing several others. However, he found that the occasions which provoked the strongest criticism and dissent were mostly marginal.

On broader issues he had much of the community behind him, and he was making solid progress in the area which he had placed at the top of his priorities – education. He became more relaxed and began to feel he was among friends. The hostility of the JC abated, and when William Frankel was succeeded as editor by Geoffrey Paul in 1977, he believed that he had found a veritable ally. He was also happier with his immediate entourage.

The Chief Rabbi had an extravagant faith in imports. He himself had gone abroad in pursuit of his career, as did many of his abler colleagues, which left him with the ingrained belief that there was no real talent in Britain, especially in education. Thus where a vacancy occurred, he often turned to America, to Canada or to Israel, but he eventually reconciled himself to home-grown products. He was particularly fortunate in the appointment of Moshe Davis as manager of his Jewish Educational Development Trust (of which more later) and director of his office.

Davis, who was tall, lean and hawk-nosed, with bushy eyebrows, a dandyish moustache and a ribald sense of humour, had served as a soldier during the war and as a chaplain to the forces after the war and seemed to combine sacred and profane elements in his make-up without any apparent sense of conflict. He was, among other things, a gifted preacher. He had helped to run a small, family-owned airline, which proved too small to be viable, and was director for a time of the education department of the Jewish National Fund, at which he was very successful.

He was shrewd, energetic and capable, a man of the world, which the Chief Rabbi was not, and he knew and understood the community, which the Chief Rabbi did not (though he was learning fast). Davis was able to save him from small errors of judgement, which might have had large repercussions, and to advise him on how to couch even unpalatable statements in palatable language. He had a wide range of contacts, some of whom were to prove invaluable to the Chief Rabbi's educational schemes. He also enjoyed good connections with the JC and was able to forge a happier relationship with the editor, though, as we have noted, by the time he joined the Chief Rabbi's office in

1972 relations had already improved and Jakobovits himself had become more self-confident and sure-footed.

The Chief Rabbi has many friends but few intimates, which some ascribe to aloofness but which is in good part due to shyness, diffidence and even a slight awkwardness, for he is never quite sure how he will be received. He is also, like his father, extremely mindful of the dignity of his office, which makes it difficult for him to unbend, but he was usually at ease in Davis's company and could discuss personal issues and private problems and treat him as a member of his own household.

They had different attitudes and very different personalities, but found many things in common. Davis was also able to approach him with a candour which would have been unforgivable in others, for though the Chief Rabbi is prone to self-criticism, he does not take kindly to reproof from outsiders, though sometimes dark murmurings were heard that he assumed too much authority and exercised too much influence.

The Chief Rabbi is Jewry's representative to the outside world and his dignified bearing, his courteous manner, his ability to find the right word for the right occasion and the warmth which he brings to his relationships made him a natural ambassador. He was often quoted in the national press and appeared with increasing frequency on radio and television. He was becoming a revered national figure, all of which enhanced his standing among Jews.

In May 1973, Israel celebrated its silver jubilee and he addressed a special service to mark the occasion in St John's Wood Synagogue. The place was packed and the mood was festive. There was much to celebrate. It was almost six years since the triumphs of the Six Day War. Israel was passing through a brief golden age and his speech reflected the sense of thanksgiving and pride with which the community regarded the achievements of the Jewish state:

> In but one generation, Israel has already become the world's leading centre of Torah learning and intensely religious living; proportionately it has given a haven to more refugees than any other country in history; it has achieved greater ethnic integration and equality for the most diverse tribes in two and a half decades than the advanced civilization of America did in 100 years.... Its leaders and diplomats are men and women of outstanding ability and dedication; its army has earned the respect of friend and foe alike, and its contributions to the development of other emergent nations have set a rare example of a struggling nation stretching out a helping hand to sustain the struggles of others....

One factor cast a shadow over the event. It was hoped that the different factions in the community might join in saluting Israel at its silver jubilee at one united service, but the efforts in that direction proved unavailing. The Orthodox would not attend a service in a Reform or Liberal synagogue,

Reform or Liberal clergy would not be allowed to participate in an Orthodox service, while the extreme Right did not think that the emergence of Israel was an event worth celebrating at all.

Five months later, on Yom Kippur, the Jewish world was at prayer, when news came that the Egyptians had crossed into Sinai, that the Syrians were advancing in the Golan and that Israel was once again in peril. The Chief Rabbi's phone was already ringing when he got home and he had hardly broken his fast before he was caught up in the organization of an emergency campaign. In the next few days he attended an endless succession of meetings and rallies. All the divisions which had riven the community seemed piffling and irrelevant, and he once again came to the fore as the acknowledged leader of British Jewry.

It also showed in dramatic form how far Jewish life in the Diaspora was dominated by events in Israel, and how far events in Israel affected the Chief Rabbi's standing in his own community, but, as we shall see in a later chapter, the effects were not always positive. The Israel he had known before the Yom Kippur War was not the Israel he came to know after, and he watched the changing mood of the country with the deepest misgivings.

Nine years later with the outbreak of the Lebanese War, when Israel was not even remotely in danger, the Chief Rabbi knew in his own heart that in this instance she was the aggressor. The onslaught from the media, however, was so fierce and one-sided that the Jewish community felt threatened, and he could not therefore voice his reservations – in public at least – about the whole operation and felt compelled to assume a defensive role.

The Chief Rabbi, in fact, operates on two levels. On major issues he generally speaks for, and is regarded as the spokesman of, the entire community – we shall look at the exceptions in a later chapter. On minor ones his influence is more limited and, as we have seen, he is prey to all the fractiousness and bickering which goes with parochial life, for the smaller the cause the fiercer the resentments; and if the larger causes generally bring out the larger man, the smaller ones bring out the smaller man and display some of his limitations of character.

They also – though he would be loath to admit it – rather weary him, and there were times one could almost hear him cry out in the words of Moses: 'How can I myself alone bear your cumbrance and your burdens, and your strife?'

Scenes from Clerical Life

SOME of the Chief Rabbi's duties and privileges are defined in writing, others are governed by convention, but they vary with the character of the incumbent and, indeed, with the character of the ruling laymen.

Unlike his predecessors Jakobovits has not had to contend with the over-lordship of powerful and overbearing laymen. Sir Isaac Wolfson was in some ways every bit as autocratic as Sir Robert Waley-Cohen, but, unlike Sir Robert, he believed in the rule of rabbis. As we have seen, this did not mean that Jakobovits had it all his own way, but the interference he suffered, if irritating, was minimal.

There is a Chief Rabbinate Council consisting of twenty-three members drawn from congregations recognizing the Chief Rabbi's authority and contributing to the maintenance of his office, which meets once a year and from which is drawn a sub-committee of five called the Chief Rabbinate Consultative and Advisory Committee, which meets as and when required and which is basically a committee of overseers. Under previous incumbents the overseers oversaw; this is no longer the case.

The Chief Rabbi is required to consult with the Committee to enable lay leaders 'concerned with and responsible for the general administration of their synagogues to gain a greater understanding of the religious considerations on which the Chief Rabbi bases his ultimate and unfettered decision'.

Jakobovits is eminently approachable and any lay leader anxious to discuss a religious issue with him is free do so. Many have done so, occasionally in fairly acrimonious terms, but formal sessions of the Committee on such matters are a thing of the past.

More important, the Chief Rabbi is required to consult the Committee on 'any public pronouncement proposed to be made on behalf of, or in relation to, the Jewish community either in his own name or in association with other Jewish bodies'. The clause derives from a time when lay leaders were nervous of anything which might be uttered on behalf of the community and which might possibly expose it to controversy. Such nervousness is by no means a thing of the past, but that clause too has gone by the board.

There used to be an area of no-man's land between the spheres of influence exercised by the Chief Rabbi and laymen which was sometimes the occasion of bitter dispute, but which has since been abandoned to the Chief Rabbi without a shot.

Jakobovits, though always happy to retreat to the sanctuary of his study, takes a lively interest in what is happening in the world and occasionally he feels moved to make statements, some of which have excited national and international headlines, and not a few of which have upset even his own followers. It could be argued that he made them in his private capacity, but it is not an argument behind which he has himself ever sheltered, if only because he is aware that a public statement made by a public figure can never be regarded as a private aside, and that all his utterances are ex cathedra. He enjoys this freedom not because he brooks no interference, but because there has been none.

The chairman of the Consultative and Advisory Committee, and as such the chief overseer, is the president of the United Synagogue, but where Sir Robert was president for decades, presidents now tend to serve for a mere three years. Since becoming Chief Rabbi, Jakobovits has seen six presidents come and go – Sir Isaac, Alfred Woolf, S. S. Levin, George Gee, Victor Lucas and Sidney Frosh – though Frosh may stay on for a second term to help Jakobovits's successor settle in. Such transitory figures were not in a position to challenge his authority even if they were inclined to do so, which, on the whole, they were not.

The Adlers, Hertz and Brodie dealt with laymen who, in the main, were not observant and who, in some instances, believed in the Chief Rabbi rather more than they believed in God. Jakobovits has had to deal with laymen who, in the main, were, or are, positively Orthodox and who, therefore, rarely presume to question his authority. If he enjoys greater power, it is not because he is more assertive than his predecessors – in some ways he is less so – but because he is subject to fewer restraints.

All of which does not, of course, mean that he never seeks or takes advice. When faced with a legal problem, for example, he will consult Lord Mishcon or Lionel Swift QC (a nephew of the late Dayan Swift). On medical issues he would pick the brains of the late Lord Cohen of Birkenhead and the late Lord Rosenheim, and now often consults Professor Robert Winston. On political issues he can turn to any of half-a-dozen Jewish parliamentarians. Geoffrey Paul often advises him on publicity and he has ready access to leading authorities – some of whom are his personal friends – in almost every imaginable field. Yet when faced with a serious problem his instinctive reaction is to turn to the ancient codes rather than to any living individual, and in a sense his principal adviser is Maimonides, whose counsel, he believes, is as relevant now as it was 800 years ago.

Jakobovits had always argued that the concentration of authority in the hands of the Chief Rabbi had reduced synagogue clergy to the role of functionaries. One of his first acts on assuming office, therefore, was to form what he called a 'Cabinet' – the first members of which were the late Rabbi Morris Nemeth, Rabbi Solomon Goldman, Rabbi Morris Unterman and Rabbi Cyril Harris. He entrusted them with 'portfolios' or 'departments' to cope with various responsibilities usually discharged by his office, though retaining a supervisory role in the direction of them all. The fact that he was introducing a form of Cabinet government, however, did not mean that he planned to become *primus inter pares*.

He also warned that there was a crisis in the recruitment of suitable clergy and wanted the whole status of rabbis to be reconsidered. As an immediate measure he called for higher salaries. 'If you pay peanuts,' he said, in one of his less felicitous asides, 'you get monkeys.'

At the same time, he felt that rabbis were a little too secure in their jobs, which was perfectly true, for a rabbi once installed can only be removed for high crimes and misdemeanours, and sometimes not even then, and several clergymen used their posts as sinecures. He did not recommend the American practice of giving rabbis contracts which come up for renewal every two years, but he believed that they should be encouraged to move on at least every ten years, both for their own sakes and that of their congregations. 'I can tell you from my own ministerial experience', he said, 'that ten years is normally about as long as you can be creative in a congregation. After that you begin to stagnate.'

The rabbis, in the main, preferred to stagnate and were aghast at his proposal. There were even murmurings about a possible strike. He has not been particularly sympathetic with strikers even in industrial jobs and has always argued that anyone discharging a holy office was debarred by the very nature of his work from withholding his services.

In the end there was no strike and the rabbis were able to obtain definite benefits without making any definite concessions, but in the event they took his advice to heart and it is now rare for a rabbi to remain in anything other than a top job for more than ten years.

No Chief Rabbi has done more to advance the welfare and status of his colleagues. Whatever vows an Orthodox rabbi has to take, poverty is no longer one of them, and he enjoys about the same income as a university professor. As a result, there has been a considerable improvement in the number and quality of young men entering the profession.

The Cabinet system operated most effectively both in relieving the Chief Rabbi and in strengthening the influence of his office. He also used it as a consultative body on major religious policies, but some colleagues occasionally demurred, and Rabbi Cyril Harris, then of St John's Wood and now Chief Rabbi of South Africa, complained that the authority vested in the Cabinet was illusory, that the Chief Rabbi never listened to their advice and that they were not free to use their own initiative.

The Chief Rabbi's own feeling was that most of his colleagues were not always ready to use even the initiative they had. The ingrained habits of a century do not change overnight and when anything vaguely important cropped up they brought it to his door.

Part of the trouble was that members of his Cabinet received only a nominal fee, so that Cabinet office hardly amounted to promotion and could sometimes amount to a headache. Even so, there was always jostling to fill any vacancy which occurred.

The Chief Rabbi also wanted to improve the career structure of his clergy. One could move from a smaller synagogue to a larger one, from the provinces to London, but there was no rank between puisne rabbi and Chief Rabbi, except that of Dayan (judge of the Chief Rabbi's Court).

The Court, or Beth Din, as it is generally known, is composed of authorities in the *halacha*, some of whom have served as congregational rabbis, and the office of Dayan carries both a higher salary and a superior status.

The entire bench of judges (or Dayanim) were in sight of retirement when the Chief Rabbi took office, and they have all since been replaced, but United Synagogue rabbis were hardly given a look in. Of the five members of the old Beth Din, three had served United Synagogue congregations. Of the four members of the new one, only one has done so, while the other three are from areas of the community which have never even recognized the Chief Rabbi's jurisdiction.

Dayanim – who were originally known as the Chief Rabbi's ecclesiastical assessors and were paid by him out of his own pocket – are appointed by the United Synagogue on the recommendation of the Chief Rabbi, so that the offices are virtually in his gift. The fact that they are nearly all from the far Right may suggest a determination to pull Anglo-Jewry towards stricter Orthodoxy, an aim which he would not in fact deny, but which, he claims, had nothing to do with the appointments. He was looking for the best people available irrespective of background and believes he has found them. His Beth Din, he claims, is 'now widely acknowledged as one of the world's leading assemblages of rabbinical expertise and Jewish juridical power', which is indeed the case, but he has nevertheless effectively moved it outside the career structure of the United Synagogue.

A few years after he took office Jakobovits confessed that he sometimes had his differences with his Dayanim, which may have been due to the fact that they were, as he put it, his elders, 'at least in age, if not in knowledge'. To which the late Dayan Swift, who was not renowned for his reticence, retorted: 'As far as the general sittings of the Beth Din are concerned, the Chief Rabbi has never participated since his appointment and has thus had no opportunity to differ from us.'

This was perfectly true, but misleading. The Beth Din meets five times a week to discuss such routine issues as divorce, conversion and the supervision of the dietary laws; though the Chief Rabbi is ex-officio head of the Court, he rarely attends its formal sittings. He is, however, often in touch with Dayanim both individually and as a group on specific issues and there is a regular process of consultation between them, but it is true that his relationship with the old Beth Din was less happy than with the new one.

The former was composed of Rabbis Grossnass, Lew, Rapoport, Steinberg and Swift, all of whom had grown old in the service of the community and who thought they knew its strength and its weaknesses. They were therefore not entirely happy with the sudden intrusion at their head of a much younger man who was virtually a stranger to Anglo-Jewry. A certain timelessness, not unrelated to the character of Jewish law, also pervaded their deliberations, while Jakobovits was in a hurry to get things done. Four of the five were of East European origin, and the fifth, though born in England, was trained in an East European yeshiva, and they felt that their chief was not quite one of them. Neither, indeed, was his predecessor, Dr Brodie, but he had the saving grace of being an English gentleman, which Jakobovits was not. He was also not their match in scholarship so that they could, to an extent, patronize him. They could not patronize Jakobovits and at first a certain amount of friction ensued. Dayan Swift, a brilliant speaker and a vigorous and colourful person-ality, who felt that his talents had never been fully recognized, could be particularly awkward, but even so a harmonious working relationship did eventually evolve between them.

With the new Beth Din, it is the Chief Rabbi who has grown old in service to the community, while his colleagues are the newcomers. One of them, Dr Lerner, is his contemporary, while Rabbis Ehrentreu, Berger and Kaplin are all much younger, and all four, as we have seen, were his nominees. They are also rather less testy as individuals and the Chief Rabbi regards them not only as trusted colleagues but as personal friends, yet in a way he has less control over them than he had over their predecessors.

Hitherto, while some Dayanim were more scholarly than others, they were all in theory equal and the Chief Rabbi was their unquestioned superior. However, when Rabbi Ehrentreu joined the Beth Din in 1984, he was given the title of *Rosh*, or head, of the Beth Din, and by formally raising him above his colleagues and increasing his authority, the Chief Rabbi has in some ways diminished his own.

That is not the Chief Rabbi's view of the situation. Ehrentreu was his own nominee and he is happy with his appointment. 'My relations with him and the entire Beth Din', he says, 'have been, and continue to be, far better than with any of his predecessors. I attend more frequently than I used to, and the Dayan always insists I preside.' He cannot recall a serious disagreement with him, nor does he feel that his appointment has in any way diminished his authority.

Ehrentreu, who was born in Frankfurt in 1932, is not only a great scholar, but a forceful personality, articulate, clear-headed and ambitious. He was for some years head of the Manchester Beth Din and was only prepared to move if he was accorded the same rank in London. Though the superior status which it suggested need only have been nominal, with Ehrentreu it has been actual and, with all the affection and respect he has for the Chief Rabbi, he regards the status of the Beth Din as almost autonomous. To that extent, therefore, the Chief Rabbi's authority has been diminished.

The Chief Rabbi is concerned with the general principles of Judaism, while the Beth Din deals with the actual application of Jewish law, with the small print. Where people are unhappy with their verdicts, they often turn to the Chief Rabbi as a sort of court of appeal. He may then join with the Beth Din to examine the old evidence afresh or to weigh up any new evidence which has come to light and, if occasion demands it, he may invite his colleagues to reopen a case.

There were often complaints that the old Beth Din was too rigorous in its interpretation of Jewish law, but the new is, if anything, worse, and if the former, so to speak, chastised the community with whips, the latter has done so with scorpions. Thus, for example, where the old was content to see that the food served at Jewish functions was kosher, the new also insists on kosher wine, and it has given hints that it may even insist on kosher milk.

In earlier times there was the danger that milk from clean animals might be mixed with that of unclean ones, such as asses or sows, so that milking had to be supervised. As it is difficult to change ancient usages in the light of changed circumstances, milk for Jewish consumption must, strictly speaking, still be supervised; hence 'kosher' milk. However, laws are sometimes allowed to lapse and the idea of kosher milk had, as far as Anglo-Jewry was concerned, fallen into disuse. The Chief Rabbi's predecessors were content to use ordinary milk, but Jakobovits has always used only kosher milk and it will no doubt insinuate its way, if not into most Jewish homes, at least into all kosher functions. All of which may seem of very slight import, but anyone who dismisses such trivialities as trivial does not understand the nature of Orthodoxy.

It must be said that the Chief Rabbi has never insisted, or even implied, that his own level of observance – which is very strict – must become general. If one searches his sermons one finds frequent exhortations to a higher level of conduct, but no specific prescriptions; on the contrary, he has often insisted that Jewish observance, and Judaism itself, can only be spread by example.

At the same time, there is no evidence that he has tried to check the efforts of the Beth Din to push the community to the right, if only because he himself has always had reservations about middle-of-the-road Judaism.

Writing in 1956, while still Chief Rabbi of Ireland, he was fairly critical of what he called

> the much lauded Anglo-Jewish predilection for a 'mellow form of Jewish observance' – a moderate, conservative brand of Judaism which, it is claimed, combines the virtues of tolerance and tradition.
>
> Lacking a separate philosophy to inspire it, this typically Anglo-Jewish expression of Judaism is characterized by negative rather than positive ideals. By raising the art of compromise to an ideal per se, it shuns all tendencies to extremism without, however, at the same time finding or emphasizing new values to supplement those modified in the process of accommodation.

The 1950s are not the 1980s and the community has been transformed in the intervening decades. This has, of course, been part of a worldwide trend, but the Chief Rabbi has never been afraid to challenge a trend, however widespread, where he finds it unwholesome. In this instance, however, he was not only happy to go along with it, but he has done everything to encourage it with the result that it may have gone further than he intended.

His ideal was the sort of German community inspired by the teachings of Samson Raphael Hirsch, which his father had served and in which he had been brought up; but, as he observed in a lecture in 1971, it was a spent force even by then. Hirsch's Orthodoxy, though strict and unyielding, was outward-looking and of this world. The new Orthodoxy, though equally strict and unyielding, is inward-looking and of the next, and he is beginning to feel that there was, after all, possibly something to be said for compromise as 'an ideal per se'.

To that degree he has softened slightly over the years and we shall see in a later chapter the extent to which he is ready to compromise. That readiness is not, as yet, shared by his Beth Din.

What is ironic about the whole situation is that while the Beth Din has become almost autonomous, the Chief Rabbi is still, in the last resort, held responsible for its decisions. He is a little like the political head of a government department who is answerable to Parliament for the actions of his civil servants, but has only limited control over them. The following is an example.

In 1977, Paula McKenzie Wilson, a twenty-three-year-old Newcastle girl, while on a visit to Israel, enrolled as a volunteer at a kibbutz. She found herself drawn to Judaism and, after going through a rigorous study programme, was converted under the auspices of Chief Rabbi Shlomo Goren, who stamped her certificate, 'Not Valid Outside Israel'. That was the first complication.

A little later she married a member of the kibbutz called Cohen in a Reform synagogue, which was the second complication.

Anyone called Cohen is presumed to be – unless he has evidence to the contrary – a descendant of the Temple priesthood. Such descendants are not allowed to marry converts, which is why they resorted to a Reform synagogue. The prohibition, however, is one of the hybrids peculiar to Jewish law, which is to say that one shouldn't do it, but if it's done that's the end of it, and any children of such a union are Jewish.

The Cohens had three children in the next few years and had no difficulties whatsoever, but in 1988 they moved to Newcastle, where their troubles began. They sent their eldest boy to the local Jewish school. Questions were raised about his origins, upon which the local rabbi took the matter to the Beth Din. The Beth Din, basing itself on documents received from Jerusalem, ruled that the boy was not Jewish and could not be given religious instruction. Mrs Cohen protested and, when her protests were unavailing, she wrote to the *Jewish Chronicle* and *The Times*.

In the past her letter would have gone unheeded for the Beth Din felt no need to explain its judgements or even to communicate with the public at all. The Chief Rabbi, however, believes that the public has a right to know and decisions are now explained and, if necessary, defended by the court registrar, Rabbi Berl Berkovits, who is himself a trained lawyer (and who has since become a Dayan of another ecclesiastical authority). Berkovits replied that in essence Mrs Cohen had brought her troubles upon herself, first by knowingly entering into a forbidden marriage, and secondly by ignoring the provision of the conversion certificate and moving to England.

(One should add that Rabbi Goren later declared the conversion null and void because she had married a Cohen, though again there is no known case of a conversion being nullified, and there is serious doubt whether a conversion can be nullified; in this, as in so much else, Rabbi Goren seems to be a law unto himself.)

An angry correspondence ensued in the pages of the *Jewish Chronicle*. It was asked how someone could be Jewish in one country and not in another; and if Mrs Cohen and her children were Jewish – and they were treated as such in Israel – what possible grounds were there for treating them any differently in England? The matter, confined initially to the pages of the Jewish press, was soon taken up by the national press.

Jakobovits is extremely sensitive about the issue, which, he believes, is being manipulated by people anxious to discredit Orthodoxy and his office. He feels that he cannot defend himself properly because of the complexity of the case, its delicacy and the confidentiality which surrounds it. He also points out that Mrs Cohen's case is by no means unique and that if she had been more patient and less contentious, it might have been resolved by now.

Mrs Cohen, for her part, has waived all claims to confidentiality, but the whole issue has been mishandled from beginning to end by Rabbi Goren. It is difficult for one Chief Rabbi to question the wisdom of another, even though, as we shall see, Goren himself has never felt inhibited about questioning the wisdom of anybody.

In some instances people bring their problems directly to the Chief Rabbi rather than to the Beth Din and he is particularly interested in cases of adoption, marriage and divorce. Like his father, he is often moved by the plight of *agunoth*, women who cannot remarry because their husbands are missing or who refuse to divorce them, but, like his father, he is not always able to help them. The *halacha* can be, and often has been, modified through a process of reinterpretation, which amounts almost to innovation, but such innovations have been rare in recent times and are becoming rarer.

The Chief Rabbi tries to explain his attitudes in frequent letters to the *Jewish Chronicle* or through a spate of publications, the most notable of which is *L'Eylah*, a twice-yearly journal founded by him and now edited by Dr Jonathan Sacks, the principal of Jews' College. Well written, attractively produced and imaginatively edited, it tries to present what might be called the acceptable face of Orthodoxy and is avidly read even by those who find the very idea of Orthodoxy unacceptable.

Most synagogues employ a minister and a cantor, the first styled rabbi, the other reverend (though he is generally referred to as the *chazan*). Both have their own ideas of their place in the ecclesiastical firmament, which may not always coincide, and friction can sometimes ensue. Or a rabbi may fall out with a colleague, or with his synagogue wardens, or even with his wife; or synagogue wardens may fall out among each other. In each instance, the Chief Rabbi may be asked to restore peace.

He is, indeed, the ultimate pacifier and is regarded as a sort of Solomon cum Ombudsman. He had some foretaste of this when he was Chief Rabbi of Ireland, but if every Irish Jew felt he had a claim on his time, there were only some 5,000 of them. British Jewry is eighty times as large and problems pour in with every post, while his phone never stops ringing. The Chief Rabbi has given an inkling of some of the dilemmas in *L'Eylah*. For example, here is one from the medical director of an infertility advisory centre.

A mother, after considerable difficulties, eventually conceived and was convinced that the child was going to be a son. When it proved to be a daughter, serious psychiatric problems ensued, and when she contemplated having another child, her psychiatrist wrote: 'It would be absolutely disastrous for her to have another female child. I fear she would have a complete mental breakdown.' To which the medical director, himself an observant Jew, added: 'I am not keen to see this couple to give infertility treatment if she eventually does conceive, has an amniocentesis to determine foetal sex and then sees another specialist to insist on a termination of pregnancy should the foetus be female.'

The Chief Rabbi replied:

I do not know what is meant by fear of 'a complete mental breakdown'. If this includes a hazard, however remote, to the life of herself or anyone else, by suicidal or violent tendencies, then this would be a valid ground for termination. But I doubt that such a danger can be realistically established.

It would seem to me that the fertility treatment should be proceeded with in any event. Once a pregnancy is achieved, there is always a fifty per cent chance that the foetus would be male. There is the further possibility that by then, perhaps through intense counselling, she will accept the prospect of giving birth to another girl. If not, there is always time to assess her condition *then*, and to make a decision based on the circumstances prevailing at that time. I think a decision in advance should be avoided.

Not all the problems he has to face are of that order. Some are a form of light relief and the late Moshe Davis once gave a possibly fanciful inkling of them:

'Chief Rabbi, I'm a pious, God-fearing Jew but I've got five daughters, the eldest is thirty already and I can't get her off my hands...'

'Chief Rabbi, have you heard our new cantor? He has a lovely voice, but he can hardly read a word of Hebrew and I'm not even sure if he keeps Shabbos...'

'Chief Rabbi, we used to be a large and united congregation; unfortunately the new rabbi you suggested is emptying the synagogue ...'

'Chief Rabbi, our rabbi and *chazan* keep quarrelling in front of the whole congregation. Is there any way in which we can get rid of them both?'

'Chief Rabbi, I'm Jewish and my wife was sort of Jewish, but she's been dead for nearly a week now and they won't let me bury her in the Jewish cemetery...'

'Chief Rabbi, you don't know me, but I want to be cremated and the rabbi says over his dead body...'

'Chief Rabbi, when my late husband passed away I reserved a plot right next to him; now I see they've buried his first wife there...'

'Chief Rabbi, I've been teaching in ... without complaint for sixty-six years, and suddenly they tell me I'm too old...'

'Chief Rabbi...'

Jakobovits has secretaries to cope with unwelcome calls and callers, but he does not like to make himself too inaccessible for he believes it is part of a rabbi's job to suffer nuisances gladly.

Some of the questions addressed to him give startling insight into the extent to which ancient prohibitions have been revived. Thus, for example, Mrs Jo Wagerman, headmistress of a Jewish comprehensive school which is run under the auspices of the United Synagogue, wrote to ask if she could form a girls' choir. Men are cautioned against listening to a woman's voice raised in song (there is nothing against women listening to men singing), so the question was not entirely academic.

The Chief Rabbi replied that there was no reason why such a choir should not be formed, but warned that solo performances before 'mixed audiences of pupils, teachers and parents' should be avoided. The ruling shows the extent to which the Chief Rabbi tries to be lenient. Many of his colleagues would have said 'No'.

The Chief Rabbi is expected to keep his clergy in order, which, on the whole, is not too arduous a task, though some people think he performs it with excessive leniency.

No officiant can be appointed to a synagogue under the Chief Rabbi's jurisdiction without a certificate from the Chief Rabbi testifying to his 'religious and moral fitness'. In many instances his opinion is sought long before an appointment is even considered.

Ten years ago he established a placement committee through which almost all London, and some provincial, appointments are now made, but even so few major synagogues would take on a rabbi without sounding out Jakobovits on the suitability of the man. It is a matter to which he gives a great deal of thought, but not everyone appointed with his approval has been found worthy of his trust.

The Chief Rabbi puts his failure rate at about five per cent, some would put it higher, and some of the failures have proved fairly dramatic. Thus one highly lauded candidate appointed to a plum job had to abandon his pulpit within a few months of taking office for what can only be called conduct unbecoming a rabbi and a gentleman. Another rabbi was disciplined – though many felt he should have been dismissed – for dabbling in dubious property deals. A cantor was required to resign after beating his wife to a pulp. These are all incidents which have reached the public ear. There have been others which the Chief Rabbi was able to check before they got out of hand, or at least before the public got to hear of them.

The Chief Rabbi likes to think well of his men, especially his fellow clergymen, and takes such recurrent evidence of human frailty deeply to heart as if it in some ways reflects his own shortcomings as a spiritual leader.

He also likes to keep in touch with every part of his far-flung parish. No sooner was he installed in office than he went on a pastoral tour which took him to every major Jewish community in the British Isles and not a few minor ones, to the Jewish day schools, the universities, the youth movements and even HM prisons. He makes twenty to thirty trips outside London in the course of a year and several abroad and he has lectured or preached in most parts of the globe.

Since assuming office he and his wife have paid six visits to Australia and New Zealand and four to South Africa. He generally goes to America about twice a year and is often in Israel for rabbinical or academic conferences. He is president of the Conference of European Rabbis, which takes him frequently to Europe, and in all he must have logged over a million miles in the past twenty years.

His visits to America and South Africa are mainly lecture tours. He is often in Israel because he is on the board of governors of four universities as well as the Shaare Zedek Hospital in Jerusalem, though he is also summoned to special rabbinical conferences. His visits to Australia and New Zealand arise out of his role as Chief Rabbi of the British Commonwealth.

In 1974 he and his wife were the guests at the centenary celebrations of the Sydney Great Synagogue. It was a glittering occasion. The Chief Rabbi addressed over two thousand worshippers in a congregation which included the Governor-General, Sir Zelman Cowan (who later became provost of Oriel College, Oxford, and who is himself Jewish), party leaders, church dignitaries and eminent figures from all walks of life.

Their visit to Sydney was followed by a tour of Melbourne, Canberra and Perth, and the three major cities of New Zealand. His speeches were widely quoted in the national press and they were greeted by enthusiastic crowds

Julius Jakobovits's and Paula Wreschner's engagement photo, 1919

Immanuel, Lotti, George and Joseph, 1929

Lotti

Julius Jakobovits on holiday with
Immanuel and Lotti

Rabbi Jakobovits at the Wailing
Wall, Jerusalem, 1947

Immanuel and Amelie's wedding day, Paris, 1949

Chief Rabbi of Ireland, with mother, wife and four children

Chief Rabbi of Great Britain: enjoying a pipe in his garden, although he has
since given up smoking for religious reasons

With Elie Wiesel

Relaxing on a foot-plate

With David Ben Gurion and Duncan Sandys, 1964

With Menachem Begin and James Callaghan

With Mr and Mrs Thatcher, March 1985

On holiday in Caesarea, 1989   Greeting Her Majesty The Queen

With the late Moshe Davis en route to Moscow, 1975

The Jakobovits children assembled for their father's introduction to the House of Lords, 9 February 1988. Left to right: Elisheva Hamburger, Aviva Adler, Shoshana Turner, Esther Pearlman, Rabbi Shmuel Jakobovits and Dr Joel Jakobovits

About to take his seat in the House of Lords, flanked by his two supporters, Lord Young (left) and Lord Mishcon

everywhere they went. The entire tour was a personal triumph and if, as the former Chief Minister of the Sydney Synagogue claimed, the Chief Rabbi's jurisdiction in Australia was 'a fluid notion', it became rather less fluid as a result of the tour.

'I am not an empire builder nor do I seek to expand the exercise of my jurisdiction,' the Chief Rabbi has said, but where his help is sought he feels obliged to give it. And it frequently is sought both by rabbis and laymen — by the latter, perhaps, more than the former, if only to settle the squabbles commonplace among the former. He is also in great demand as a speaker.

He can, if need be, speak off the cuff, and does so quite felicitously, but he takes his audience, large and small — and they tend to be large — seriously, and every speech he makes is the result of prolonged cogitation. Wherever possible, he likes to introduce a new thought to his audience. The right expressions do not always come easily to him and it can take him weeks to prepare a lecture and days to prepare a sermon, but then, as he has often argued, 'nothing worthwhile comes from nothing'.

Every rabbi is expected to visit the sick, comfort the bereaved and help the fallen, and while it is generally presumed that the Chief Rabbi is too busy to do the same, Jakobovits has rarely excused himself from such duties. If he or his wife cannot attend in person, they will often send a letter and both will go a long way to perform a small service.

Whenever a major Jewish organization — and no Jewish organization thinks of itself as minor — holds a public function, usually in the form of a large and expensive meal in a large and expensive setting, places are usually reserved at the top table for the Chief Rabbi and his wife, and both usually feel obliged to attend, though in recent years they have tended to avoid the meal itself.

And then, of course, there are Barmitzvahs and weddings, to say nothing of state occasions like banquets for visiting dignitaries, and ambassadorial receptions. There is no duty so pleasurable which does not become a chore when repeated three or four times a week and the Sabbath assumes a special significance for him if only because it is the one occasion when he can be assured of the company of his own wife, children and grandchildren in the privacy of his own home. He sometimes wonders how public figures who do not keep the Sabbath manage to keep their sanity.

He does not allow the welter of routine or official duties to obscure his priorities. He regards his main task as the furtherance of Jewish education. He has, as we shall see, been closely involved in the creation of a major new Jewish secondary school, and the nearer the plans approach fruition the greater the demands they make on his time.

His day begins at seven, when he rises to attend prayers at the local synagogue in St John's Wood, which is about ten minutes' walk away. This is the nearest thing he has to physical exercise. He will scan the morning papers, go through his mail over a snatched breakfast and answer letters by dictaphone in his chauffeur-driven Volvo on the way to and from his office, and even there he is often interrupted by phone-calls.

His mornings are usually occupied with meetings and interviews. He then goes home for a frugal lunch, usually a fried egg or a piece of fish. He is not fastidious about food. 'He eats anything you put in front of him,' says his wife, with something like chagrin (though he admits to a weakness for cream cakes). He was taken ill shortly after coming to London and now, on doctors' orders, has a nap after lunch. He will then continue to work from his pleasantly appointed, book-lined study overlooking his garden.

Visitors are numerous and frequent: a rabbi from Brazil, another from South Africa, a whole delegation of rabbis from Israel or Australia, or groups of visitors from New York; all are made welcome.

The Chief Rabbi and his wife entertain almost as frequently as they are entertained, cardinals, bishops, diplomats, judges, lawyers, newspaper editors, politicians, writers, artists, industrialists and bankers, all mixing easily and freely. Lady Jakobovits reckons that they have entertained over eight thousand guests since coming to London. They have a suite of stately drawing-rooms, but, when people drop in unexpectedly, she is not at all abashed to invite them to a meal round the kitchen table.

Kosher food is expensive – kosher meat, for example, is about twice the price of its non-kosher equivalent – and their hospitality, as we shall see, brought on a financial crisis because they had no entertainment allowance. They now receive one.

By British standards, and certainly by church standards, the Chief Rabbi is generously paid. He gets about £40,000 a year plus free accommodation and a car; it is also rumoured that he doubles his salary through his American lecture tours, but this is a wild exaggeration. He can, on occasion, command a fee of about $5,000, but he usually gets less than half of that. As Lady Jakobovits often accompanies him on his trips, the fees do not in fact always cover his expenses, and his lecture tours arise out of a yearning to teach rather than a yearning for money. They also allow him to visit family and friends in Baltimore, New York and Los Angeles at frequent intervals, but in net terms they bring in less than £5,000 a year.

His visits to Australia and elsewhere are usually paid for by his hosts. The whole cost of his office – which includes the Marriage Authorization Office – is about £250,000 a year, which is mainly borne by the United Synagogue, though provincial and overseas communities also make their contribution.

He is out of the country for about three months in the year, but when at home he will try to snatch an hour for private study, almost furtively, as if indulging in something improper.

His office hours are unrelated to his working hours. He often has meetings in the evening, and he is frequently disturbed by phone-calls, sometimes deep into the night, for Americans do not always appreciate the time difference between New York and London and some callers have no sense of time at all. And then there is always unfinished business: a speech to prepare, a lecture to complete, calls to make, advisers to consult, books to write, proofs to edit, letters to sign.

He likes to put in an occasional appearance in the House of Lords and has to date spoken on questions like immigration, medical ethics, education, the Human Embryos Amendment Bill and, most recently, the War Crimes Bill.

He takes particular pains with every word he utters, firstly because he has the highest respect for the House of Lords as a forum, and no matter how arcane the subject it is likely to contain someone who is a world authority on it, and secondly because he is still a rare bird and anything he says is given undue prominence. He is also nervous of saying anything which could be wrenched out of context, for it could redound not only on himself but on the entire community, and so he writes and re-writes, drafts, and re-drafts, and sometimes finds himself composing speeches in his dreams.

As a public figure he has always had to take certain minimal precautions over his personal safety, but Arab terrorist campaigns have put him in the front line. Since the attempt on the life of Ambassador Shlomo Argov in 1982, he has been hemmed in with security guards and given a long list of dos and don'ts — mostly don'ts — which seriously impair his freedom of movement. It also means a careful vetting of guest lists and, in spite of the numbers he entertains, his house is not quite as open as he would have wished. He suffers such restraints dutifully but not always cheerfully.

At first he found the restrictions irksome, for there have been red alerts during which he could not even go to synagogue, but he has learned to live with them and now looks upon his guards as members of his family.

His job, in other words, is extremely demanding and, as he has often confessed, he might have found it impossible without the support of his wife.

10

The Rabbi's Wife

JEWISH tradition barely accords any formal function to a rabbi's wife, and, in so far as it does, it is a retiring one. Rabbis' wives, it suggests, should be seen but not heard, and preferably they should not be seen either: but as there are few specific guidelines on the matter, each wife is more or less free to assume any role she chooses. Lady Jakobovits, as we shall see, has assumed a great many, but the one in which she has particularly excelled is that of public relations officer to her husband, and many people believe that he would not have got where he was without her.

'The trouble is', she explains, 'he's very shy and very modest and never says a good word for himself, so I say it for him.'

They are an obviously happy couple. The affection between them radiates across the length of a room and he will never pull her up in public – perhaps not even in private. However, he sometimes winces when she enlarges on his qualities.

'That he's brilliant everyone knows, but nobody knows how good and helpful he is, the way he puts himself out for people, how deeply he cares and how hard he works. That's why I got so upset when he was attacked in the early years.'

She goes through the papers before breakfast and, during their first years in London, there were occasions when he returned from synagogue in the morning to find her on the stairs in tears.

'He doesn't seem to be bothered by criticism, he takes it all in his stride. He even takes praise in his stride. I wish I could be more like him.'

'How did you meet?' the Queen once asked her.

'Through mutual friends,' she said.

'Funny,' said the Queen, 'that's how I met my husband.'

Lady Jakobovits is happy with her role, even if it has turned out to be more onerous than she expected.

'A girl should think twice before marrying a rabbi,' she says. 'Her time isn't

114

really her own. She must always be ready to give of herself and not everyone is cut out for it.'

As for herself she had always hoped to marry a rabbi or a doctor, for she believed that both callings involved the husband and wife as a team. Certainly her own marriage was to offer abundant scope for her energies.

If she had the chance she would start a school for rabbis' wives, for they have so much to learn and so many things to do, and they do it — as she did — by a process of trial and error. Only one of her four sisters married a rabbi; the others would not hear of it because of the demands which would have been made on them. Of her own four daughters only one is married to a rabbi, 'but he doesn't do it for a living', she is careful to add. 'He's an accountant.'

Amelie Jakobovits was born in 1928, in Ansbach, Germany, where her French-born father was district rabbi. She recalls it as a small, charming town with friendly people and crowded with churches and monasteries. Her early childhood was particularly happy and, as her father was transferred to Paris when she was only eight, she has no memories of anti-Semitism.

If her father was French, he tended to be Germanic in outlook, in his studiousness and the rigour of his religious observance, yet he combined it all with a great tenderness and an improbable romanticism. If her mother was German, she took to Paris as if it were her natural home.

'She was very religious, of course, but she was a gay, light-hearted woman. We kept open house and never knew who would turn up, or how long they would stay, but somehow managed to make everyone feel at home. Everybody loved her, and I like to think that I'm a little like her.'

Her father was called up for military service on the outbreak of war, leaving them on their own, and when the Germans invaded France in May 1940 they fled on one of the last trains out of Paris. The train was so crowded that there was literally no room to move and hardly any room to breathe. They hoped they were heading south, but they were not even sure of that, for the train seemed to be shunted in all directions. There were four of them in the family by then, the youngest only three months old. The journey seemed to go on forever. They hesitated to alight at one of the many stops because they were not sure how far the Germans had advanced, and they were running out of food, but then, nearly a week after they had left Paris, the train pulled into the small town of Albi in the Pyrenees and the name rang a bell. In one of the intermittent letters which Mrs Munk had received from her husband, Albi had been mentioned, so they quickly scrambled out.

The place was teeming with refugees from all over France and from further afield, and they were given temporary shelter at a special camp set up by the authorities.

The next morning Amelie borrowed a bicycle and set off in search of her father. She eventually located him in a large army camp on the outskirts, but was not allowed to see him. She returned crestfallen to her mother. Along the way she paused to ask someone what day it was, for she had lost all sense of time, and was startled to discover it was Saturday. She had, albeit unwittingly, desecrated the Sabbath and was racked with guilt even though she appreciated that the times were far from normal.

Rabbi Munk was demobilized after the Franco-German armistice and the family eventually moved to Nice, which was then under Italian occupation. The town was flooded with Jewish refugees, but Lady Jakobovits recalls that the Italians treated them very decently. Their accommodation was cramped, but they rarely went cold or hungry, and they felt secure. But in September 1943, after the Italian surrender, the Germans occupied the town and immediately began rounding up Jews for deportation.

The Munk family had made friends in the neighbourhood who helped to hide them. As the months passed, however, their situation became precarious and they felt that they were endangering both themselves and their protectors. One night, under cover of darkness, they made their perilous way across hills and forests towards Switzerland. There were six children in the family by then, including twins, a boy and girl aged thirteen months.

They were hiding in a forest near the Swiss border when the boy, normally a placid child, began crying. Nothing the parents could do would stop him. They were then startled by the sound of rapid footsteps in the undergrowth and a soldier appeared. They thought that they had been discovered, but the soldier was Swiss. He had heard the child crying and thinking that he had been abandoned, crossed the frontier to bring him over; instead, he found two adults and six children cowering in the darkness. He helped them all to cross and they eventually found shelter in a refugee camp near Geneva.

In spite of the hardships and hazards, Lady Jakobovits looks back on her days in occupied France with something like nostalgia. 'There were terrible stories about Nazis and collaborators,' she says, 'but I can only tell you that everywhere we went the non-Jewish French people treated us with sympathy and kindness. You wouldn't believe how helpful the people we met were, and at great risk to themselves. There was a shortage of everything, but even so they managed to get us kosher food. They weren't so nice in Switzerland, even though it wasn't at war, and even though everything they gave us was paid for by the American Joint Distribution Committee.'

The family returned to Paris early in 1946 and found that, although their flat had been requisitioned, everything had been left undisturbed, even to the needle in a sock which her mother had been darning six years before.

Her father took no pride in having survived where so many others had perished and told his children not to talk about the war years. Amelie found that as her own children grew up they wanted to know more and more about them and she could no longer remain silent. She regards the fact of survival as a source of obligation, though she is also anxious to repay to others some of the kindness she has received herself. 'We are obviously saved for something,' she adds. 'I'm not sure what, but it wasn't just to have a good time.'

There were seven in the family by then and their circumstances were fairly straitened. There were many mouths to feed and a new dress or suit for one or another of the children sometimes meant a financial crisis. Fortunately, the Government began to pay special allowances to large families and her mother received more from the allowance than her father from his salary.

Amelie was nearly eighteen, without an education to speak of, for her schooling had been disrupted by their wanderings. But where the lack of a formal education is a source of hang-ups in others, she has learnt to come to terms with it. 'Of course, I'd have loved a good education and to attend a girls' seminary like my daughters, and to go on to university. I'd have liked to be a dentist, but I've still somehow been able to manage without.'

In retrospect, she finds that the war years, in which she had to fend for herself at a very young age in hazardous circumstances, were an education in themselves and have possibly stood her in better stead than a formal education might have done.

She is not, in fact, as totally unschooled as she suggests, for she received a good Jewish education from her father. She also has a shrewd intelligence, a perceptive eye, a lively curiosity and is not cramped by inhibitions. She manages to hold her own even in the most formidable company. Indeed, the more formidable the company the more welcome her interjections. Where her husband weighs every word carefully and can sometimes be ponderous, she shoots from the hip, and her remarks have sometimes saved a pleasant social gathering from degenerating into a seminar.

The more senior Dublin matrons, who had warm memories of Rabbi Herzog's wife – a large, bustling, matriarchal figure – did not quite know what to make of the vivacious young wife of their new incumbent, with her French manners, her new-look French clothes and her elegant coiffures. One day they asked if they could come and see her.

A delegation consisting of four ladies, all hatted and in their expensive best, duly arrived. She served tea and they made polite conversation, but every now and again they lapsed into silence and exchanged nervous glances over their cups. Finally, one of them cleared her throat and made a little speech. Every word sounded as if it had been rehearsed.

'Forgive me, Mrs Jakobovits. I hope you don't think we're being personal. We much appreciate all you are doing for the community, but when Rabbi Herzog was Chief Rabbi before the war, his dear wife, bless her, always had her head covered; in fact, she wore a wig. We thought that perhaps ...'

Almost before she could finish, their hostess — who was not totally unprepared for the speech — raised a finger to her forehead and pushed her wig back as a man might push back his hat. The sort of wig normally worn by pious, Orthodox matrons in those days resembled a roughed-up doormat, and it had not occurred to them that anything so elegant could have been artificial.

Jewish law requires married women, out of modesty, to keep their hair covered. The law used to be largely ignored in England, even among the wives of Orthodox rabbis, but it was taken seriously on the continent. Amelie took it as axiomatic that, once married, she would wear a wig. Now she has four.

'They save hours in time and a fortune on hairdressers,' she says. She does not deny that some wigs worn by Orthodox matrons are a good deal more attractive than the hair they hide, but argues that rabbis never expected Jewish women to look like drabs. This view is strongly supported by her husband, who cites numerous passages from the Talmud on the need for women to look their best so that, for example, while men may not even shave while in mourning, women are at liberty to put on make-up.

This does not, of course, answer why, if women are expected to look their best, they should have to cover their hair at all, but it is not the sort of contradiction which troubles her. Tradition demands it and she conforms to it.

She takes great care with her appearance and has her own distinctive style. She has an ample wardrobe and likes bright, lively colours, which would seem flashy on anyone else, but she somehow gets away with them.

Her Dublin sojourn was dominated by the demands of her family, for she had five children in fairly rapid succession: Yoel in 1950, Shmuel in 1951, Esther in 1954, Soshana in 1955 and Aviva in 1958. Unlike her husband and herself, her children all received good Jewish names, none of which, however, sound particularly outlandish to English ears.

Jewish law, certainly as interpreted by her husband, frowns on contraception, but, in any case, she was from a large family and wanted one herself. She feels that any hardships involved from having many children are more than outweighed by the compensations. In that respect she was more Catholic than the Catholics around her.

'I find it hard to imagine what sort of lives people can lead with only one or two children. It's not fair on the children.'

She does not regard expense as a problem because, from what she could see, the size of families tended to be in opposite ratio to incomes.

She took charge of financial affairs, as she still does: 'Mano's not very practical and doesn't understand money, and if I didn't keep an eye on things we would be left without a penny. Father was the same.'

His Dublin salary was not princely, but life in Ireland was not expensive. She could afford both a maid and a nanny so that she was rarely house-bound.

'I think my mother-in-law, after what she'd been through, thought I was spoilt – not that she ever said so, but she could say a lot without saying anything.'

As the Chief Rabbi's wife she was invited to preside over various organizations, which bored her. 'When I belong to something I want to be active. I have never enjoyed sitting on top tables and receiving bouquets.'

At first, she was handicapped by language difficulties. She quickly picked up enough English to unveil plaques and open bazaars, but her husband liked to interview young couples before their wedding and she would speak to young brides on the duties of married life, some of which were of a fairly delicate nature.

It was generally known, for example, that according to Jewish law husband and wife had to stay apart during her period of menstruation. What was less known was the fact that they had to continue to be apart for seven days thereafter and that they could not resume marital relations until the wife had immersed herself in a ritual bath. Moreover, any show of blood round the vagina was thought of as menstrual, so that if the bride was a virgin – as brides usually were in those days – it meant that once the marriage was consummated, she had to be separated from the groom for about twelve days.

The laws had virtually lapsed in the British Isles, but her husband attached the greatest importance to them and she felt the same. However, it was difficult to put them over without a full command of English. She nevertheless persevered.

They entertained every engaged couple to dinner on the Friday night before their wedding and her easy, uninhibited manner enabled her to cope with the most intimate matters without blushing herself or occasioning a blush in others. She does not know how many of the brides took her message to heart, but she still meets people who recall those Friday night visits with affection.

They enjoyed immense hospitality, but the drawback to being Chief Rabbi, or even a Chief Rabbi's wife, was that such hospitality tended to be rather formal and a little stiff. People were usually on their best behaviour in the presence of clergy.

'You don't have to be good, I used to tell them, be natural. It's difficult for a rabbi's wife, even for me. People either put you on a pedestal, or look at you as something holy, and I keep telling them, you should know me better than that, but it doesn't seem to make any difference.'

Yet she was happy in Dublin. She liked the country, the people and the way of life.

'The fact is,' she says, 'if you're married to the right person you can be happy anywhere, and if it was left to me we would never have moved, even though my brothers and sisters were now married and living in America and my parents were planning to retire there, but I could see there was not enough scope for my husband in Ireland.'

That was also the opinion of her sister-in-law Lotti: 'There was only about a year between them, and they were very close. I was supposed to be a bit like her and I like to think that's why Mano was attracted to me. She thought America was the place for him. It was she who helped organize his American lecture tour, and when he came out on the tour she saw to it that he met the right people. We gave ourselves ten years when we came to Dublin and, in any case, we knew we'd have to move once the children grew older, but if it would have been left to Mano nothing would have happened. It was Lotti who got things moving.'

They had numerous friends in England who urged them not to go to America. 'They thought that if Mano came to England, or even remained in Ireland, he would eventually become Chief Rabbi. I mentioned it to my father and he said that if the Almighty should decide that he will be Chief Rabbi of England, he'll become Chief Rabbi wherever he is.'

Her arrival in New York, laden with luggage and children – the oldest was eight, the youngest a babe in arms – was something of an anti-climax. Lotti had helped to find them a rarity, a town house right in the middle of Manhattan, on Fifth Avenue and Central Park: '"You'll love it," said Lotti. I did not. It was large and dark and gloomy, and creepy, with lifts and dumb-waiters, and a musty smell, as if they never opened a window – not a place for a family with young children. I boarded out the children with my brother and sisters and wouldn't move. A good job too. I later heard that somebody had been murdered in the house but they never found the body, so it was going cheap.'

They were eventually offered two adjacent flats in East 62nd Street, which were less than ideal, for the synagogue did not feel it could go to the expense of knocking them into one. But she quickly adapted them to their needs.

'I arrived from Dublin in what I thought was the height of fashion, but Myrtle Hirsch, whose husband more or less founded the synagogue, took one look at me and put her hand to her eyes. She helped me choose a new wardrobe.'

Mrs Hirsch, one of the most elegant dowagers in New York, still thinks of her as if she were her own daughter: 'We took to her the moment she came. She was like a little Dutch girl, fresh, innocent, but she adapted very quickly. She was soon at the centre of everything and helped to make a family out of the congregation.'

Most of the members were some twenty to thirty years their senior and regarded the rabbi and his wife as children. Yet, in a sense, she and her husband were the parents of the congregation, he as spiritual mentor and guide, she as helpmeet.

In Britain, congregations engaged only the rabbi and treated any help they might receive from the wife as a bonus. In America, and certainly in the Fifth Avenue Synagogue, she was part of the deal; in any case, she and her husband had always worked together as a team from the day they married.

The congregation began with eleven members. Anything new in America has its immediate appeal, but the rabbi and his wife were expected to play their part in attracting new members, which they readily did, though the element of salesmanship involved came more easily to the latter than the former. Jakobovits can seem stand-offish when he is in fact rather shy, whereas she has no hesitation in sailing into any company and making lasting friends among total strangers. The numbers grew from week to week and within a year or two they almost had to put up 'House Full' notices.

Lady Jakobovits unhesitatingly ascribes the growth to her husband's personality and preaching. To use an expression of one of his congregants, 'He wowed them', but so did she. If his Irish connection added to his appeal, her French connection added to hers.

As in Dublin, they kept open house so that their flat became an adjunct to the synagogue. They were fortunate in that the synagogue was comparatively small and could only hold about three hundred worshippers, so that each new member became, and remains, a personal friend.

New York itself took some getting used to, its colour, its clamour and its size. Dublin was a village in comparison. But where Dublin Jewry formed almost an invisible minority, New York was almost Jewish. In Dublin, they had been isolated not only by the fact that he was a rabbi, but by their level of Orthodoxy. In New York, such Orthodoxy, if not ubiquitous, was not uncommon. In Dublin, a social invitation could be a source of embarrassment, for they could never be certain how kosher their hosts were. In New York, if a home was kosher at all it was strictly kosher. On the other hand, Dublin had been a step up in economic terms, while New York was a step down.

The fact that the congregation was largely composed of millionaires did not mean that the rabbi was paid a fortune. The synagogue itself was not generous, even though individual members were and showered Jakobovits and his family with expensive gifts – one couple arriving for dinner came laden with an entire dinner service.

He was paid a good deal more than in Dublin, but the money bought a good deal less. In Dublin, school fees were nominal; in New York, they seemed astronomical. They did not find it all that easy to feed and clothe their five children and sometimes made do with hand-me-downs from wealthy friends. In Dublin, they had two servants; in New York, they could not always afford a daily help. But more important, in Dublin they occupied the same economic milieu as most of their parishioners, while in New York they existed on a different plane. Within the gilded purlieus of the Fifth Avenue Synagogue they were the nearest things to paupers.

But once they got used to the place they loved it. They were in a metropolis again, which may have meant little to Jakobovits but meant a lot to his wife. It was almost like being back in Paris. She felt less hemmed in and there was a wider choice of friends and acquaintances.

Moreover, she had sisters, brothers, brothers-in-law and sisters-in-law living nearby; her parents, too, eventually settled in Brooklyn. The children, who had hardly anyone to play with in Dublin, now found themselves surrounded by cousins and they received a level of Jewish education that they could not have obtained anywhere else in the world. Her husband was feted as one of the outstanding Orthodox rabbis of his generation, and she herself was becoming somebody in her own right. New York, as far as she was concerned, was new Jerusalem and thus, when he was invited to become Chief Rabbi of the United Hebrew Congregations of the British Commonwealth, her heart sank.

She did not want to go to England; neither did the children. The boys in particular had reached a stage in their schooling which could not be interrupted, and she now had a sixth child only a few months old. However, she realized that her husband had got about as far as he could get in America, while the office of Chief Rabbi offered a new challenge and greater scope. She was torn between her wishes for her family and herself and her ambitions for her husband.

Jakobovits was never a man for quick decisions. If anything he is a man for slow ones and his wife was not disposed to hurry him, if only because her own mind was not made up. He would rise in the morning determined to go, reach out to phone Sir Isaac, hesitate and then spend the rest of the day in further cogitation.

He consulted colleagues and friends, but what perhaps settled the matter was an exchange of letters and phone-calls with his father-in-law, whose opinions he had always valued and who not only told him that he should go to London, but that he was obliged to go.

Sir Isaac had booked a suite for them on the *Queen Mary* – in fact, the suite he normally occupied himself on his transatlantic crossings – and the better part of their congregation came on board to see them off.

'All with huge bouquets and presents,' she recalls. 'I thought the ship would sink under their weight. It was like a wedding, but it was difficult to part with so many close friends whom I thought I might never see again, and family too. We were leaving our two dear boys behind. I was in tears most of the time.'

They were two days at sea when there was a knock on the door and a steward entered staggering under a huge floral arrangement fringed with shamrocks. A second came laden with Irish whisky. A third followed with *green* bagels and smoked salmon – a St Patrick's Day surprise from their former congregation. They had, presumably, been unable to get green salmon.

To Jakobovits, Britain was something of a homecoming, the scene of his early struggles which he could now regard with nostalgia; to his wife and family, it was a foreign country, and a dank and inhospitable one.

It was not easy to get used to. In New York, they were surrounded by relatives and friends. In London, they hardly knew anyone and the children in particular felt isolated.

New York had the colour and exuberance of a Jewish city. London had its Jews too, but they were somehow more restrained and less Jewish. It was also colourful and indeed swinging, but its joys were not the sort to appeal readily to a Chief Rabbi and his wife.

A well-wisher took her for a tour of Carnaby Street; it left her singularly unimpressed.

In New York, they had first-class – if expensive – Jewish day schools. In London, they found schools which offered a good secular education, or a good Jewish one, but none which offered both.

But what depressed her most was the house.

'A dungeon,' she recalls.

Dr Brodie, who was childless, had used the house as his office and it had lost the warmth and intimacy of a home. The garden too was a mess. She spent many an afternoon sitting in the gathering dusk, gazing out gloomily on the bedraggled plants and wondering what on earth had made her move.

In New York, the phone hardly stopped; here it hardly rang.

She felt utterly alien. She somehow thought that Ireland had given her a taste of England, but London was not Dublin, the English were not Irish and, more particularly, English Jews were not remotely like their Irish co-religionists and even less like their American ones. She and her husband were received with every courtesy, but it fell short of actual warmth.

Lady Wolfson was the first to come to the rescue. She brought in an interior decorator, who went over the house from top to bottom and introduced new furniture, furnishings, curtains and carpets. The upheavals seemed endless, but by the time he finished the place was a palace.

It is still an impressive abode with a suite of three large reception rooms and two kitchens (one for milk dishes and the other for meat) on the ground floor and a book-lined study and bedrooms upstairs. No expense was spared in the refurbishing because everyone thought that Sir Isaac was paying for it, but the bill eventually landed on the desk of the treasurer of the United Synagogue.

The children soon made friends, but Lady Jakobovits herself felt isolated, especially as she still had a small baby at home. However, she cheered herself up by taking her young family along on her husband's frequent pastoral tours.

'It's what you expect when you make a new start,' she recalls, 'but I was still unhappy. There was Lady Wolfson, of course, who couldn't have been kinder, but we were hardly in the same social bracket and, understanding as she was, I couldn't pick up the phone and pour my heart out to her.'

And then she was introduced to Erica Lawson, an energetic and purposeful woman, who was the wife of a London property developer. 'Erica was a wonderful friend. She still is. She knew everybody and everything, and once I got to know her London was open to me.'

They were frequently entertained and entertained frequently, not only because her husband's position called for it, but because they had always kept the door open, until she discovered, to her horror, that they were in debt.

The Chief Rabbi's salary was £7,000, which was a substantial sum in 1967 and which sounded like a lot of money to her, especially as they had free accommodation, but they had six children, with four in fee-paying schools and a fifth in university, a certain style to maintain and no entertainment allowance.

The Chief Rabbi himself had a limited understanding of money. His wife had always managed the family finances and, with her French upbringing, she had always managed them well, but the very opulence of her surroundings had undermined her sense of thrift. She discovered that the more one had, the greater the circumference of one's needs, and for the first time in her life she was running an overdraft. The very word smacked of profligacy. She felt as if she had committed a mortal sin, and she panicked.

What made it worse was that she could not even discuss the problems with her husband for she felt that he had enough worries as it was. When she confessed her troubles to a friend, she was told tartly: 'If you can't manage on seven thousand a year, my dear, you'd better look for another job!' Another friend, however, came to the rescue with a loan, and eventually she received an entertainment allowance. The crisis was over. But she also had worries of a more lasting nature.

Her first concern was always her husband. In Dublin and New York, he had been received with friendship and acclaim. In London, she felt, he was greeted with hostility, not by the United Synagogue or his colleagues, but by the *Jewish Chronicle.* 'They belittled him or ignored him and never had a good word for him. Mano got used to it, I didn't.'

Her feelings about her husband, she claims, do not arise merely out of wifely loyalty. If he is wrong, she is the first to say so (though only in private), but in this instance she felt — like him — that he was the victim of a vendetta. 'They could no longer take it out on poor Rabbi Brodie, so they took it out on him.'

The rifts caused by the Jacobs Affair had not quite healed. Jakobovits regarded himself as a bridge-builder, but any attempts at an accommodation with the Left brought fire from the Right, while any concessions to the Right brought fire from the Left; and some of his actions and utterances provoked fusillades from all directions.

'Quite honestly, I didn't know what people wanted from him. It was so different in New York, so different, and for the first two or three years I was as unhappy in London as I've been anywhere in my life. It was so cold, so damp, so unfriendly.'

As always at such times, she drew on the philosophy imbibed from her father, who argued that no day is so dark as to be without its lighter moments. 'Clutch at the light moments', he would say, 'to brighten your darkness.'

Her natural *joie de vivre* gradually reasserted itself, the attacks on her husband began to ease off and, a little to her own surprise, she began to enjoy London.

In 1972, their eldest daughter Esther, a tall, attractive girl, got married. She had attended the Hasmonean Girls' School in north-west London and had then gone on to the Michlala seminary in Jerusalem. She met her future husband Chaim Pearlman, an accountant with the Bank of England, before she finished her course and was only eighteen when she married.

The Chief Rabbi has often denounced large, lavish weddings, but in this instance — as in the weddings of all his daughters — he was not quite able to practise what he preached. The reception was held in the Festival Hall and they had nearly two thousand guests.

'We had to invite representatives from here, there and everywhere,' says Lady Jakobovits, 'and as we weren't always sure who represented what we ended up by inviting everybody. We didn't want quarrels or upsets.'

But if the wedding was large, it was not lavish. The fare was frugal and, by the time the reception was over, some guests repaired to the Savoy on the other side of the river for a meal. The wedding dinner itself was a small, family affair held in the privacy of their own home.

Esther is now the mother of eight children. Her husband, a graduate of Cambridge and Ponovesh Yeshiva (a major seat of Jewish learning in Israel), has since left the Bank of England to go into private business and is a part-time rabbi at the Machzike Hadath Synagogue in Golders Green; he thus somehow manages to serve both God and Mammon.

In a sense Lady Jakobovits is now the queen of British Jewry. She likes to be called 'Lady J' and is not ashamed to admit that she is thrilled by the title. However, no one would suggest that she has been changed by it and she has never assumed, and is incapable of assuming, the airs of a *grande dame*. In that sense, and in that sense only, the prognostication of her mother-in-law that she would never be a lady was well founded and she often wonders how she got where she is.

When she and her husband were the Queen's guests at Windsor Castle, she kept asking herself, as they were led from one stately chamber to another: 'Amelie Munk, what are you doing here? You should be at home darning socks.'

It was the same when her husband was made a peer: 'I couldn't believe it. Mano a lord? Me a lady? My children hons? What's happening?'

'We have been everywhere,' she recalls. 'This palace, that palace, the Guildhall, Downing Street, many times, and it still feels like a dream.'

When they attend state dinners kosher food is, of course, provided, but embarrassing situations can sometimes arise. When they were dining at Windsor, all the guests had identical crockery, only the kosher portions – brought in by an outside caterer – were twice as large.

She frequently has a dozen or more people to dinner herself, politicians, prelates, lawyers, academics, journalists, and prefers to do her own cooking – 'nothing fancy, the sort of things mother would have made' – but brings in help to wait at table and clear up. A hostess, she feels, should be at the table along with the host.

Her husband, while insisting that a woman's first priority is in the home, does not like to see her in the kitchen, and she tends to sneak in and out – almost furtively – when he's not about.

'He doesn't like to see me in an apron either,' she adds. He likes the benefits of domestic life without the evidence of domestic drudgery.

She is at ease in any company and can make anyone feel at ease. 'Everybody likes to think that you're interested in them, which is easy for me, because I'm interested in everybody.'

Her life is built round her husband, not merely because Jewish custom demands it, but because all her instincts commend it. Any plans she may have, large or small, have to fall in with his.

'If he has to go abroad I try to go with him, and I've been to Australia, New Zealand, South Africa, everywhere. It's easier now that the children have grown up and left home, but when they were smaller I had someone in to look after them. Not that I ever neglected them, but Mano always comes first.'

She makes the point so emphatically that it almost sounds like her watch-word.

Her day begins about seven, when her husband brings her a cup of coffee in bed before setting out for morning prayers in synagogue. She comes to life quickly and spends about half an hour over prayers herself.

Jewish woman are not, strictly speaking, required to pray daily, but neither are they required to desist from it, and she finds the experience comforting. She is a deeply devout woman, has much to be thankful for and feels that it is not a bad thing to begin the day with a word of appreciation.

By the time she has made breakfast, her husband is back from synagogue. They breakfast together – 'nothing elaborate, continental rather than English. I watch my weight, he watches his time' – and go through the morning mail.

Every time they have a grandchild – and they've had thirty-four to date – the letters come flooding in and she answers them all personally. She also sends notes of congratulation to her innumerable friends every time they have something to celebrate, and every time a major festival approaches she makes a point of either writing or phoning them.

Her phones start early in the morning and rarely stop. There are four in the house – some ring, some squeak, some croak – and they sometimes all go at once. Occasionally she may conduct two or three conversations simul-taneously. She also has a portable phone, which is rarely out of her hand.

When they first came to London she was importuned by several dozen organizations to serve on their committees. 'I was very frank with them. I am not a top-table person, I said, and if you only want my name on your letter-heads the answer is no. If you just want me to serve as an honorary this or that, the answer is again no, but if you want me to be active then the answer is yes.' She in fact serves on nearly a dozen committees, including the

Association of United Synagogue Women, Jewish Care and the women's division of the Joint Israel Appeal, though perhaps her favourite is the Jewish Marriage Council. 'Mano's baby,' she says proudly.

She is also a lively, amusing and colourful speaker and is in great demand on public platforms.

Like her husband she regards the family as the foundation of Jewish life, as the foundation of all civilized life, and she is disturbed by the soaring divorce rate. 'Even in our circles,' she adds dolefully. 'One quarrel, one rough patch, and it's all over.'

If pressed she will admit that, in common with most couples, even she and her husband have their differences: 'Not often, and nothing serious, and we soon make up. I don't know, perhaps girls are too romantic these days, or too spoilt, but one angry word and they reach for their lawyers. And parents interfere too much. When I got married my mother told me quite plainly: "You're off my hands now. Any problems you'll have are yours not mine." I wish all mothers were as sensible.'

In general she is more concerned to make marriages than to mend them.

There was a rabbi who acted as a sort of honorary marriage broker to the ultra-Orthodox community and worked on the principle that if one party is male and the other female, and both are Jewish, then the foundations were there for a happy marriage. She is rather more discriminating. 'I have to know them well, not only the boy and girl, but their parents. Among Jews you not only marry a wife, you marry her family, and if their backgrounds don't match there could be trouble.' But if they do match she takes immediate action.

It's an old Jewish game. God, according to legend, was the first match-maker. In terms of success she is possibly the second. She began in Paris when she was still single, continued in Dublin and proceeded at an accelerated pace in New York. In London, while her own children were of marriageable age, she was under some restraint, but now that they are all happily married she proceeds without inhibitions. Sometimes she approaches the parents. More often she will tackle their offspring and her manner is disarming and direct: 'Look, I've got this most marvellous girl for you. I don't want to say too much about her because you'll find it all out for yourself, but this much I can tell you, she's just the girl for you. Give her a call, tell her I said so.' She does not recall an occasion where her advice has been ignored.

She does not claim that all the expectations she aroused were satisfied or that every marriage she instigated was happy, but she has enough successes to her credit to look back on her efforts with gratification.

She did not have to exercise her talents where her own family was concerned for one of her daughters married at eighteen, two at nineteen and the fourth at twenty-one. Her two sons also married young.

'They were all love-matches, but if I would have had to find them husbands or wives, I couldn't have done any better.'

All their children are very Orthodox – more so, in some respects, than they are – and it is now quite customary in such circles for the husband to devote himself entirely to sacred studies while he is supported by his wife or her parents. However, it is not the sort of custom which commends itself either to the Chief Rabbi or his wife. 'We haven't got that sort of money, and we do not have that sort of attitude. All the boys either had a profession or were well on the way to getting one.'

The eldest son, a graduate of Baltimore Yeshiva, Johns Hopkins University and University College, London, is, much to the delight of his father, a doctor. He specializes in gastroentorology, lives in America and has eight children. The second, a rabbi, is an editor in a rabbinical publishing house, lives in Jerusalem and has four children. All the daughters live in London and, to date, have had twenty-two children between them. One son-in-law, as we have seen, is an accountant-cum-rabbi. Another is an actuary with Prudential Assurance. A third is a doctor. The fourth is an estate agent. All four studied in yeshiva and all spend as much time – perhaps more – on the Talmud as they do in their professions.

Some of the grandchildren are now old enough to study Talmud and family gatherings round the Sabbath table sometimes assume the character of a tutorial.

'Mano loves that, it's his greatest joy. He got pleasure enough from studying with his children, but the greatest pleasure of all is studying with your grandchildren.' Especially male grandchildren, she might have added, for the Talmud is a male preserve, though her daughters, having studied in various seminaries, also like to join in the discussions. Evening meals can sometimes extend late into the night.

Her husband is occasionally criticized for his negative attitude to women and she feels that this is one area in which he has been totally misunderstood. 'It is not negative at all. He believes that men and women have different roles and, if anything, he thinks the woman's role is the more important.'

Her husband has never taken any important decision without consulting her and she thinks this is true of most Jewish families. Even if women may not hold important offices, the influence they exercise is enormous and sometimes crucial.

She does, however, allow that women could be given a greater say in communal affairs and to that end she has founded the Association of Synagogue

Ladies' Guilds. On her insistence, women were consulted on the appointment of the new Chief. Voting, however, was limited to men, as it is whenever a synagogue appoints a rabbi. She does not pretend to be happy with the position, but if her husband insists that the law would not allow it – which he does – she, for one, is not disposed to argue.

On the other hand she shares his hostile attitude to feminism. 'There he's right, absolutely right. There are women who want to change the world and don't even know how to run their own households.'

She would not go so far as to say that the women's libber is a failed wife or mother, but she does believe that there is something lacking in her make-up, such as religious belief, or a tendency to seek fulfilment in the wrong place.

She certainly has found fulfilment. She is a women who feels good about herself and has ample grounds for doing so, and who is happy with the role, or roles, she has assumed. She is self-confident without being strident or assertive, but she finds it difficult to imagine the situation of women who are less happily placed. Like her husband, she is too prone to draw general conclusions from her particular circumstances and, although she has a disarming way of stating her case, her attitude does sometimes smack of complacency.

She used to regret the fact that she did not go to university but is not sorry now, nor is she sorry that none of her daughters acquired a professional qualification. As far as she is concerned, wife, mother and, eventually, grand-mother are qualifications enough. Though, as a matter of fact, one of her daughters is a gifted calligrapher, while the others are involved in Jewish education.

She has an entire wall of her home – the 'naches wall' (wall of joy), she calls it – taken up with photos of her children and grandchildren. The photos form an attractive display and the grandchildren themselves are extraordinarily like their parents and grandparents. It would seem as if the Chief Rabbi and his wife have somehow contrived to transmit not only their customs and values to their progeny, but their facial characteristics. A Jakobovits child or grandchild is unmistakably a Jakobovits. As far as she is concerned, they are her finest achievements, for although she has always taken her public duties seriously, she has never allowed them to interfere with the claims of her family.

The children are even more proud of their parents than the parents are of the children, not only in the obvious sense that they are proud of their achievements, but in the feeling that they have been everything parents should be. Both were always busy, but neither was ever remote. The mother, though affectionate, did not hesitate to slap them down where necessary, and the father, though affable, could be stern. He did not mind high spirits but would not tolerate *chutzpah*, though his reproof was always verbal.

Their upbringing was didactic, though they learned more from the example of their parents than from their teaching; they, in turn, are trying to transmit the example they received.

As we note elsewhere, they do not belong to synagogues under their father's jurisdiction, but are in no way apologetic for it, for, as one daughter observed, their father attends the United Synagogue because it is part of his job. If he did not, he would attend the same sort of synagogues as they do. Nor are they apologetic that none of their children attend school under their father's jurisdiction, because they are not the sort of schools which they attended themselves.

They were fairly isolated over the Sabbath festivals when they lived in St John's Wood because most of their friends were in Golders Green and Hendon, some three or four miles away, though they sometimes walked over to see them. Now, accompanied by their children, they often make the trek in the opposite direction to visit their parents.

They are all on the phone to their mother two or three times a day and can't wait till their parents finally retire so that they can have them round the corner. British Telecom will be the poorer for their move.

Lady Jakobovits is now in her early sixties – 'one of the disadvantages of being married to a public figure is that everyone knows your age' – but has worn well.

Her wigs have their advantage, for if she wants a new hairstyle she sends one of her old wigs round to the hairdresser or buys a new one – 'no sitting around under hair-dryers for me'. Although she does not like shopping, she spends a considerable amount of time in the shops, not because she has a large wardrobe, but because she has fastidious taste and is careful with money.

Her husband likes her to look good and, as we have observed, quotes numerous passages which not only permit, but positively insist, that women should make the best of themselves. It would not be difficult to find passages which take a contrary view, but in this area, certainly, he is no hardliner.

They frequently have to go to public banquets, which he usually finds tiresome but which he nevertheless attends out of a sense of duty. She loves them and approaches them with the bright-eyed avidity of a young girl about to attend her first ball.

There is something mildly theatrical about her manner and she will readily confess to a love of display and most of the things which make up the good life. Normally when talking of 'a Mother in Israel' one looks to the Bible for comparisons, but she tends to evoke memories of Maupassant.

She is, to an extent, her husband's representative in this world and will read books and magazines which he would not, attend plays which he could not, and keep him in touch with passing fads and fancies, but, like her husband, she is a mass of contradictions and combines her exhibitionism, gaiety and even epicureanism with deep personal piety.

The highlight of the week for her, as for him, is the Sabbath with its glow of candle-light, hymns, ancient ceremonies and mellow rituals. Yet one is sometimes left with the impression that within the pious matron there is a naughty girl trying to get out.

The impression is probably misleading for, with all her worldly airs, she can, like her husband, be very innocent and more than one affair has steamed away under her very own nose without her being even remotely aware of it. But there too she is like her husband, for she likes to think well of people and needs more than circumstantial evidence before she will change her opinion of them, and where the evidence is irrefutable, she will look for mitigating circumstances. A sinner has to be very sinful indeed before he is classed as such in her eyes.

She is, with all her *joie de vivre*, a serious person with deep feelings and profound convictions. She has gravity without *gravitas* and is able to retain her light-hearted ways precisely because her attitudes are underpinned by faith.

She is formidable and, indeed, *formidable*, religious without being sanctimonious, prefers perfume to incense, has high standards herself without being censorious about the failings of others, and gives the impression that Judaism not only can be fun, but jolly well should be.

No one has added more to the gaiety and colour of Anglo-Jewish life. She will be a hard, if not impossible, act to follow.

(11)

Healing Faith

WITH the possible exception of rabbis no profession features so prominently in Jewish lore as doctors. For many centuries the two were, in fact, combined and one of the most celebrated of all rabbis, Maimonides (1135–1204), was also one of the foremost physicians of his age.

Judaism, while not overlooking the next world, is largely concerned with this one, as may be seen from its preoccupation with longevity. Only one of the Ten Commandments – Honour Thy Father and Thy Mother – offers actual compensation, which is 'length of days'. All Israel is also promised – in the words of the *Mishnah* – 'a portion in the world to come', but one does not have to strive officiously to get it and there is a general presumption that if we look after this world the next one will look after itself.

Judaism makes many and sometimes impossible demands on its adherents, but only in extreme circumstances does it expect them to forfeit their life for their faith. It does not make a virtue out of martyrdom. Divine ordinances, said the Talmud, were made so 'that man should live by them and not die by them'. That, indeed, is a guiding principle and there is hardly a Jewish law, however important, which is not suspended where a life, however unworthy or tenuous, is at stake.

Moreover, a history of persecution tends to make survivors self-conscious about their very being, as if obliged to keep themselves in good working order. As a result, the Jewish concern with health amounts almost to an obsession.

A large part of the Mosaic Law is concerned with the laws of hygiene, quarantine and cleanliness, and one of the most fundamental duties of Jewish life is visiting the sick. It is also a sin to hazard one's health needlessly so that most rabbinical authorities, for example, agree that it is forbidden to smoke. Jakobovits, who used to enjoy a pipe, put it aside the moment he became aware of the ruling.

Amongst Jews, as amongst others, faith and medicine have always intermingled and it is difficult to know where the one finished and the other began. The priests were the first doctors and the brass serpent held aloft by Moses, 'so that if a serpent had bitten any man, when he beheld the serpent of brass he lived', was to become the symbol of the medical profession.

The study of medicine formed part of the curricula of the ancient talmudic academies, though the main stress was on social hygiene and preventative medicine rather than cures. Once the universities were open to Jews, medicine proved to be the most popular of all callings, partly because of the high standing it enjoyed in Jewish society, partly because it always assured a livelihood and partly because it was a portable skill. Though the calling is now less popular than it used to be, there are still few Jewish families without a doctor in their midst. In Jakobovits's own family there are five: a brother, a son, a son-in-law and two nephews.

He himself, as we have seen, was drawn to the subject almost by chance. Once he got caught up in it, however, it became a major preoccupation, and he has produced not only a pioneering book on Jewish medical ethics, but a succession of pamphlets and newspaper articles, which keep up to date with the many advances in medicine.

He explained his interest in a preface to his book:

In the past, the human inventive genius served mainly to aid nature in the amelioration of life. Now it bids fair to supplant nature, replacing it by an artificial, synthetic existence in which the deepest mysteries of creation are not only laid bare but subjected to the arbitrary whims of mechanized man. ... There can be little doubt that, of all practical sciences, it is pre-eminently medicine with which Judaism historically and intellectually enjoys a natural kinship, and to which Jewish law is best qualified to address its reasoned, pragmatic rules of morality. For many centuries rabbis and physicians, often merging their professions into one, were intimate partners in the common effort for the betterment of life. The perplexities of our age challenge them to renew their association in the service of human life, health and dignity. Indeed they challenge Judaism itself to reassert its place as a potent force in the moral advancement of humanity.

This work is a modest attempt at helping to meet that challenge.

The attempt was, in fact, far from modest, for it is a comparative study of the attitudes of all the major civilizations to the medical problems of their age, from the God-physicians of ancient Egypt to the God-physicians of our day, or rather to the physicians who, given half the chance, would, he feared, assume the role of God.

In a way his book was inspired by the presumptions of the medical profession and he approaches the doctor with a mixture of awe and suspicion. He marvels at their skills but fears that, like other scientists, they could be carried away by their own discoveries. He explained:

So long as the practice of medicine was rigidly controlled by the Oath of Hippocrates, the occasions for religious 'interference' were relatively few and unimportant. The Oath provided that the honourable physician would limit his art to healing the sick. Today the area of medicine has extended far beyond the classical definition and includes acts which require a moral rather than a medical assessment.

It is precisely that which he tried to provide.

It is a lucid and searching work, wide in scope, readily accessible to the intelligent layman and rich in intriguing detail. He shows, for example, that the first reference to artificial insemination was mentioned in the Talmud some 1,700 years before it was heard of elsewhere. In Jewish law a High Priest can only marry a virgin and the rabbis, in debating whether he could marry a purported virgin who happened to be pregnant, concluded that he might on the grounds that she could have been impregnated while bathing in waters previously used by a man. He also shows that oral contraceptives composed of various herbal ingredients mixed in wine were known to the talmudic sages, but they permitted their use, possibly because there is no evidence that they ever worked.

There is something of a tradition among Jews that the fee which may be exacted for a service is in inverse ratio to its importance, and some sages doubted whether a doctor — like a rabbi — could charge a fee at all, because healing the sick was a religious duty. Some rabbis argued that one could charge a fee for treatment but not for instruction, though Maimonides, who was, of course, himself a doctor, mentions no such restrictions. There is, however, universal agreement that no pauper could be denied treatment because of his poverty, which meant in effect that the rich could be surcharged for the needs of the poor and some communities organized a form of socialized medicine.

The rabbis also prescribed limits on prescription fees and called for a division of labour between doctors and apothecaries, on the grounds, presumably, that a doctor who was also an apothecary might be tempted to over-prescribe.

There is a curious outburst in the Talmud, 'to hell with the best physicians', which may suggest a certain rivalry between the profession of rabbi and that of doctor. Isaac Lampronti, an eighteenth-century sage who was both rabbi and doctor, held that the outburst was directed at surgeons because 'they exceed, or fall short of, the proper measure when letting blood, according to their limited intelligence, thus killing their patients'. Jakobovits suspects that it was provoked not so much by professional incompetence as cupidity. The saying is generally believed to apply to doctors who are convinced that they know best and will not defer to a superior authority. No important commentator took it to apply to the profession as a whole and, as we have seen, it has certainly not affected the Jewish attitude to doctors.

What happens where doctors differ on the need to violate a particular Jewish law, as they did even in ancient times (more so, it would appear, than in modern times)? The view of the doctor with the most grievous prognosis is taken. But more than that, where the patient himself yearns for a remedy which might involve a breach of Jewish law, but which his doctors feel is unnecessary, the patient's view prevails, which suggests that Judaism is almost a prescription for hypochondria.

One might have thought that the really true believer would have resigned himself to any malady he might have suffered as a divine punishment for his shortcomings, which was, indeed, the attitude of some small Jewish sects, but they, not surprisingly, died out.

Jews in general had, and have, a healthy belief in health as their natural due and, far from reconciling themselves to disorders, will not readily reconcile themselves to a negative diagnosis. Hence the numerous jokes about the Jewish quest for 'a second opinion'. And hence the law allowing the patient himself the final say on what he needs.

This attitude, as Jakobovits shows, is deeply rooted in Jewish teachings, for 'it was the prerogative and duty of man to harness his intelligence and the resources of nature in his conquest of disease', so that healing and the search for remedies became positive duties.

The book is in many respects painfully honest, for the author must have been tempted to follow the example of Maimonides and skip over the numerous practices born out of darkest superstition which one can find in the ancient texts. He does, however, try to suggest that, where they exist, 'they were almost all of Babylonian or Persian origin', and that 'in general the Talmud largely retained the biblical hostility to superstition'. This is not, however, the same as saying that it is free of superstition, and he, for example, acknowledges that both the talmudic sages and rabbis of later generations readily accepted the efficacy of amulets and other occult devices. Thus, for example, while Judaism regards witchcraft as a capital offence, it allows a recourse to magic where it is thought it might save life, even if only through auto-suggestion.

He also faces up to the fact that some of the remedies for different disorders suggested in the Talmud are absurd, and quotes with approval – or at least a lack of disapproval – the observations of Sherira Gaon, a tenth-century commentator, to the effect 'that our sages were no physicians; they only recommended that which experience had proved useful. Their counsels in this field are by no means laws. You must not, therefore, rely on medicines mentioned in the Talmud.'

Most Orthodox rabbis, when faced with something plainly irrational in the Talmud, will suggest either that it should not be read literally or that it has hidden meanings beyond our comprehension. Jakobovits is too honest for that and argues instead: 'It is not, of course, the task of theology or religious leadership to correct all human illusions and errors of scientific judgement, and it would be illogical to hold the teachings of religion responsible for such fallacious beliefs as are strictly outside its province.'

Yet if these 'fallacious beliefs' on scientific or medical matters are expressed by rabbis, whose words on religious law are said to be divinely inspired, are they not inseparable from the religion itself? The Chief Rabbi's answer to that is, where the rabbis touch on Jewish law they are indeed inspired, but that their comments on medicine amount to no more than incidental asides and carry no doctrinal weight. It is not a convincing argument and may explain why no rabbi before him cared to enlarge on the subject.

His book is concerned with general principles rather than particular situations, the most general principle of all being that nothing should stand in the way of the relief of suffering or the preservation of life.

Thus, for example, while the churches took quite literally the curse pronounced upon Eve in Genesis III: 16 — 'In pain shall you bring forth children' — and agonized over the use of analgesics to relieve labour pains, it posed no problems to rabbis, some of whom — as Jakobovits shows — even recommended sterilization of mothers who feared the pain of further births.

Difficulties can, however, arise in marginal cases. The Sabbath laws, for example, may be set aside in cases of serious illness. But what constitutes a serious illness? The rabbis will almost invariably defer such matters to the judgement of the physician, but Judaism is concerned not only with the needs of the living, but the dignity of the dead, and there the rabbi can sometimes clash with the doctor.

'Jewish law', we are told, 'condemns any undue interference with the corpse as an execrable offence against the dead', but that law, in common with most others, can be set aside where there is a patient 'at hand' who can derive immediate benefits from an autopsy. Where the benefits are less obvious or direct, as in the use of cadavers in anatomy lessons or for medical experiments, opinion is divided. Although Jakobovits is usually content to quote different opinions without intruding his own, he in this instance has little hesitation in siding with the doctors:

The need for autopsies to conquer some of the worst scourges, such as cancer and heart disease, is, according to medical opinion, incontestable. Indeed any autopsy, nowadays, however routine, is more likely to help in the saving of life than in any 'at hand' case permitted two hundred years ago when medical science was primitive by comparison and the prospect of any meaningful results yielded by an autopsy was negligible.

When it comes to contraception he is rather less lenient, as may be seen from a paper he read before the ninth conference of Anglo-Jewish Preachers in 1951:

The popularity of contraception has opened the door wide to immorality and marital faithlessness, to the eradication of all traces of sanctity, refinement and self-control from life on a scale which even the ancient heathens probably never knew. Man has become a brutalized addict of selfishness and convenience, and he forgets that, in the end, he has to pay a far higher price for his failure to maintain the ideals of moral and ennobled life than would be incurred by co-operating with God in the normal generation of life.

His belief was to be amply confirmed some thirty years later by the eruption of *AIDS*.

All his subsequent researches and, indeed, observations have merely confirmed him in his view. He anticipated the swinging Sixties, the permissive Seventies and the agonizing Eighties.

The first of all commandments in Scripture, as we have seen, is 'be fruitful and multiply' and, according to Jewish law, the least that a couple can do, therefore, is to replace themselves. Birth-control is tolerated only where the physical or mental health of the mother is threatened, or there is the probability of a defective child, but even here there are restrictions. The use of condoms is forbidden as a form of onanism though female contraceptives are treated more leniently.

Artificial insemination from a donor other than the husband is forbidden. Some rabbis regard it as a form of adultery, but, more important, because all children sired from one source are half-brothers and sisters, the possibility of incest is greatly multiplied. A few authorities find even the use of the husband's sperm unacceptable because it would involve masturbation.

Jakobovits regards the whole process with misgivings, not only because of rabbinic prohibitions, but because he fears that 'the generation of children would become arbitrary and mechanical, robbed of those mystic and intimately human qualities which make a man a partner with God in the creative propagation of the race'.

For the same reasons, with all his stress on large families, he is unhappy about the resort to surrogate wombs, for they too could reduce the mysteries of propagation to a type of stud farming and usurp the functions of the Creator. It would also raise the question of who is the real mother of the resulting child, the egg-donor or the womb-owner?

On abortion he shows that Judaism is more lenient than the church in that it puts the fate of the mother above that of the child. He quotes the *Mishnah* to the effect that where the mother's life is at stake, the embryo 'may be dismembered in the womb limb by limb – since her life has priority over his'.

The mental state of the mother should also, according to some authorities, be taken into consideration, though Jakobovits tends to be wary of psychology and psychologists. He also allows that abortions may be permissible in cases of rape and incest, but not for fear of deformity, unless it is well founded, though he cites authorities who would object even then.

'Both before and after birth', he writes, 'an abnormal child, whether the defects are mental or physical, enjoys the same title to life as a healthy child, quite apart from the chance that an abortion might eliminate a perfectly normal child.'

He rejects absolutely any idea that the woman is somehow the final arbiter of what to do with her body and he believes that no abortion should be allowed without the guidance of a rabbi.

Jakobovits has been a rabbi now for fifty years and, apart from his stress on Jewish education and medical ethics, there is no subject that preoccupies him more than what he calls the 'vanishing Jew'. He sometimes overstates his case, especially as he is prone to use figures in an area where it is almost impossible to obtain reliable data, but he quotes them so often that they have acquired something of the consistency of fact.

In 1968, he was told by the Israeli Medical Association that there were at least 40,000 abortions a year in Israel, most of them on healthy mothers who would almost certainly have had healthy children. He argues that over two million Israelis have thus, as he puts it, been 'smothered in the womb' since 1948.

He points out that British Jewry has decreased by about a quarter in the past twenty years, while he quotes data put out by the Harvard Center for Population Studies to suggest that, given present trends, the six million Jews in America will be reduced to 10,420 by the year 2076.

His solution to the problem, like his solution to almost every problem, is the cultivation of a religious conscience, 'through nurture in the spiritual treasures of our faith'. Where this prevails, he argues, 'parents cheerfully raise large and happy families, blessed with children who are generally immune to the scourges of crime and vice as to the erosion of assimilation, preserve their dignity even in physical deprivation, and who assure Jewish survival by heeding Rachel's timeless cry, "Give me children, or else I die."'

In London, he points out, Hassidic day schools grow by twenty per cent a year purely through natural increase, while the Hassidic communities of Brooklyn, Stamford Hill, Bnei Braq and Jerusalem double their number every eight years, so that their future is assured, but he can see none for the rest of Jewry, not even for the sort of modern Orthodoxy with which he is associated.

Some of his figures are contradictory. There are, for example, at least 100,000 Hassidic Jews in America and if present trends continue – which is to say, if they double in number every eight years – there would be a hundred million of them by 2076 and not the 10,420 projected by Harvard, but there is never any certainty that any given trend will continue so that the projection of demographic figures is always a fanciful exercise.

He also has a rather idyllic view of the sort of 'dignity' one finds in homes overrun with children. Nor does he give sufficient weight to the high incidence of abnormality in ultra-Orthodox families arising partly out of their very size, partly because bearing children to the utter limits of one's child-bearing age invites abnormality, and partly through in-breeding, but there is no gainsaying the fact that the main body of Jews, far from accepting the injunction to 'be fruitful and multiply' seriously, are not even replacing themselves.

By far the best argument for a large family is his own, but neither his example nor his exhortation have borne much fruit. Even rabbis in synagogues under his own jurisdiction rarely have more than two or three children – though younger rabbis are proving to be more fecund – and he has more or less reconciled himself to the thought that in so far as Jewry has a future in this world it lies largely with Jews who have their eyes on the next one, and that the sort of this-worldly Orthodoxy, which he upholds and perhaps exemplifies and which was summed up in Hirsch's expression '*Torah im Derech Eretz*', has had its day.

It is one of the reasons why he is so hostile to Jewish feminism. He has never underestimated the ability, intelligence or zeal of Jewish womanhood, and while he has encouraged their greater involvement in communal life, he believes that nothing they could add to the well-being of the community is remotely equal to the contribution they could make as wife and mother.

To those who ask whether such matters are not best left to the individual conscience, he retorts:

What kind of considerations is the conscience to weigh in reaching a reasonable conclusion? Every person is bound to be an interested party in the verdict on the size of his family.... How, therefore, can the individual conscience, called upon to make capital decisions of this magnitude, avoid the bias of convenience, expediency or other ulterior motives in arriving at the right conclusion? I have yet to hear an even remotely reasonable answer to these questions, whereby the individual conscience would turn out to be anything more than a glorified substitute for selfishness.

All of which suggests a rather cynical view of how a conscience works. No man needs a conscience to tell him how best to butter his bread, and conscience comes into play where one's self-interest come into conflict with a higher awareness of what one knows to be right. What Jakobovits is saying is that one's so-called higher awareness is really self-interest masquerading as conscience and that, in the last resort, only rabbis can be trusted to say what is right or wrong. One's conscience is meant to enforce laws, not to make or unmake them, at least in the Jewish view as he understands it.

But that is only part of it. One can also be torn between the demands of conscience and the demands of one's faith and, as we shall see, even the Chief Rabbi is not quite able to resolve the conflicts which thus ensue.

Judaism has never laid great stress on numbers and many rabbis comfort themselves with the thought that even if there will be fewer Jews, they will be more Jewish in outlook and in their way of life. Jakobovits himself has never underestimated the importance of quality, but he also believes in quantity and is distressed by the obvious signs of numerical decline to the point where it threatens Jewish survival. The issue appears and reappears in his work on medical ethics, and intrudes upon almost everything he writes, and if one cannot always accept his arguments it is difficult not to admire his persistence.

He has, for all the calls on his time, kept abreast of the major developments in his field and, while he preserves the traditionally positive Jewish attitude to anything which might preserve life or enhance the quality of living, he is frankly startled by some of the advances. Thus, when giving evidence to the Warnock Committee on surrogate motherhood in May 1984, he felt compelled to point out that 'the sanctity of life, the dignity of every individual, the inviolability of marriage and the distinctiveness of all natural species' were even more important than the treatment of infertility. He added:

The erosion of the family-founded marriage as the basic unit of society is a greater social and moral evil threatening the stability of society and its fundamental values than the suffering of individuals caused by disease or childlessness. Hence relief of such suffering must never be purchased at the cost of impairing the sanctity of marriage as the sole legitimate agency for the procreation of children.

It was not a view shared by the Committee. When it published its report later that year, he expressed his misgivings in a long article in *The Times*. He did not share its positive attitude to surrogate motherhood, no matter how carefully controlled. What he found particularly indefensible was 'the considered refusal to limit access to treatment for infertility to legally married couples'. This, he felt, was 'an intolerable affront to the most precious element of the Judaeo-Christian heritage, and would cause incalculable harm to children deliberately conceived under such conditions'.

The report, he concluded, was not only permissive, but short-sighted, and he could envisage 'human life, generated from test-tubes and Petri dishes, sustained by artificial food and drugs, and terminated by unplugging some life-support machine. . . .'

He lost no opportunity to warn against the dangers which could arise from 'experimentation with the very building blocks of life – test-tube babies, frozen embryos, cloning and genetic engineering' and called for legislation which would give the Government an overview of all work in this field.

'We don't mind playing God as long as it is to right defects,' he said. 'We believe God wanted us to use our ingenuity to alleviate suffering, to correct faults in nature. But as soon as it is used to improve nature – that could be catastrophic for the human race.'

It is a neat formulation from which one might conclude that while plastic surgery to correct an actual deformity would be in order, a nose job would not. Such operations are, however, permitted where, for example, they would make it easier for a woman to find a husband, but then the rabbis have always regarded spinsterhood as a fate worse than death and their permissiveness in the matter could come under the heading of saving life. What is rather more surprising is their readiness to allow even men who are not obviously deformed to resort to cosmetic surgery. Their leniency in this matter – which is manifestly not shared by Jakobovits – contrasts harshly with their strictness elsewhere and is at odds with their many injunctions against vanity.

The Chief Rabbi's concern with medical ethics is one of the issues which brought him to national prominence and his work on the subject both as contained in his book and in many subsequent articles has occasioned keen debate, both within the community and without, for many of his opinions are open to argument.

Is it, for example, ethical to lay stress on large families in a world which is already grossly over-populated?

The Chief Rabbi has three answers to that, the first of which is rather startling. The law to be fruitful and multiply, 'according to most rabbinic authorities' – and he does not seem inclined to argue with them – 'is altogether not incumbent on "the sons of Noah" [i.e. non-Jews]'.

The second is that Jews, far from adding to the pressures of population, are on the way to extinction. 'When Jews will threaten the world's food supply with over-population', he writes, then different arguments would apply.

The third is to be found in Jewish history. A small and persecuted race which has been decimated over the centuries, he argues, not only has the right, but the duty, to replace itself. In any case, he is concerned not so much with growth as with survival. But his work also raises larger issues which he has not attempted to answer, at least directly, and which brings us to the question we have raised earlier, the conflict between conscience and faith.

How ethical is Jewish medical ethics? In broad terms, as he shows, it not only conforms to the highest standards of humanity, but it evolved the very values on which those standards are based, yet he sometimes quotes opinions which are in conflict with one of the most sublime precepts of Judaism, 'Love thy neighbour as thyself.'

If the commandment 'be fruitful and multiply' is a moral imperative, and everything in the Chief Rabbi's work suggests that it is, can there be one law for 'the sons of Noah' and another for the sons of Abraham?

He has no problems with that and invokes what he calls 'the perfectly ethical principle of *noblesse oblige*', which is to say that Jews, being chosen, have to assume harsher burdens.

But there are other issues which are more awkward. One may, for example, desecrate the Sabbath where a life is at stake, but the Talmud argues that the life must be worth saving, and the rule, therefore, does not apply to pagans or non-observant Jews. This suggests that while all lives are precious in the sight of God, some are more precious than others, depending on the moral ends they serve.

Such a precept goes against every principle of medical ethics and is clearly in breach of the Hippocratic Oath, and Jakobovits himself observes that it is ignored by the overwhelming majority of even religious doctors. He does not feel moved to challenge the ruling, but he is clearly uncomfortable with it, and one does not have to read between the lines to discern his own attitude to it.

Similarly most Orthodox rabbis, basing themselves on the ruling of an eighteenth-century sage, are adamantly opposed to the use of Jewish bodies for dissection or medical research, though they are not opposed to Jews enjoying the benefits of such research. Is that ethical?

'Yes,' he replies, 'as long as the religious scruples of the deceased are respected', but the fact remains that even where a Jew has no scruples on the matter and actually leaves his body for medical research some exponents of Jewish law demand that his wishes be ignored.

There are five universities in Israel, four of which have medical schools, but the fifth, Bar Ilan, being religious hasn't, because of the Jewish laws against dissection. (Yeshiva University, New York, which is, of course, also religious, does have a medical school, and a very good one, but then it is not dependent on Jewish cadavers.) Again Jakobovits's own view may be discerned from the fact that he has a close association with the Ben Gurion University in Beersheba, whose medical school has a department endowed in his name.

He claims in the preface to his book that Jewish law is 'reasoned, pragmatic and moral', which in general terms may be true. It is largely true of the attitudes he himself brings to bear on the subject. It is, however, not true of all the authorities he quotes, but he is careful to explain that in writing his book his role is that of expositor rather than commentator, and that he does not presume to pass judgement on the opinions of others. The opinions nevertheless raise some awkward questions.

He is, as we have seen, troubled by the rapid advances in science and he has voiced much of the unease which the public feel on the subject. Who, he asks in his foreword, 'will control the physician and the growing army of other scientists'? His answer would no doubt be the rabbis. But who will control the rabbis?

Even the Talmud does not have an answer for everything and when faced with an insoluble problem it resorts to the expression 'teyku', meaning it will be answered when Elijah comes. There is more than one teyku implied in the Chief Rabbi's work, but they fit within an ancient tradition.

12

Tidings from Zion

LORD Jakobovits did not begin life as a Zionist, but then few Jews did. In common with all devout Jews, he prayed thrice daily for the return to Zion, but people addicted to prayers do not normally expect them to be answered, at least not in their own lifetime. (Rabbi Maimon, Israel's first Minister of Religion, an erudite and witty man, lamented: 'For two thousand years we prayed for a Jewish state, and it had to happen in my lifetime.')

Zionists have always been energetic, articulate and excellent publicists, so that one sometimes has the impression that Zionism engaged the sympathies of the entire Jewish world from the moment it was born, whereas it appealed only to a minority even in the main centres of Jewish life in Eastern Europe, while in countries like Germany it hardly made any headway at all.

It attracted a great deal of attention because it was an exciting idea, especially to Christians brought up on the Bible. To most Orthodox Jews, it was a heresy, especially as it tended to be anti-clerical in spirit, while others were inclined to treat it as an irrelevance.

When Chief Rabbi Hermann Adler received Herzl, he listened to him with courtesy but dismissed his ideas as 'an egregious blunder'; and while Zionist leaders struggled desperately to find a 'night-shelter' for the Jewish victims of Russian persecution – Herzl was even ready to consider Uganda as a refuge – most of the victims themselves found perfectly adequate shelter in the United States of America. If the doors of America had not clanged shut to Jewish immigrants in the 1920s, there would have been no Jewish state.

Zionism became a mass movement after the rise of Hitler, but it was slow to grow even then, and Jakobovits was only converted to Zionism at the age of twenty-six after a visit in 1947 to what was then Palestine.

As he noted in *Chayenu*, the now defunct journal of the Organization of Religious Pioneers, it was an overwhelming experience. 'I felt humbled by the idealism, the valour, the hardship and the intense Jewish purpose of my brethren in the Land. A longing to join them was sparked in my heart.' This was not mere rhetoric, and there is little doubt that had he not been invited to become Britain's Chief Rabbi he would now be living in Israel.

At the same time, he was already troubled by the Jewish attitude to the Arabs: 'I missed sustained efforts to replace, or at least accompany, the show of strength by goodwill and reassurance.' His anxieties, he recalls, were 'curtly dismissed as defeatist and condemned almost as heretical', but he was young, inexperienced and little-known and they attracted meagre attention.

It was quite otherwise when he became Chief Rabbi and, so to speak, made his remarks ex cathedra.

In 1968, a year after he assumed office, he made a BBC broadcast on the eve of Passover and touched on 'the unspeakable misery of the refugees — whether Arab refugees displaced from their homes in the Holy Land, or deprived Jews in and from Arab lands'. Many Jewish listeners could hardly believe their ears. They were aware of the plight of Arab refugees, but did not think it was a Jewish problem, and certainly not a Jewish responsibility, and they felt that for their own Chief Rabbi to draw attention to it, and in the course of a Passover address, when all Jewish thoughts are normally directed to the suffering of the Israelites in Egypt, seemed almost perverse.

He returned to his theme six months later in the course of a New Year address, again on the BBC, when he referred to 'the cries of despair from Arab refugees drained of all human dignity in the world's worst breeding ground of hate'. Worse was to come.

For all his reservations about the treatment of Arabs and Arab refugees, Jakobovits was fairly hopeful that in the course of time their situation would improve. Like everyone else he was immensely heartened by the triumphs of the Six Day War and the religious revival which followed, and he believed that the territories gained in the war would prove to be useful bargaining counters in an eventual peace settlement. As the years passed, and opinion hardened against making any territorial concessions at all, he became less sanguine, but hesitated to voice his opinions.

In 1977, Menachem Begin, after thirty years in the wilderness, became Prime Minister of Israel with the help of the religious parties, and one of his first acts was to encourage the creation of new settlements in the occupied territories. There were, however, groups, most of them religious, who felt that he was not going far enough or fast enough and who called not only for large-scale settlement but for outright annexation. They were vociferous in their assertion of Jewish rights, but seemed oblivious to the fact that the Arabs too had their rights. The Chief Rabbi denounced their attitude as a betrayal of Judaism.

He was anxious to show that Orthodoxy was not monolithic on the issue and that it could be just and humane, but he was in those days a lonely voice.

The *Jewish Chronicle* had for long had misgivings about the directions of Israeli policy and, in June 1978, it reiterated them in bold terms, which were more or less summarized in the opening paragraph:

What is difficult for Israel's friends to say without being accused of treachery – but which must be said – is that, being at the heart of the conflict, no solution can be effective without doing justice to the strivings for some sovereign Palestinian entity. Anything short of this recognition is bound to keep feeding the frustrations of the Palestinians and their supporters everywhere, erupting in continual terrorism and threats, and acts, of aggression.

The Chief Rabbi had discussed the issue with Geoffrey Paul, who had become editor of the paper the previous year, and with whom he had built up a warm relationship. He agreed with every word of the editorial and sent him a letter both to commend his views and to enlarge on his arguments. It was a long letter, but perhaps its most telling points were contained in one paragraph:

Obviously, for religious Jews, settlement in Israel has a special dimension as a religious ideal.... But by the same token their conscience must be particularly sensible to other, perhaps overriding religious imperatives, too, such as the pursuit of peace as Judaism's highest ideal; to the preservation of life which suspends all other laws; to the inhuman condition of thousands of Palestinians in wretched refugee camps, whatever and whoever the cause; to the justice of some Arab claims even when they conflict with ours; and, above all, to the Jewish character of Israel which would be vitiated by retaining a large Arab population within her borders, especially when on present demographic trends Jews would be a minority within the next fifteen years.

The *New York Times* picked up his letter and gave it a two-column spread under the heading, 'British Chief Rabbi Assails Israel for Hard Line on Mid-East Peace.' It was also taken up in the Israeli press and other papers, while the *Jewish Chronicle* itself was overwhelmed by a torrent of letters, most of them angry.

The angriest letters of all, however, came from America, mostly from Orthodox quarters. In Britain, at least, they had read his remarks in a Jewish paper. In America, they appeared in the general press, which compounded his sins and sharpened the fury. Some of the letters simply hurled abuse and even obscenities. One accused him of 'treachery', another asked him to resign, a third called him 'the new Neville Chamberlain of 1978'.

The Chief Rabbi felt that the furore was perhaps due less to what he said than to the slant given to his words by the press and he complained of misrepresentation to the *New York Times*. His letter to the *Jewish Chronicle*, he protested, 'contained no word of criticism of the Israeli Government. It referred to the "intransigent stance" by some "religious elements" (not by "Israeli political leaders", as your report states), contrasting this with the stance of "moderation" of many other Jewish religious leaders.'

He protested a little too much, for although some 'religious elements' had indeed taken up an intransigent stance, the policies they were supporting, and which he denounced, were those of the Israeli Government. He was soon to have rather better grounds for complaints about misrepresentation.

In February 1980, he invited about a dozen London-based Israeli correspondents to an informal lunch. He felt that the Israeli press gave inadequate coverage to the Anglo-Jewish community and he hoped to suggest various aspects of Jewish life which, he believed, deserved their attention.

They listened courteously to his suggestions, but when he invited questions they showed little interest in the subjects he raised – which confirmed his point – and turned instead to a subject he had not raised, namely his attitude to Israel and the occupied territories. He was never afraid to explain his convictions, even at the risk of repetition, and reiterated his view that the Palestinian issue lay at the heart of the Arab–Israeli conflict:

There are many who believe that an accommodation with the Arabs will never be found. I do not and cannot share this despair. If I did not have absolute faith that some time in the future – in ten, fifteen or even twenty years – an understanding with the Arabs would eventually be reached, I would rather salvage what can be salvaged and we might as well liquidate the state, for it could not forever prevail against a hundred million Arabs in a hostile world.

He added that Israel should give up nothing until the Arabs had shown that they could live with her in peace, and that all options – including a demilitarized Palestinian state – should be open for negotiation only after ten years of peace. He was opposed to any redivision of Jerusalem, but thought that room could be found for sovereign enclaves, including the Moslem Holy Places, along the lines suggested by the Mayor of Jerusalem, Teddy Kollek, and he did not see why such enclaves should not form the capital of whatever Palestinian entity might emerge. It was a visionary scheme, far too visionary for most Jewish tastes, and, as he recalls, 'within hours, the storm broke'.

Furious calls flooded in from Israel on 'the shocking and astonishing' remarks reported on Israel Radio. The following morning, under the headline 'LIQUIDATE ISRAEL NOW', an Israeli paper reported that he had, among other things, advocated a Palestinian state, expressed support for the PLO and 'agreed to Jerusalem becoming an Arab capital'. Other reports were even more far-fetched.

The word 'liquidate' was not happily chosen, for with its loaded associations, it had a startling impact even when used in context and, as in the above example, it was frequently wrenched out of context and provoked anger and dismay.

The Israeli press fulminated. Over the next few days the normally liberal and fair-minded *Jerusalem Post* carried three sharply critical articles, two by staff writers and a third by his former rival for the office of Chief Rabbi, Dr Louis Rabinowitz. President Itzhak Navon expressed surprise at his remarks, while the Education Minister, Zevulun Hammer, commented: 'If he said it, it typifies a Diaspora outlook.'

Shlomo Goren, the Ashkenazi Chief Rabbi, summoned a special meeting of the Chief Rabbinate Council to castigate him publicly for 'undermining the eternal right of the Jewish people to Eretz Yisrael, the land of its fathers'.

However, the Sephardi Chief Rabbi, the venerable Ovadia Yosef, dissociated himself 'from the strong unseemly words' of his Ashkenazi colleague, and Rabbi Menachem HaCohen, a Labour Member of the Knesset, said: 'Good for him; let's hope he will not be frightened by his own boldness.'

If the reaction of all religious hawks was violent, the American religious hawks, as always, were the most violent of all. An invitation to lecture in Omaha was withdrawn, while a lecture he was to have given in New York was cancelled after threats of disruption from Meir Kahane's Jewish Defence League.

In South Africa, he was condemned by Chief Rabbi Bernard Casper from his Johannesburg pulpit, and in Australia, the Sydney Beth Din – nominally under his jurisdiction – declared that 'to express views on future relationships between Israel and the Arabs ... one must have in-depth knowledge and skill in political judgements which are not usually possessed by rabbis'. They could have said that again.

Some of the rabbis who denounced him in public later apologized in private; others, after looking around them, pulled him aside to whisper their support in his ear.

The doyen of American modern Orthodoxy, Rabbi Joseph Soloveitchik, who had some sympathy with his views, advised him to ignore his critics and act as his conscience dictated, but otherwise he remained silent.

Several eminent Orthodox figures applauded both his courage and his sentiments, but there was not one rabbi among them. Even those who, in some respects, shared his outlook, had run for cover. He was completely alone. It was, in some senses, his finest hour, but it was a shameful one for the brand of Judaism of which he was, and is, one of the principal exponents.

He has always argued that one does not have to be in the majority to be right and that the Jewish people was a proof of this fact, but to be in a minority of one, even when shored up by unflinching convictions, can be unpleasant.

Three months later, he was asked by the Egyptian Embassy in London if he would give an interview to Mokram Mohammad Ahmad, managing editor of the semi-official Cairo daily *Al Ahram*. After what he had been through with the Israeli journalists, he might have been forgiven for refusing to receive an Arab one, but he was advised that such a refusal would be discourteous. He finally agreed to see him, subject to one stipulation. He wanted Ahmad to let him check any report he might make of their conversation to make sure that it was balanced and accurate. Ahmad readily agreed, and the interview proceeded without a hitch.

Jakobovits made the points he had made before, but in more guarded terms, adding a few home truths about the nature of Palestinian terrorists and the enormities they had perpetrated against unarmed civilians. Six weeks passed and he heard nothing further from Ahmad, which did not worry him unduly, and he presumed that he had not found their conversation sufficiently newsworthy for publication.

Then early one morning as he was preparing to set out for synagogue, a BBC man came to his door with an Associated Press report of his interview, which had just appeared in *Al Ahram*. Minutes later his phone began ringing. The report had already been broadcast on successive news bulletins in Israel and had caused widespread fury.

The next day *The Times* carried a front-page story from Tel Aviv under the heading 'BRITAIN'S CHIEF RABBI VILIFIED IN ISRAEL', to the effect that 'the Rev. Shlomo Goren, the Chief Rabbi of Israel, today ferociously attacked Dr Immanuel Jakobovits, the Chief Rabbi of Britain, and called upon British Jews to cast him out'. It then quoted Goren verbatim: 'I call upon the rabbis in the world and the Jews of Great Britain, who hold the city of Jerusalem and the land of Israel sacred, to spew this dangerous man from our midst.'

Goren, a former chief chaplain to the forces, was a warrior priest, a robust, spirited figure rather than a spiritual one, a fiery patriot, a very considerable scholar and a living proof that scholarship does not always go with sagacity.

In the meantime, the Chief Rabbi was still in the dark as to exactly what he was supposed to have said. When he did find out, he could understand the fury for, as he put it, 'the article put words into my mouth I had never uttered and projected views, by exaggeration or embellishment, I had never held, whilst skirting the major points I had made in our conversation on the need for Arab moderation if any progress towards real peace was to be made'.

It did, however, have one benign effect. Goren's outburst united British Jewry behind him. In a way it was like the public's reaction to the Jacobs Affair. People were less interested in the arguments than in the fact that a cherished institution was under attack; in the end, even those opposed to the Chief Rabbi felt compelled to take his side.

Also, among British Jews criticism of Israel, even before Begin assumed power, was never regarded as a form of blasphemy. The *Jewish Chronicle* itself tended to voice its reservations about Israel's policies in muted terms, but it opened its columns to contributors who were fairly outspoken, so that the Chief Rabbi's remarks — even as misreported — came as less of a shock than elsewhere in the Jewish world, especially America.

The experience, however, was rather intimidating and he emerged chastened, if not contrite, a trifle more cautious in his relations with the press, a trifle more hesitant about appearing in or on the media.

Once his name began to feature in the headlines, he was invited to appear on various chat-shows, but he did not feel that they were an appropriate platform for the sort of message he had to convey. He was also asked to take part in Robin Day's *Question Time*, a programme he much admired, but had to decline once more because he found it too political. He had trouble enough with controversies within his field without wishing to excite controversy outside it.

He was also trying to raise large sums of money to build new Jewish day schools and was dependent on the generosity of private donors, most of whom tended to be well to the right of the Zionist spectrum. While this had never prevented him from saying what he had to say, he saw no point in outraging them without good cause.

He had preached on the need for rabbis to improve their public relations skills as long ago as 1957, when he presented his six-point programme to the Conference of European Rabbis in Amsterdam. The time was long past, he said, when the words of rabbis were virtually accepted as the word of God and they could lay down the law without fear of contradiction. Rabbis now had to reason, to argue and to explain, and he urged that 'every major rabbinate should have attached to it an efficient public relations officer who should act as its spokesman in the press and elsewhere'.

The nearest thing the Chief Rabbi had to a public relations officer was his own wife, who exercised her task with great aplomb in the sense that she charmed any journalist who set foot in her house. Moshe Davis, the executive director of his office, had good press connections, but he was not a trained journalist, and the Chief Rabbi, in the main, handled the media himself. His judgement, at first, was less than sound, but he gradually acquired the necessary confidence and skills.

The Jewish rhetorical arts, as displayed in the pulpit, do not encourage economy of expression. The sermon is, first and foremost, meant to teach and

151

it does so through various embellishments, each of which are in effect a form of reiteration, on the principle that if a thing is worth saying, it is worth saying repeatedly, so that those trained in the spoken word do not translate comfortably into print. Jakobovits was no exception, but over the years he managed to attain both clarity and concision. He was, however, slow to understand the exigencies of reporting and editing and the tendency of even serious newspapers to go for the newsworthy rather than the relevant.

He was aware that not even the *New York Times* could carry a whole interview verbatim (though it sometimes reads as if it does), but he did not always appreciate the difficulties of compressing a long speech into a few short paragraphs, for compression necessarily highlights and can give a slant to an utterance which the speaker never intended.

The difficulties are compounded in translation, especially into a language as cryptic as Hebrew which lacks the wealth of nuances available in English. Moreover, anything said seems bolder when read, so that the Chief Rabbi's first reaction when seeing his words in print was, 'Could I have said that?' In the case of *Al Ahram* he did not, for that was a simple case of wanton misrepresentation, but he was in other respects fairly faithfully reported. There were, however, two occasions when he felt compelled to consider legal action.

The first was in October 1980, when the right-wing South African *Jewish Herald* published a report of an article by him, under the heading 'UK CHIEF RABBI AGAIN SPEAKS FOR PLO', when in fact he had denounced it. The paper was compelled to publish an apology and a correction.

The second was in July 1981, and it arose out of a comment in the same paper by the former Chief Rabbi of South Africa, Louis Rabinowitz. Jakobovits had received a knighthood in the Birthday Honours list, which led Rabinowitz to suggest that he had probably expected a peerage, because his declaration 'that the Palestinians were justified in claiming East Jerusalem as their capital' had encouraged Lord Carrington, the Foreign Secretary, to put forward a similar plan.

The Chief Rabbi had, of course, made no such declaration and wrote to the *Jewish Herald* to say so. But it was only after the threat of legal action that it published a withdrawal:

Rabbi Rabinowitz has apologized for his imputation and we are happy to say that if there is some suggestion by Rabbi Rabinowitz of some collusion between the Chief Rabbi and Lord Carrington – the basis for the suggestion being that Rabbi Jakobovits had hoped he might thereby acquire a peerage – it is wholly without foundation.

Rabinowitz subsequently wrote to him privately, saying that in his Yom Kippur sermon that year he had referred to the sins committed in speech and in writing, adding, 'and since I always try to apply my preaching not only to my congregants but to myself also, I humbly beg your forgiveness, as I did that of the Almighty, for any such sins I have been guilty of with regard to you'.

Rabinowitz, as we have seen, had good reason to believe that he would be elected Chief Rabbi of Britain and, when he was passed over, became a frustrated and embittered man. He was a mass of contradictions. If comparatively liberal on religious and South African issues, he was far from liberal in his Zionism, and after the Six Day War he opposed any idea of withdrawal from the occupied territories, even though they exposed Israel to the danger of becoming another South Africa. He was thus the exact opposite of Jakobovits, who, though liberal when it comes to Zionism, is conservative on domestic British issues and resolutely die-hard on religious ones. From which one might infer that the Chief Rabbi is also a mass of contradictions, but, as we shall see, his views on Israel are entirely in keeping with the general body of his beliefs.

By 1982, the controversies he had excited over Israel were largely forgotten. Then, as if to confirm everything he had warned about the attitudes of the Begin administration, came the invasion of Lebanon.

At first, however, he, in common with everyone around him, believed that the objectives of the operation would be limited and its duration brief, so that he had no difficulty in defending it.

Moreover, not only the interests of Israel were at stake. The campaign in the media against the invasion was so fierce and sustained that Diaspora Jewry felt threatened. Newspapers received a torrent of hate-mail. Synagogues and other Jewish institutions rushed to take extra security precautions, and a police guard was placed round the Chief Rabbi's home. It was as dark an hour as he had known since assuming office and in rushing to defend Israel he was basically defending his own community.

He complained of 'the patently verifiable misinformation spread in the Western media, with PLO-inspired reports on more people rendered homeless than there are inhabitants in the region', and, as he pointed out, far more Palestinians and Lebanese had been killed by their fellow Arabs than by Israelis. Israelis, he said, were 'shocked beyond belief by the present outcry against them compared with the silence of the Christian world when the PLO terrorized and massacred tens of thousands of fellow Christians'.

All of which was perfectly true, but some of his other arguments were disingenuous. The Falklands War had broken out at about the same time and he claimed that he could see 'no greater moral objection to military action for "peace in Galilee" to protect the lives of tens of thousands of citizens than to such action by Britain to secure the freedom of 1,800 islanders 8,000 miles away'; but while the '1,800 islanders 8,000 miles away' had actually been overrun by a hostile power, the people of Galilee had not, nor was there the remotest possibility that they would be.

Even more improbable was his repetition of the Israeli Government claim that the PLO had the power to carry out the extermination of Israel, for the entire Lebanese adventure, as he knew himself, was the outcome of trends against which he had warned privately and publicly over several years. Yet while Israel was under universal attack, he felt instinctively bound to rush to her defence so that his arguments were not, perhaps, as well considered as they might have been and at times were downright preposterous.

All this occurred in the early stages of the invasion, when Israel's claim that it was a defensive action did not seem entirely spurious. As Israel advanced deeper into Lebanon, he found the efforts to justify it a physical, moral and emotional strain. When a friend, Shear Yashuv Cohen, Chief Rabbi of Haifa, suggested that he, in common with other Diaspora leaders, was not doing enough to present the 'simple and basic facts' to the public, he replied with some heat: 'While I appreciate the gravity of your challenge to me "to explain the simple and basic facts of the situation" to the wider world, I am surprised by your assumption that this is simple and that I have not so far done so.' And he went on:

My greatest anguish in this crisis, frankly, is the bankruptcy of our own spiritual leadership, notably in Israel itself, in addressing ourselves to our own people. Blaming everything on others while maintaining a stance of complacent self-righteousness, we seem to have departed completely from prophetic tradition. Indeed, it is mainly the religious element which supports and keeps in power a government which has set Israel and the Jewish people on the present course, leaving it to the secularists to articulate the Jewish conscience and to salvage the Jewish honour. What a perverse reversal of our roles!

Then came the siege of Beirut and the massacres at Sabra and Chatilla, which for a moment seemed to confirm his darkest fears about Israel. But he drew comfort from the fact that the news had brought 400,000 Israelis out in a massive demonstration of protest against the war and was further reassured when President Navon called for a judicial inquiry into the massacres. He was among the few Orthodox rabbis to support the idea of an inquiry and among the very few to acclaim its findings.

To Begin, Sabra and Chatilla had been a matter of 'goyim killing goyim', but while the inquiry showed that Jewish troops were not directly involved, Defence Minister Ariel Sharon and some senior officers bore indirect responsibility for the massacres. Israel was thus not completely absolved. Jakobovits drew reassurance from the thoroughness of the inquiry and its essential fairness.

It showed that even at a time of crisis and divisions, the teaching of the prophets still had currency in the Jewish state, even if they were rarely echoed in the preaching of the rabbis.

Jakobovits should by then have been sufficiently familiar with the attitudes of his Israeli colleagues not to have been surprised by anything they said or failed to say, but he liked to think that the trauma of Lebanon might have induced a more moderate outlook, which it did in some instances. Among others, however, it had the contrary effect and he confessed that he was 'flabbergasted by this betrayal of the Jewish commitment to justice'.

As we have seen, he was, in common with most Jews, shaken by the storm of abuse unleashed against Israel as a result of the invasion. He was not, however, troubled by the fact that people expected a level of conduct from Israel which they did not expect from her Arab neighbours. If anything he saw this as a tribute, because he too expected more of her; but if he could not overlook the one-sidedness of the media, he thought it was 'neither true nor wise to attribute such discrimination simply to anti-Semitism'.

It was not true, he said, because he knew any number of prominent individuals with anti-Zionist feelings who were warmly disposed towards Jews, 'respecting them as fellow citizens, denouncing any manifestation of anti-Semitism, staunchly supporting the cause of Soviet Jewry and similarly identifying with Jewish concerns'. (He might have added that there were also any number of people with anti-Jewish feelings who were warmly disposed towards Israel.)

It was also unwise, because he felt such attributions were self-fulfilling and helped to breed anti-Semites. He also believed that it tended to 'undermine Jewish confidence in the basic decency and tolerance of the society around us, and thus contribute to Jewish insecurity'.

Zionists argue that the world is full of Jew-haters and that only Israel offers refuge from their hatred, while the Orthodox accept the endemic nature of anti-Semitism almost as an article of faith and seek refuge in divine beneficence. Both now pointed to the international reaction to the Lebanese invasion as a proof, if proof were needed, of their belief, and both were therefore outraged by the sight of a Jew, and especially a rabbi, giving voice to misgivings about Israel. If they dismissed any critic of the Jewish state as an anti-Semite, they regarded any Jewish criticism as an example of self-hatred. Jakobovits was thus subjected to further vilification to which, however, he was by then inured.

The Chief Rabbi was to repeat his reservations about Israel's policies in later years but they caused no further excitement, partly because they were by now familiar, partly because they were more widely shared, but largely because many of his misgivings were confirmed by events. If anything the line he has always espoused has become the new Orthodoxy – but not among Orthodox rabbis.

Jakobovits, as a leading exponent of the *halacha*, once described the principles on which it worked. The source of the law, of course, lies in Scripture and the Talmud, but both are subject to interpretation; as there are many interpreters, one generally tends to rely on a consensus of rabbinical opinion. As the opinions accumulate, he explained, some interpretations fall away while others harden as part of the binding norm, and thus, with very few exceptions, all new interpretations, 'derive their validity ultimately from their implicit or explicit assent by the majority'.

Now when it comes to retaining the West Bank and Gaza there can be no doubt that of those rabbis who have ventured an *halachic* opinion on the matter, the majority insist that not an inch may be returned to non-Jewish hands. A few rabbis – including the former Sephardi Chief Rabbi of Israel, Ovadia Yosef – have suggested that the territory could in some circumstances be returned if only because lives are more important than land. Jakobovits is the only Orthodox rabbi of any eminence who has argued openly, repeatedly and vehemently that territory not only can be returned for the sake of peace, but should be; he has even contemplated the creation of a Palestinian 'national entity'.

The *halachic* grounds for his arguments, which he explains in considerable detail, are immaterial. The important thing is that in this instance he is prepared to defy the consensus and maintain his lonely stance.

But why on this issue and no other? Because with all his religious convictions he is basically a pragmatist and draws his political beliefs not so much from Holy Writ as from Jewish life. In a word, he believes in Orthodox Judaism because it works.

He is aware that there are Orthodox crooks, Orthodox philanderers, Orthodox gangsters, Orthodox drug-dealers and Orthodox cut-throats, but they are the exceptions. As far as he is concerned, their purported Orthodoxy merely adds an extra dimension to their infamy, but does not contradict the inherent beauty of Orthodox life.

And indeed the life of the truly Orthodox Jew is, in many ways, exemplary. It begins and ends with study and prayer, and it demands piety, rectitude, industry and self-denial. Not everyone can live up to it, but the very effort to do so brings its own benefits and it is a matter of common observation that the typical Orthodox community, if not a brotherhood of saints, is industrious, sober, law-abiding, peaceful and caring. The only area where he feels they can be faulted as a group is in their attitude to the Arabs, where, it seems to him, they fall far short of the ideal demanded by Scripture, for where he looks for amity he finds hatred, and where he looks for justice he finds oppression.

He also has an irreducible belief in the universal dimension of Judaism as defined by Samson Raphael Hirsch, which is completely absent from the teachings of his Israeli colleagues and from many of his American ones, and he ascribes the absence to two 'cataclysmic' events in recent Jewish history, the first catastrophic, the second constructive.

The first was 'Germany's betrayal of civilization, culminating in the Holocaust', which 'produced a terrible disillusionment with all Western culture and science', so that one can no longer assume the inevitability of progress or enlightenment. The second was 'the rise of Israel as a political reality and the primary focus of Jewish life and thought', which, he believes, 'has largely removed the dynamic' of Israel's mission to humanity and, as a result, 'all our energies are fully engaged in the mission to the Jews, not to mankind'.

It says something for the particularist streak even in the Chief Rabbi that he overlooks a third cataclysm which pre-dates the two he has mentioned, namely the First World War, for if the belief in the inevitability of progress and enlightenment died anywhere, it was in the fields of Flanders and the marshes of Poland.

Jews suffered dreadfully, not only in the Great War itself, but in the Russian civil war, in which they were massacred by the thousand and whole communities were devastated, especially in the Ukraine. But it takes more than an ordinary degree of suffering to temper Jewish optimism and it was not finally stifled until the Holocaust.

The Chief Rabbi's own optimism, however, remains basically untouched, as does his belief in the Jewish mission. If anything it has been reinforced by the events of the past fifty years, for he sees in the unique, if tragic, experience of the Jewish people the confirmation of a unique destiny, and it was his hope that once Israel had surmounted the immediate threats to her existence, she would emerge as a model of everything a state should be.

'For me,' he once declared, 'the urge to make a salutary impression on the world constitutes the heart of Zionism ... the prophet's vision of the Jewish return to Zion was invariably linked with Israel's universal purpose. Salvation was deemed indivisible; there would be none for Israel without encompassing all mankind as well.' Israel, he believes, has lost sight of this mission.

His views have led some people to ask whether he is a Zionist at all. If a Zionist is someone who regards the Jewish Diaspora as a passing phenomenon without legitimacy or purpose except as an extra-territorial pressure group to further the interests of the Jewish state, then he is not, and never has been, a Zionist, for he has never believed – to use his own words – in 'anticipating, or actively working for, the eventual disappearance of the Diaspora in the foreseeable future'. That much would be said by many other Jews who think of themselves, and are thought of, as Zionists, but he goes further:

My understanding of the Conditional covenant does not allow me to regard Israel as indispensable to the future of Jewish existence. That Jewish life without Israel is unthinkable, yes; but impossible, no. Had the assumption of such impossibility prevailed at any time in the past, the Jewish people would no longer exist. Hence, I believe it is neither historically correct nor ideologically healthy to promote such an assumption by allowing Zion to circumscribe the outer limits of the Jewish mystique or the capacity to survive.

The Diaspora to him is thus 'an eternal remnant of the Jewish people no less authentic than Zionism', and he could not sacrifice one for the other.

His reference to the 'Conditional covenant' touches on his belief that the Children of Israel were granted possession of the Holy Land on condition that they lived as a holy people. Their failure to do so in the past led to their expulsion and exile, and he is by no means convinced that they will succeed in doing so in the future.

All of which might suggest that his Zionism is of a luke-warm variety, but this is not the case, for, as he has repeatedly said, 'I subscribe unreservedly to the centrality of Israel in Jewish life today and seek to translate this into the conduct of our religious and educational affairs.'

Zionism has an established place in the curriculum of every school under his jurisdiction and he rarely misses an opportunity to encourage young people to make their home in Israel.

He may not have succeeded in this respect in New York, but then he had very few young people in his congregation. In Britain, however, the outflow — partly through his efforts — has been considerable both in numbers and quality, and it is one of the reasons why the community has shrunk so rapidly in recent years.

He gives his time and energy to a host of Zionist causes, whether as governor of the Hebrew, Bar Ilan, Ben Gurion or Haifa Universities, or the Shaare Zedek Hospital.

There have been years when he has visited more Israeli institutions than British ones, and he has certainly been instrumental in raising more money for Israel than for domestic causes. However, with all his devotion to the Jewish state, he believes that Jewish leaders must take account of the possibility, however remote, that Israel may not be here to stay, so that even if they question the legitimacy of the Diaspora, they cannot afford to neglect it. His views taken together are such as to alienate him from almost every group around him.

'Secular Zionism', he feels, 'starts with an historical error and culminates in a contemporary illusion,' the error lying in the belief that one can maintain a claim to Zion, while dismissing the religious foundations of Zionism, while the illusion lay in the belief that Israel could prosper by merely being a nation like other nations: 'For me, Zionism is as unthinkable and as meaningless without Judaism as without Jews. If Zionism were to become just a Jewish national liberation movement, seeking a state for Jews like any other, it would destroy rather than fulfil the uniqueness of the Jewish people.' This may all be true, but many Zionists were weary of Jewish uniqueness and yearned for a Jewish state so that Jews could be a people like any other.

Nor can he accept the non-Zionism or the anti-Zionism of the ultra-Orthodox, who believe that the restoration of Zion must await the coming of the Messiah and who, as he puts it, regard the foundation of Israel – religiously speaking – as 'a non-event', so that they will not even offer up prayers for its welfare.

But he is even less happy with those religious Zionists who think the Messiah is at hand, see proof of his imminence in the military triumphs of Israel and are indifferent to the impact on world opinion which the actions of Israel might have. Such an attitude, he believes, is not only short-sighted but represents 'the almost complete suppression of our universal commitment ... a shrinkage of the Jewish message and purpose which comprises both our assigned role as moral pioneers and our image among the nations'.

He drove this point home in the course of a lecture at Bar Ilan University – the very heartland of modern Israeli Orthodoxy – in 1980:

Hunted and spurned though we were by the nations, we always saw their salvation through our impact on them as an essential to the scheme of our own Redemption. A messianism limited to Jews was inconceivable to us. ...

This concern is now out of fashion – and, I must add, particularly in religious circles. We have become introverts, all but disengaging ourselves completely from the moral commitment to the outside world which features so prominently in the prophetic tradition.

He rejects absolutely the idea that Zionism would or could solve the Jewish problem and offers abundant evidence to show that it has, if anything, been made more intractable. It has not, he believes, even tempered the pressures of anti-Semitism, but has merely changed its focus.

He also has misgivings about the efforts of the religious parties to establish the rule of heaven here on earth. Where other Orthodox rabbis were jubilant at the fine showing of the religious parties in the 1988 Israeli general election, he was filled with foreboding.

He favours a Torah state based on religious principles, yet firmly rejects the idea of a theocracy for he believes that religion should be spread by example rather than fiat, and he feared that the religious parties might use their gains to extort new privileges, impose new restrictions and thus provoke new hatreds.

He is thus vehemently opposed to the very existence of religious parties and questions their achievements, for he believes that by dabbling in the murky sea of Israeli politics they compromise their spiritual aims and often alienate the very people whose interests they claim to serve.

He cannot divorce the character of Orthodoxy from the actions of the Orthodox. It is almost as if they remained peace-loving, tolerant and benign only as long as they were impotent, and that once in power, or even within sight of power, they have become as assertive and aggressive as anyone else, only more so, if only because they believe they are acting in the name of God.

He has never argued that God could be left to fight His own battles, but it seems to him that those who purport to do so, far from sanctifying the divine name, are desecrating it.

But what pains him even more than the aggressiveness of the Orthodox is the thought that the moral high ground once occupied by the prophets is now held by the secularists, the very people who, in other contexts, he has denounced as the enemies of Judaism. It strikes at the very basis of his creed, which is why he feels compelled to make his lonely stand if only to show that rabbis too can be on the side of justice. He believes that as long as they are in the minority, Orthodox Jews and their leaders will have to choose between power and influence, between legislation and education, and between coercion and persuasion. They cannot have both and he prefers the latter.

Jews have often had to tread a lonely path among the nations, and his own efforts to uphold the teachings of the prophets against the dominant trends even in Orthodox Jewish life has meant that he has often had to walk a lonely path among Jews. Such an attitude calls for inordinate courage but, as he has repeatedly shown, he can be courageous on large issues, even if he is sometimes pusillanimous on small ones.

13

Holy Writ

*T*HERE is a line in Proverbs: 'Of the making of many books there is no end', which sounds like a complaint, but the Chief Rabbi has taken it to mean that through writing many books one attains immortality. I write therefore I am; I have written therefore I was.

In the beginning was the word, and also the end. But it must be the written word. The spoken word can be so much noise, but the written word enjoys something like sanctity in Jewish lore. According to legend, God revealed the art of writing only on the eve of the first Sabbath as one of the last acts of creation.

The sermon, as far as the Chief Rabbi is concerned, no matter how carefully considered and well phrased, dies the moment it is uttered; the written word, no matter how banal, lives, if only in obscurity. Therefore, he was hardly established as a rabbi, and barely familiar with English, before he began to appear in print.

His first published article – on the influence of the yeshiva on Jewish life – appeared in 1940, when he was nineteen. Others began to appear shortly after the war when paper was still rationed and publications – especially Jewish ones – were few and thin. One of the first things he did on becoming Chief Rabbi of Ireland was to produce a local magazine and publish an *Irish Jewish Year Book*.

In Ireland, he had a parish of over 5,000, few of whom would be found in synagogue on a normal Sabbath; his magazine was, therefore, a means of addressing absent friends and preaching to the unconverted. It also helped to keep the community together. In New York, he eventually had a parish of about 300, most of whom he saw every week, but there too he produced his own magazine. He made his motivations clear in the preface to his second book, *Journal of a Rabbi*:

The instinct of self-preservation, nature's most powerful urge, manifests itself in diverse ways. It provides trees with barks; it makes birds sing to attract their mates, and it sends salmon up-river to spawn in safety. It animates the physiology of love

161

and hunger and pain to reproduce and preserve and protect life against decay and oblivion. The drive for self-preservation also makes authors write.

His first book, *Jewish Medical Ethics*, published in 1959 – which we considered in an earlier chapter – was a work of original scholarship. His second book, published in 1965, was not, and again he was frank about his motives:

Upon the appearance of this book I shall enter the twenty-fifth year of my pulpit career. With the spoken and the written word serving as the tools of my vocation, my output of sermons, addresses, articles and letters during this period has been considerable. This volume is an attempt to rescue some of these from oblivion, to assign some permanence to speeches which are often ephemeral and 'but as yesterday when it is passed' and to writings hidden away in some dusty periodicals.

The anxiety to preserve his utterances for posterity may seem immodest, but as he explained: 'The implied claim to literary survival and attention lies less in the intrinsic value of my thoughts than in the rather unusual nature of my experience, of my subject matter and sometimes of my way of thinking.'

His experience has not been all that unusual. He has been a wanderer, as have many rabbis. Nor is there anything out of the ordinary about his subject matter, except that he displays a range of curiosity uncommon in an Orthodox rabbi. However, there is something quite amazing not in his way of thinking, but in the constancy of his thoughts. One can go right through the entire corpus of his written work – which, if one includes newspaper and magazine articles, is huge – and find that the ideas he had in 1947 and 1957 were still extant in 1990.

Thus, for example, the 'Blueprint for Rabbinic Leadership', which he delivered at the first Conference of European Rabbis in 1957, is substantially the same blueprint he offers to young rabbis now, except that he has tested it to the full in the course of his own career and finds that it works. Similarly, the sermons he gave on the thirteenth and fourteenth anniversaries of Israel's independence would not have been wholly out of place on her thirtieth or fortieth anniversaries. There have been refinements in argument, and certainly there have been improvements in style and greater economy of expression, but no changes in sentiment.

Such constancy can be regarded in two ways. Either he has never developed, or he has, so to speak, sprung fully grown from the brow of Zeus (if one may be forgiven the metaphor).

Here they are, all the concerns which he was to make familiar on pulpit and platform, in newspaper and magazine, on the air and off it – the Jewish mission as a light unto the nations; the importance of education; the inroads of secularism; the spirit in an age of materialism; Zionist chauvinism (written even before Israel became independent); medical ethics; vanishing Jews; the dangers of extremism; obligations as opposed to rights; prayer as a means of self-improvement; family fidelity; chastity – all carefully argued and patiently explained.

His constancy derives largely from his concern with basic issues and the guidance of basic texts, Scriptures, the Talmud, Maimonides and others. His mind is not closed to external influences and new ideas, but he weighs them against the old and often finds them wanting.

An immutable faith combined with a stubborn temperament does give rise to immutable attitudes, so that in essence he is not all that different from most strictly Orthodox rabbis, except that rabbis with his range of scholarship and powers of exposition generally veer towards the great talmudic academies and transmit their knowledge to successive generations of students, whereas he has chosen to remain in the outside world and in the outside world such constancy does seem phenomenal.

His third book, *The Timely and the Timeless,* published some ten years later in 1976, is composed largely of sermons and addresses, some of which had already appeared in pamphlet form or in magazines, so that their inclusion in the book represents their third incarnation; but, one must add, the material is often too good 'to be hidden away in some dusty periodicals'. It is cogent and perceptive and forms a lively record of his responses to the more dramatic events of the decade, including the Six Day War, the reunification of Jerusalem, the centenary of the United Synagogue, Israel's silver jubilee, the Munich massacre, the Yom Kippur War, and the record of his own visit – the first by a Chief Rabbi – to the Soviet Union. Read in tandem with his previous book, one can trace his evolution as an orator.

His standing as a speaker is due less to the cultivation of natural gifts than to the triumphs over natural handicaps. He has none of the qualities which make one a natural orator, neither a relaxed manner, nor a pleasant voice, nor a facility for words. His manner was tense, his diction flawed, his voice harsh and, when excited, it rose to a scream. Yet he has always managed to hold his audience and eventually has acquired an international reputation as a speaker. How did he do it?

First of all he learned to temper his language, to excise the more florid expressions, to make them less wordy and orotund. He has learned to control his voice, and it has become less harsh and more mellow. He has developed a sense of humour and, where occasion permits, he can be witty, though he has restricted the temptation to which many of his colleagues have fallen prey of acting as a stand-up comedian. He takes his audience, no matter how small, seriously and takes immense pains with everything he says (which is another reason why he feels tempted to save it for posterity). He rarely talks off the top of his head, so that even where one disagrees with him, he always gives food for thought. He has an immaculate sense of occasion. And finally there is his compelling presence – one sits up and takes notice before he even begins – his fierce convictions and transparent sincerity.

However, this means that the speeches can seem a little flat when reduced to writing, without the occasions which inspired them, without the presence of the man or the fervour of his delivery. Yet the nuggets abound.

'I am sickened to the heart by the spectacle of some Jews who, having previously betrayed their God and betrayed their religion, are now publicly calling upon their fellow Jews to betray their people.'

'In the final analysis, we suffer or prosper as a nation, not through the capricious conduct of others but only through our own failure and merit.'

'The mere fact that a tiny people restored to a little land, with few natural resources, continued to be at the very heart of the major political, economic and strategic upheavals besetting the entire world, affecting the fortunes of super-powers and small nations alike, is itself the surest indication that the millennial drama of God's special relationship with Israel is far from played out.'

'Far from having solved "the Jewish problem", the Jewish state has highlighted it. The "abnormalcy" of the Jewish condition – with all its attendant prejudices and dangers – has now been extended from individual Jews and scattered Jewish communities to the Jewish people as a whole.'

'In the Diaspora, many Jews have found vicarious refuge for the expression of their Jewish identity in the existence and support of Israel. For them, living as Jews by proxy has conveniently replaced the personal discipline of Jewish living.'

'... the dynamics of Jewish history are governed more by spiritual forces within the Jewish people than by physical factors inside or outside it.'

'... the Hebrew prophets are without heirs today; the why and wherefore, the questions on how to put the jigsaw pieces of our jumbled world intelligently together remain unanswered. The perplexed are not guided, at least not by any corporate voice of the national Jewish conscience, and the imperatives of Israel's moral impact on human affairs are altogether ignored in an abrupt disengagement from the prophetic ideals of Judaism.'

'What Judaism is it that I will teach and defend ... the Judaism which will never be in accordance with the times until the times are in accordance with Judaism.'

'The world today is plagued by a restiveness which springs from the constant incitement and agitation, focused only on demands.'

'The moment society or groups of individuals are prepared to come to terms with injustice to say, "it's too bad; we will have to learn to live with it", then they will indeed have to live — and suffer — with it....'

It was possibly these phrases which induced Lord Weidenfeld to take the Chief Rabbi aside to suggest that he write a full-blown autobiography. Jakobovits, however, regarded *The Timely and the Timeless* as an autobiography of sorts, for he lives through his words and ideas and he thought that by giving his responses to the events of his day he was saying enough about himself. But the personal self, the man behind the writ, remained elusive and Weidenfeld hoped for something more. In the event he did not get it.

What the Chief Rabbi offered was a compilation of his previous writings and speeches on Zionism, which would have been a third book roughly on the lines of the previous two, but Weidenfeld was less indulgent than his previous publishers and it was put to him that such a work 'would lack reader-appeal'. A compromise evolved in the form of a semi-autobiographical volume, published in 1984, called *If Only My People* ... and sub-titled 'Zionism in My Life'.

The rather odd title comes from the opening verse of Psalm 81: 'If only My People would Hearken unto Me, and Israel walk in My ways, I would soon subdue their enemies and turn My hand against their adversaries.' The book draws heavily on his previous articles and speeches, but, with a few exceptions, they are not mere reprints, and the plaintive tone of the title tells half the story.

He foresaw many of the difficulties now faced by Israel, warned how they might arise and suggested what steps might be taken to avert them, but his case, though strongly argued, has been consistently ignored.

He describes successive meetings with prime ministers and party leaders, Golda Meir, Itzhak Rabin, Menachem Begin and others, and though he was always well received he did not have the feeling that the counsel he offered weighed heavily with them. He used one particular occasion to illustrate this point.

In 1975, the United Nations, on the initiative of the Arab states, aided and abetted by the Soviet Bloc and numerous Third World states, passed a resolution condemning Zionism as racism. United Nations resolutions hostile to Israel were commonplace, but none, as the Chief Rabbi observed, 'could compare in virulence to this one'. Prime Minister Rabin immediately convened an international conference of Jewish leaders in Jerusalem to counter its effects and Jakobovits was among the few rabbis invited to attend.

He gave immense thought to the occasion and prepared a ten-point plan calling for the spiritual mobilization of Israel and the Jewish people, which he sent to Rabin in advance. He then reinforced each of his points verbally, but he felt as if he was talking to himself.

Israel is a far more religious society than England, and the religious elements in the country are far more powerful than their English counterparts, but the opinion of rabbis was rarely sought on the basic issues affecting the nation, and Jakobovits found that he was more instrumental in shaping the ideas of a Christian prime minister than of a Jewish one.

Many pages of the book are devoted to the Arab–Israeli conflict, but he is more concerned with friction among Jews:

... at the present time the dangers of polarization and extremism leading to major reversals in Jewish fortunes are acute and ominous. I remain unshaken in my belief that the key to stability and progress, certainly in the on-going realization of the Zionist dream, lies above all in restoring Israel's spiritual visions. To achieve this, as well as to preserve Israel's unity, two main impediments must be removed: the politicization of the religious elements and the secularization of the rest.

He closes with a trenchantly phrased summary of his views:

Anything less than Israel's uniqueness renders the Jewish state disposable and Jewish survival meaningless.

More to be feared than anti-Semitism is the fear of anti-Semitism if that fear becomes the major cause of Jewish identity and activity.

A smaller and more intensely Jewish Israel is both safer and more ideal than a greater Israel in which the Jewish majority and its Jewish ethos are increasingly at risk.

The less coercive religious legislation there is, the more religious Jews will be.

Israel's moral fibre cannot withstand constant erosion by the denial of traditional Jewish education to two-thirds of all children, by progressively replacing idealism with materialism, and by encouraging sole reliance on military strength.

He repeats some of the arguments made in his earlier books, but with good reason, for many of the problems he noted then, far from abating, had become more acute, for as he says in what is almost a final remark: 'Neither religious discipline nor national sovereignty can be permanently imposed by force on hostile majorities. Such force must in time disaffect the ruled and brutalize the rulers.'

Three years later the *Intifada* erupted. The drawback to being a prophet of doom is that one is so often proved right.

The Chief Rabbi has complained of 'the severe curtailment of opportunities for literary and scholarly work imposed by the ceaseless procession of public commitments which, however necessary, and expected of leadership, distract the mind and divert one from academic pursuits'.

Chief Rabbi Hertz was able to produce a highly regarded and widely used translation and commentary on the Pentateuch, but he was less accessible and less approachable than Jakobovits, nor was Israel in existence in his day. There are years in which Jakobovits spends more time in Israel or on Israeli-related issues than Hertz spent on communal affairs.

Hertz's study was his redoubt and to approach him while he was busy on his magnum opus was like approaching a lion in his den. He regarded his written work as his major preoccupation. Jakobovits's literary efforts, on the other hand, are the products of snatched hours, but even so a bibliography of his published work prepared by Mrs Ruth Goldschmidt-Lehman, a former librarian of Jews' College, covers some five hundred items and extends to over sixty pages. Snatched hours, however, are all right for the sprinter rather than the long-distance runner, hence the multiplicity of pamphlets rather than books, and hence the two books largely consisting of pamphlets.

(He has also produced a more specialized work called *Jewish Law Faces Modern Problems*, published by the Yeshiva University, which, though having a linking theme, consists largely of regular articles he contributed over a period of eight years to *Tradition*, founded by his friend Norman Lamm, which is basically the house journal of modern American Jewish Orthodoxy.)

His book on Jewish medical ethics, as we have noted, began life as a university thesis. *If Only My People . . .*, therefore, represents his only sustained literary work, and has not only a linking theme, but a consistency of style and a uniformity of treatment. Opus two and three were made books, compilations. Opus four is a written one.

He speaks of the book as 'the only autobiographical work' he is likely to write. It is autobiographical in the sense that every book tells one something of its author, and it suggests that he prefers to be known through his public stance rather than his private life. It is also more revealing than opus three in that he describes the conflicts which his views provoke, so that one gets passing glimpses both of his humanity and of his fortitude, but the man himself remains almost as elusive at the end of this book as at the end of his previous volume, which he also described as a sort of oblique autobiography.

We shall have more books yet, if only because his flow of pamphlets on topics as varied as human fertilization, religious responses to the Holocaust, new priorities on the Orthodox agenda, AIDS and ethical guidelines for an ageing Jewish world continue unabated and most of them deserve a more permanent form. There are also his regular contributions to *L'Eylah* — which we have touched on in another chapter — which might be called a rabbi's casebook and which could constitute a fascinating work in its own right, if only he could learn to be a little less discreet. He will also no doubt be approached by publishers to enlarge on the various major controversies in which he has featured in recent years and he may well be tempted to yield to their importunities.

In the meantime, he is at work on the revision of Singer's Prayer Book, which is to Anglo-Jewry what the Standard Book of Common Prayer is to the Church of England and is used in synagogues under his jurisdiction.

Services in Orthodox synagogues are conducted almost entirely in Hebrew, which to most worshippers is a foreign language, and the Rev. Simeon Singer (1848–1906), minister of the New West End Synagogue in the final decades of the nineteenth century, produced a translation which, with a few revisions, is largely in use to this day.

It first appeared in 1890 under the authority of Chief Rabbi Nathan Adler. A revised edition was produced under the authority of Hertz in 1917, and it was further revised under the authority of Brodie in 1962. There is thus almost a tradition that each succeeding Chief Rabbi puts his own imprimatur on the work, but the new – or centenary edition – as it will be known, will be radically different from its predecessors. It will have a new format and lay-out, with a revised translation by Rabbi Eli Cashdan, a noted biblical scholar, and introductory notes and commentaries by the Chief Rabbi.

For the better part of a century Singer's was perhaps the most popular translation of the standard prayer book in any language. In recent years, however, the Torah Scroll publishing house of New York has produced a new translation, together with compendious notes, which is widely used in America and has even insinuated its way into British synagogues. It is a handsome work, but the translation is vapid and, as the Chief Rabbi has complained, its introduction and commentaries do not contain a single original thought.

A standard prayer book does not offer much scope for originality, but in preparing the glosses to the centenary edition the Chief Rabbi has drawn not only on the ancient texts but on his own perceptions, which should extend its life – even in the face of American competition – well into the twenty-first century.

He has also given some thought to a larger and more ambitious undertaking.

The standard prayer book commonly in use on Jewish festivals in the United Kingdom is known as the Routledge *Machzor*, which first appeared in 1904 and which has gone through innumerable editions since. The translation is the work of many hands, including the novelist Israel Zangwill, and although it still reads well the language is often archaic and badly in need of revision. It is also almost totally devoid of notes or comments and the worshipper is offered no guidance to the significance or inner meaning of the prayers, some of which are so obscure as to be almost impenetrable. Nor is there anything to suggest how they came to take their place in the liturgy.

The Chief Rabbi hopes to make good these deficiencies by preparing a new translation with notes and comments, and with a companion volume which would enlarge on the customs and history of each festival as well as the philosophy behind such concepts as atonement, prayer and forgiveness.

The services on the Jewish New Year go on for about five hours, while those of Yom Kippur last all day, so that the worshipper has ample time for reading, and the work – which will inevitably become known as the Jakobovits *Machzor* – may prove to be his most lasting monument.

It is not, however, the sort of undertaking which can be completed in the gaps between official duties and it is one of the many projects which awaits his retirement.

Ecumenist

*T*HE Chief Rabbi, as we have observed, operates on two levels, local and national, as king of the Jews and as ambassador to the gentiles. In some respects he is rather happier with the second than the first, and he sometimes turns to the latter as a relief from the former.

On the local plane he represents a particular brand of Judaism in a community which has many brands, but on the national plane he can speak for them all (which, as we shall see, does not mean that everything he says is acceptable to them all). He is involved in a search for common ground at both levels, but he has found it at the national level while it eludes him at the local one.

Common Ground is indeed the publication of the Council of Christians and Jews, of which he is ex-officio president, along with the Archbishop of Canterbury, the Cardinal Archbishop of Westminster, the Moderator of the Free Church Federal Council, the Moderator of the Church of Scotland and, lately, a dignitary known as the 'Archbishop of Thyateira and Gt Britain', who represents the Greek Orthodox Church.

The Council, founded under royal patronage in 1942 by Archbishop Temple and Chief Rabbi Hertz, brings together the Christian and Jewish communities in a common effort to fight prejudice, intolerance and discrimination between people of different religions, races and colours.

To the Jew, the cross was for many centuries the symbol of harassment and persecution and the Jewish liturgy still includes numerous passages commemorating the martyrdom suffered by Jews at the hands of the church. There is even a prayer recalling the mass suicide of Jews in Clifford's Tower, York, in 1190.

There is also a lingering suspicion that all churchmen are at heart missionaries, who, having failed to win Jews over to Christendom by foul means, are now resorting to fair ones.

It is not the sort of suspicion which troubled either Hertz or Brodie. It has certainly not bothered Jakobovits, for he believes that Jews and Christians have not only a common foe in 'materialism, secularism, atheism and sheer paganism', but a common interest in promoting religious education, combating religious and racial discrimination, and resisting 'morally unacceptable legislation, from abortion on demand at the start of life to euthanasia at its end'.

On the other hand, he has been careful to lay down limits to co-operation and, unlike his Reform colleagues, he finds theological dialogues and interfaith services unacceptable.

'We regard our relationship with God', he explained, 'as being so intimate and personal that we could no more convey it to outsiders than we would share with others our husband–wife relationship.'

There was, he added, the further difficulty that while Christianity aspired 'to convert all human beings, uniting them within one universal religion', Judaism was content 'to remain for all time a minority faith restricted to those born into it and the few who may spontaneously seek to embrace it'. Jews, in other words, were anxious to seek common ground without compromising their own distinctiveness. He did not, however, feel that there was any contradiction between the search for unity and diversity, but that, on the contrary, it gave rise to the creative tensions which were at the source of all life.

When he was Chief Rabbi of Ireland it was said that ninety-three per cent of the population was Catholic, seven per cent was Protestant and the rest were Jewish, but if Jews were an insignificant minority, they were significant enough to excite the interest of their neighbours. Jakobovits had innumerable meetings with local churchmen, both clerical and lay, but he does not recall that he was ever invited to attend a church service.

There are Jewish authorities who have argued that Jews dare not set foot in a church, let alone attend services, and in 1965 Dr Brodie even hesitated to attend the funeral service for Winston Churchill (though he eventually went). Jakobovits takes a more lenient view of the matter and has in his time attended services on royal or state occasions, in Catholic and Anglican churches, Presbyterian kirks and Methodist chapels; he has also visited Moslem mosques and Hindu temples.

To say that he attended a service is not to say that he participated in it. The various authorities are always sensitive to the doctrinal difficulties he, and other non-Christian dignitaries, might have to face, so that, for example, the annual Commonwealth Service attended by the Queen in Westminster Abbey was – at the Chief Rabbi's behest – turned into a Commonwealth Observance, with the proceedings conducted mainly by laymen.

Similarly, when his friend Sir Sigmund Sternberg was made a Knight of the Pontifical Order of St Gregory in 1986, the investiture ceremony, in deference to his wishes, was held in the Westminster Cathedral Hall rather than in the Cathedral itself.

Such visits are rare and the occasions are always special, the most recent being the memorial service in a Scottish kirk for the victims of the Lockerbie air disaster in January 1989, which the Chief Rabbi attended not only out of respect to the victims and their families, but as personal tribute to the volunteer workers who had helped to recover the bodies.

Yet rare as the occasions are, they nearly always — the Lockerbie service being an exception — provoke the same sort of comment. From the Right comes the question: how can an Orthodox rabbi do such a thing? And from the Left: how can the Chief Rabbi attend services in a church/mosque/temple, but never in a Reform synagogue?

To the first he would answer that the promotion of goodwill was in itself a religious duty, that special occasions call for departure from normal practice, and that in making the departures he was following the precedent set by former Chief Rabbis. To the second he would reply that while the other faiths accept Judaism as it is, the Reform movement is always trying to change it, and that while everyone is perfectly aware of the difference between Judaism and other faiths, his presence at a Reform service could lead to the belief that there is no serious difference between Orthodoxy and Reform.

He is, on the other hand, perfectly happy to work with Reform rabbis in inter-faith relations, which is not the case with all of his colleagues. Thus, for example, when Pope John Paul II visited Manchester in 1982, he received a Jewish delegation headed by Jakobovits, but Dayan Ehrentreu, who was to have joined the delegation as Manchester's senior rabbi, dropped out because it included a Reform rabbi.

The Chief Rabbi deplored his action. 'It has long been agreed and accepted', he said, 'that in any top-level religious spokesmanship among non-Jews our community is united and does not carry its internal divisions into the public arena.'

Like most Jews he reveres the memory of Pope John XXIII, who worked tirelessly to improve Christian–Jewish relations and who crowned his efforts with the encyclical *Pacem in Terris*, but he has more than a passing admiration for the stubborn opposition to innovation and change shown by John Paul II.

Rabbis when faced with demands for innovation can always point to holy writ and claim, with greater or lesser conviction, that they are helpless to make changes. Popes have no such let out and, therefore, lay themselves open to pressure, sometimes even from princes of their own church. Jakobovits finds the moral stand taken by John Paul II courageous, and as Jews are never immune to the influence of external events, he feels that a conservative Pope eases his work as an Orthodox rabbi.

The Chief Rabbi is the doyen of the Council of Christians and Jews for he has shared the presidency with two different Cardinal Archbishops of Westminster, three different Archbishops of Canterbury and innumerable Moderators of the Church of Scotland and the Free Churches Federal Council. They face very different problems, but a sense of collegiality has developed between them, which in some instances has ripened into personal friendship. On balance he has perhaps been closer to the Cardinal Archbishops than the Archbishops, if only because they are more steadfast in their attitudes, and he approaches Cardinal Hume with particular respect.

'There's a glow to the man,' he says. 'Saintliness is not a Jewish expression, but when you meet him, you understand what it means.'

He also has immense respect for his Anglican colleagues. He was deeply moved by a speech made by Archbishop Runcie to commemorate the fiftieth anniversary of the *Kristallnacht* pogrom, and one passage in particular has lodged in his memory: 'Without centuries of Christian anti-semitism, Hitler's passionate hatred would never have been so fervently echoed. Without the poisoning of Christian minds throughout the centuries, the Holocaust is unthinkable.'

He knows of no prelate who has spoken in such emphatic terms and with such transparent sincerity, and he believes that Dr Runcie has shown not only a constant sympathy for Jewish feelings, but a ready appreciation of Jewish susceptibilities. He, for his part, feels that he has come close to understanding the Christian mind, yet he sometimes contemplates the Anglican world with sadness and confusion.

He has always believed that the function of the church, like that of the synagogue, is to be constant, especially in an age of rapid change, to define lasting parameters of what is acceptable and what is not so that even where people do not conform to established mores they should at least know when and how far they have strayed, and to establish a sense of continuity between the past and present.

He does not claim to have succeeded in all these respects even within his own parish, but at least he has tried. He is not aware that his Anglican colleagues have even tried, but, more than that, they do not even seem to feel that they should try. He is bewildered by a church whose very bishops question the fundamentals of their faith. What hope is there for the sheep whose shepherd is lost?

His bewilderment is shared by more than one senior churchman, and the Rev. Bill Westwood, the Bishop of Peterborough, writing in his diocesan newsletter in January 1988, said: 'Hesitation in the face of some of the moral controversies of the time has made a lot of people wonder where the Church of England really stands and has led people outside the Church to turn to the Chief Rabbi and the Cardinal Archbishop of Westminster for moral leadership in the nation.'

When he was in Ireland, he had passing differences with the Catholic hierarchy but admired its influence on the day-to-day life of the nation, the generously supported church schools and the crowded churches. He also believed that the Christian fervour of the society around them added something to the fervour of Jewish life. In England, he found himself in a largely pagan society, which venerates religion without being religious, which is in many respects deeply conservative, which fights tooth and nail to prevent the slightest alteration in the physical landscape, but which cheerfully tolerates complete transformations in the landscape of the soul.

In 1967, shortly after he assumed office, he was invited to address the silver jubilee meeting of the Council of Christians and Jews and used the occasion to launch a call for action:

I think we should address ourselves jointly to the evils and immorality rampant in our society. In the Jewish view, all spiritual leaders must assume some degree of personal responsibility for every crime that is committed by people in their care. It is our task to assure the primacy of the moral regeneration of society in the awareness of every citizen. Some years ago numerous countries banded themselves together in a colossal enterprise known as the Geo-physical Year, lavishing vast resources in brain power and finance on the exciting corporate study of the world's physical features. Perhaps we should propose the proclamation of a Geo-spiritual Year in which nations and governments will co-operate in massive research and moral rehabilitation programmes to devise effective means for the elimination of vice and crime, of marital faithlessness and immorality gnawing at the roots of our common civilization and our common heritage.

His speech was loudly applauded and widely admired. He was to repeat his call for common action on numerous occasions, but it never led to any practical results. He no longer even expects any, for he finds that if there is one thing which clergymen of all denominations have in common, it is a want of urgency, as if their preoccupation with the eternal has robbed them of all sense of time.

But he also finds in the church a diffidence verging on resignation, a reluctance to utter the name of God in public as if it were an obscenity, an unwillingness to exhort or demand. He admires the concern of churchmen with social welfare and their obvious compassion, but they no longer seem to speak of duty and responsibility. Nor is he aware of any great stress on self-control, as opposed to self-indulgence, chastity or fidelity, and it seems to him as if the impalpable, the inexplicable, the spiritual has become the unmentionable.

Thus, for example, when the deadly effects of AIDS were first publicly acknowledged, he, like everyone else, was moved by the suffering it caused. But while others were inclined to treat it as an unfortunate visitation like an earthquake, he was not afraid to point out that permissiveness was, at least, a contributory cause to the disease and suggested that in many cases the victims may have brought their misfortunes upon themselves.

Similarly he was among the few to quote Scripture on the issue and denounce sodomy as an abomination, and where others rushed to sanctify condoms, he was among the few to suggest that self-discipline could have a role in containing the disease, though – contrary to some assertions – he did not regard AIDS as a form of divine retribution.

The government publicity campaign against AIDS, he said, was virtually a campaign for promiscuity in that it told people 'not what is right, but how to do wrong and get away with it'. He suggested that the only effective defence against the disease was 'the cultivation of new attitudes calculated to restore reverence for the generation of life and the enjoyment of sexual pleasures exclusively within marriage'.

Homosexuality and even adultery, he believed, should be made criminal offences, if only as a declaration that they were wrong. There were any number of laws on the Jewish statute book, which never have been, and never could be, enforced, but which were an expression of abhorrence, and he believed that English law could benefit from doing the same.

He did not expect the churches to share his extreme puritanism – indeed, few Jews share it – but he advocated for a greater readiness to correct, to reprove, to chastise. He was aware that Christianity was more forgiving than Judaism, but it seemed disposed not only to forgive the sinner, but to dismiss the sin. Indeed, the whole concept of sinfulness seemed to have lapsed and personal shortcomings were generally ascribed to social evils, as if individuals were at the mercy of external forces and had no hand in shaping their own destiny.

All these were, of course, private reservations, but then an opportunity came to make some of them public.

Towards the end of 1985, the Church of England published a report called *Faith in the Cities* on the work of the Church in 'Urban Priority Areas'. Dr Runcie sent an advance copy to the Chief Rabbi and invited his comments.

It painted a bleak picture of poverty and hardship, decline, degradation and despair, and unhesitatingly blamed the conditions on 'the inhumane consequences of our free market economy'. The Chief Rabbi pondered on it for some time and then replied with a sixteen-page document called *From Doom to Hope*.

The report had dealt at length with the problems of minorities in what were called urban ghettos, and he pointed out that the very term ghetto 'with its connotation of squalor, deprivation and racial hatred was not so long ago applied exclusively to crowded, usually decaying, areas of Jewish settlement in the large cities'. But the Jews had nevertheless been able to transcend their circumstances, and he quoted a sermon on the subject he had given in New York in 1966:

How did we break out of our ghettos and enter the mainstream of society and its privileges? How did we secure our emancipation and civil rights? Certainly not by riots and demonstrations, by violence and protest marches, or by preaching 'Jewish power' or even non-violence. Above all, we worked on ourselves not on others. We gave a better education to our children than anybody else had. We hallowed our home life. We channelled the ambition of our youngsters to academic excellence, not flashy cars. We rooted out crime and indolence from our midst, by making every Jew responsible for the fate of all Jews. We denounced any fellow Jew besmirching the Jewish name by some misdemeanour as guilty of a desecration of the Divine Name. We did not gate-crash into the gentile environment; we made ourselves highly acceptable and indispensable by our industrial, intellectual and moral contribution to society.

Both Christianity and Judaism, he said, 'raise the relief of want as a precept of the highest religious virtue, and both regard the humiliation of worklessness as incompatible with the dignity of man', but he believed that the report fell short of 'hailing work as a virtue in itself, as an ideal to ennoble the worker and to serve society'. No work, he argued, was 'too menial to compromise human dignity and self-respect', idleness was 'an even greater evil than unemployment' and cheap labour was 'more dignified than a free dole'. Judaism, he said, 'would lay greater emphasis on building up self-respect by encouraging ambition and enterprise through a more demanding and more satisfying work-ethic, which is designed to eliminate idleness and nurture pride in "eating the toil of one's hands". . . . Any job is better than paid idleness.'

He agreed that 'the role of government in revitalizing the inner cities must be vital and indispensable', but felt that the report was 'unduly slanted against present government policies by placing all existing ills exclusively at their door'. And he concluded:

The key to the transition from doom to hope lies within the heart of man, whose confidence must be sustained in the ultimate triumph over present problems and disabilities. This must be one of the supreme priorities for planners, administrators, theologians and every member of the community, most of all the disadvantaged themselves. For patients, faith in recovery is often half the cure. For home and city-builders, the spiritual dimension is indispensable, as the Psalmist asserts: 'Except the Lord build the house, they that build it labour in vain; except the Lord keep the city, the watchman wakes but in vain.'

Although he did not say so explicitly, he found the absence of a spiritual dimension in the report the gravest omission of all.

Perhaps the most striking part of his paper was the quotation from his 1966 New York sermon, to which he might have added a passage from a broadcast he gave on the BBC in 1970: 'Jews played a leading role in sparking and supporting the civil rights movement in America and they have learnt to their cost how easily such a movement can degenerate into large-scale violence and bitter prejudice in reverse.'

In this he touched on the fact that in spite of Jewish sympathies for the blacks, Jews were regarded as symbols of white domination and were often denounced by black-power leaders as exploiters and oppressors. He did not, however, go on to suggest that Jews should therefore stay clear of civil rights movements.

'Judaism', he declared, 'clearly insists that we wipe out the evil of racial discrimination by word and deed – whether by promoting enlightened legislation or by treating our brethren with the same humanity and consideration we would wish to be accorded ourselves.'

Jews, he believed, had helped themselves by their exertions and could help others by their example, but, above all, he sought 'to replace the focus on rights by the emphasis on duties'. This, indeed, was a familiar theme, but he thought it worth repeating: 'The present imbalance between the demand to take and the willingness to give may well render the price of the resultant strife and bitterness greater than the gain in the struggle for greater equality.'

The language may have been ponderous but the words were prophetic. The race riots which broke out in Brixton, Bristol, Liverpool, Manchester and other areas a few years later showed that his apprehensions were well founded, and it was these which had led the Archbishop of Canterbury to set up his commission on the inner cities.

Nevertheless, the Chief Rabbi's response left a bad taste, certainly in some Jewish mouths, if not in the actual ghettos. It seemed to smack of smugness and complacency, and phrases like 'flashy cars' in reference to black aspirations were unfortunate, as if no Jew ever aspired to one.

His paper was, in part, born of his American experience. WASPs could not speak ill – in public at least – of ethnic minorities, but ethnic minorities could, and often did, speak ill of each other, and what the Chief Rabbi did, albeit in an English context, was to invoke ethnic privilege.

Greville Janner, Labour MP and a former president of the Board of Deputies of British Jews, who once rebuked the Chief Rabbi for being too outspoken in his criticism of Israel, now complained that he was too complacent in his references to British Jews. 'We must proclaim our excellence with some reserve,' he said.

A Jewish historian, Dr Geoffrey Alderman, went further. The Chief Rabbi, he said, had ignored 'the very different historical experiences of Jewish and black immigrants in this country'. He felt therefore that 'to tell the disadvantaged that self-reliant efforts and perseverance eventually pay off is an insult, and reflects such a lack of sensitivity that I feel Sir Immanuel should seek an early and discreet retirement. I say to him "in the name of God – go!"'

Hugo Young of the *Guardian* thought the Chief Rabbi's remarks were 'rooted startlingly in racialism', but most papers applauded his intervention, for he had said publicly what many had murmured privately. A hundred and sixty Tory MPs signed a motion on the order paper approving his remarks, and many others wrote to congratulate him personally.

The Chief Rabbi himself found the reaction to his paper strangely inconsistent. It was, he said, 'predominantly critical in Jewish quarters and overwhelmingly favourable in the general press and in the nation at large'.

Many Jewish writers – the latest of whom is Leo Abse, a former Labour MP – have treated the Old Testament as a socialist handbook, but although in Jewish law the poor have a claim on the rich, poverty has never been regarded as a state of grace and the Talmud abounds with exhortations to self-help. The Chief Rabbi's observations were thus fully in line with traditional Jewish teaching, and even more so with traditional Jewish attitudes. Most Jews in fact shared his views, but they felt uneasy at the sight of their spiritual head siding openly, indeed ostentatiously, with the political philosophy of one political party.

Jakobovits, for his part, held his ground, arguing that if precepts which he has always supported have found their way into the philosophy of one political party rather than another, he is under no obligation to disown them.

It seemed, however, that the Church of England, which used to be spoken of as 'the Tory Party at prayer', had resigned its function to the United Synagogue and from then on the Chief Rabbi came to be regarded as chaplain to the party and father confessor to the Prime Minister, and quite a few observers ascribed his elevation to the peerage two years later to that particular paper.

Dr Runcie's view of the Chief Rabbi's paper is not recorded, but it must be added that while the paper was originally prepared for private circulation it was the Archbishop himself who suggested that it be given wider publicity.

And their friendship, certainly, has remained unimpaired.

Jews tend to view his work in this field with some ambivalence for they do not regard themselves as members of a minority group. They have lived in Britain for generations, have attended its schools and universities, have served in its armed forces, absorbed its language and culture, and if they are still Jewish – after a fashion – it does not affect their status as Britons. Therefore, some of them feel that in joining with other minorities they may compromise some of their claim.

The Chief Rabbi has some sympathy with this view but at the same time feels that Jews, having made it, are obliged to work closely with recent immigrants and give them the benefit of their experience. He often quotes a verse which has coloured his attitude to both Arabs in Israel and newcomers to Britain: 'Love ye the stranger, for ye were strangers in Egypt', and he managed to include both Arabs and immigrants in his maiden speech in the House of Lords.

He began with a plea not so much for immigrants as for a consideration of the pressures which cause immigration:

There are Jewish refugees of Israel who arrived from lands under oppression by the hundred thousand in a miracle of absorption and integration and there are about the same number of Arab refugees ... who still languish in wretched refugee camps – an unspeakable tragedy of rejection and human indignity. What started as a conflict between two rights – two people claiming the same land – has now become a conflict between two wrongs, with Israel still being denied the right to exist under the threat of war and terror, and with Palestinians still denied their national aspirations.

He then urged nations to 'accommodate opposing rights before they become opposing wrongs; to befriend newcomers before they become hostile aliens; to secure decent conditions for citizens in the lands in which they live before they become frustrated minorities in places to which they are driven'.

His speech was welcomed in the immigrant press, and *New Life*, which circulates mainly among Asian readers, opened its report with the heading 'Tory Rabbi Recommends Humane Immigration Policy'. It went on:

Asians were heartened by the compassionate and compelling words of the newly appointed Lord Jakobovits.... It is with immense pleasure that we heard such a respected member of the Jewish community – supposedly close to Mrs Thatcher herself – voice deep concern over the new immigration controls. He summed up the despair of the Asian community.

He was to win further commendation a year later when Moslems took to the streets over the Salman Rushdie Affair, for instead of joining with other religious leaders in cautioning them on the nature of British democracy and the importance of freedom of speech, he wrote to *The Times* in March 1989 to declare that his sympathies were overwhelmingly on the Moslem side:

... When the Chairman of the Islamic Society for the Promotion of Religious Tolerance in the UK asked me last October to support the protest against the publication of *The Satanic Verses*, I readily agreed and he was informed that I deprecate not only the falsification of established historical records but the offence caused to the religious convictions and susceptibilities of countless citizens....

While I fully share the worldwide outrage at the murderous threat against the book's author, publishers and distributors, I stand by my view that the book should not have been published....

Both Mr Rushdie and the Ayatollah have abused freedom of speech, the one by provocatively offending the genuine faith of many millions of devout believers, and the other by a public call to murder....

We already have legislation proscribing by common consent many excesses in the freedom of expression, precious as this is. There are laws not only on blasphemy, but on pornography, libel, incitement of race hatred, subversion and breaches of national security....

Likewise there should be widespread agreement on prohibiting the publication of anything likely to inflame, through obscene defamation, the feelings and beliefs of any section of society, or liable to provoke public disorder and violence....

The Chief Rabbi's remarks on homosexuality and his paper on the inner cities had provoked strong disagreement in various Jewish quarters, but no one could deny that they were based on Jewish teaching. The Rushdie letter, however, seemed to be based on his own personal predilections, and Judge Anthony Tibber, a leading member of the Jewish community, spoke not only for himself when he retorted:

Lord Jakobovits is, of course, entitled to write to *The Times*. When he signs himself 'Chief Rabbi', it may well be thought by readers outside the Jewish community that he writes on behalf of that community or that what he is stating is Jewish law.

He does neither, and when ... he advances repressive ideas which, if put into law as he would wish, would gag strong views he does not like, I would hope that the bulk of the Jewish community would wish to dissociate themselves from him.

The Chief Rabbi, as always, was unrepentant and claimed that his letter had received a largely favourable response.

For all his sympathy with the Moslems, they differ on several fundamental issues, for while he regards the world around him with concern and hopes to improve it, they regard it with contempt and want to shun it. They are demanding not only a multi-racial society – which is in any case already a fact of life – but a multi-cultural one with their own separate, segregated schools and their own curriculum, all paid out of public funds: in other words, cultural apartheid.

The Chief Rabbi, for his part, has always accepted that the country should remain 'ethnocentrically' British, and Christian, as he explained in a debate on education in the House of Lords in July 1988: 'The principal enemy of all religion is the refusal to believe in any faith or accountability before our Creator. That leads to the moral anarchy which is now so rampant and pernicious.' He then quoted the words of his young colleague, Dr Jonathan Sacks, who had attended a Church of England school where the Jewish children had a separate assembly:

It made us, of course, acutely aware that we were different, but because those around us were taking their religion seriously, it made us consider our Judaism seriously too.... From living with those who valued their tradition, I learnt to cherish my own.... From schools that had confidence in their Christianity, I learned an answering pride in my Jewishness.

In other words, as the Chief Rabbi had often argued before, it was easier for Jews to preserve their identity in a country which was conscious of its own.

A more obvious source for contention between Moslems and Jews is the Middle East, which also has a limiting effect on relations between Jews and Christians. The Chief Rabbi has never hidden his reservations about Israel's policies, especially on the West Bank and Gaza, but he nevertheless finds it difficult to understand the Vatican's unwillingness to recognize Israel at all. When greeting the Pope in 1982 he felt compelled to observe:

While enormous strides have been made in advancing Jewish–Christian harmony, some items on our common agenda still remain to be resolved. They include the elimination of the last vestiges of religious prejudice against Jews and some residual Christian hesitation in accepting the State of Israel as the fulfilment of millennial Jewish dreams.

The Pope's reply was polite but non-committal. Some weeks later came news that he was about to receive PLO leader Yassir Arafat, which seemed to add insult to injury. The Chief Rabbi cabled:

IN SPIRIT OF OUR MANCHESTER MEETING I EARNESTLY PLEAD RECONSIDER ARAFAT RECEPTION STOP UNTIL PLO COVENANT CHANGED TO EXCLUDE AVOWAL OF ARMED STRUGGLE AND DESTRUCTION OF JEWISH STATE SUCH RECEPTION LIABLE TO CAUSE GRAVE DAMAGE TO MIDDLE EAST PEACE PROSPECTS AND TO JEWISH–CHRISTIAN RELATIONS AS WELL AS TO ENCOURAGE INTERNATIONAL TERRORISM STOP I RESPECTFULLY INVOKE THE INJUNCTION OF PSALM 122 VERSES 6 TO 9.

The verses in question begin: 'Pray for the peace of Jerusalem'.

It was a futile gesture for the meeting proceeded as planned and Cardinal Willebrands, the president of the Commission of Religious Relations at the Vatican, explained that the Pope's reception of someone did not mean he approved 'of all the ideas and actions attributed to that person', and that Arafat had expressed his opposition to terrorism and his hopes for a peaceful solution, which should involve the recognition of the rights of all peoples, particularly those of the Palestinian people for a homeland of its own and of Israel for its own security.

The Chief Rabbi had heard all this before. 'Israel', he confessed ruefully, was 'the one subject to which I found it impossible to extend my very close relations with British church leaders'. He found his Christian colleagues helpful in the extreme in combating any incidence of anti-Semitism or in alleviating the plight of Soviet Jews, 'but Israel', he said, 'never featured on our agenda'.

In 1984, a small group of Polish Carmelite nuns set up a convent in a building adjacent to Auschwitz. Many Jews were affronted by the sign of the cross hovering over the site of their martyrdom, and after widespread protests an agreement was signed in Geneva between four international Jewish organizations and four cardinals to move the convent to another site by February 1989.

When the deadline came and went and no action was taken, Jewish concern mounted, and, in July 1989, a group of Jewish zealots, led by a New York rabbi, Avraham Weiss, tried to break into the convent. They were forcibly ejected, and the World Jewish Congress immediately accused the Polish authorities of a 'vicious and unprovoked attack', as if Weiss and his followers were victims of a pogrom.

Cardinal Macharski, Archbishop of Cracow, in whose diocese Auschwitz lies, and who had earlier assured Jewish leaders that work on a new site for the convent would begin in 1990, said that he could not be seen to be acting under duress. His stand was reinforced by the Primate of Poland, Cardinal Glemp, who had never fully reconciled himself to moving the convent and who suggested that the whole affair had been gratuitously stirred up by world Jewry.

Israeli Prime Minister Itzhak Shamir did not make things any easier by accusing the Poles of 'imbibing anti-Semitism with their mothers' milk', and in the acrimonious atmosphere which ensued there was talk of breaking off all Jewish relations with the Catholic Church.

Jakobovits had, in the meantime, been striving to diffuse the issue through frequent meetings with Sir Sigmund Sternberg, a Hungarian-born philanthropist who, in a sense, has become Jewry's representative to the Holy See. In September, Glemp came on a visit to London. Sir Sigmund immediately arranged to see him. After explaining the strength of Jewish feeling on the matter, he received a written undertaking that the convent would be moved.

The Carmelite controversy had hardly been settled when another erupted over the apparent readiness of Oxfam, the international relief organization, to adopt a more positive attitude to the PLO. Many Jews who had devoted both time and money to Oxfam called for a boycott of the organization. Both Jakobovits and Sir Sigmund felt that an infelicitously worded statement had been needlessly blown up into a *cause célèbre* and, working in tandem again, they managed to contain the problem.

In May 1990, Jakobovits was invited to address the General Assembly of the Church of Scotland. He was the first rabbi to do so in the history of the Assembly and he felt very much at home for, as he observed in his opening remarks, the Jew and the Scot had a special affinity in their common devotion to the Bible.

In a brief but eloquent speech, he noted the worldwide resurgence in religious faith, but acknowledged some setbacks. 'The family', he said, 'has become a disaster area. Its widespread breakdown exacts a higher social and economic cost, by fuelling crime, drugs and drink addiction, than any AIDS epidemic.' He then came up with a novel idea: 'Perhaps we should insist on pre-marital training before we issue marriage licences.' His remarks were received with enthusiasm.

Sir Sigmund Sternberg, who has devoted a considerable part of his fortune and much of his energies over the past decade to inter-faith relations, and who is himself a leading member of the Reform synagogue, describes Jakobovits as a natural 'harmonizer' both within the community and without. 'He is', he says, 'hard-working, always helpful and available, and I cannot imagine anyone who inspires greater trust and respect.'

The measure of the Chief Rabbi's success as 'harmonizer', however, lies not so much in the actual conflicts he has settled as in the potential conflicts he has averted.

Diplomacy, especially in inter-faith relations, always involves discretion and some of his greatest achievements must thus remain unsung.

15

Bridge-Builder

*I*F the Chief Rabbi's embassy to the gentiles has been a triumph, his embassy to Reform and Liberal Jews has been rather less successful, though he is satisfied in his own mind that he has given them every sign of goodwill his office would permit.

He has, as we have seen, always sought to be a bridge-builder and his vision of the ideal community is the sort of *Judische Gross Gemeinde* which his father served and which combined all the Jewish denominations in Berlin under one umbrella. When he became rabbi of the Fifth Avenue Synagogue, he hoped to create something similar in New York.

It proved too much even for his energies and goodwill. The very norms of German life, to say nothing of external pressures, made for a certain orderliness and cohesion totally lacking in America, and he quickly discovered that there was no hope of rapprochement between the old ghetto-type Orthodoxy and the new, let alone a roof organization which would embrace the Reform movement. In America, moreover, every rabbi with tenure is king in his own domain and multiple kingships do not make for cohesion.

In London, he used his induction to display his intentions and invited all the differing elements in the community to the service. And such was his persuasiveness that they all came, from Rabbi Rayner on the extreme left to the late Rabbi Weiss on the extreme right. Then they all went away and have not reassembled since.

If he has failed, he claims that it was not for want of trying. He quickly made peace with Dr Louis Jacobs by giving formal recognition to his congregation as part of the Orthodox fold after Jacobs agreed to perform no marriage which could not be held in an Orthodox synagogue. He also agreed that Liberal and Reform rabbis should have consultative status on the Board of Deputies – a now forgotten controversy which for a time threatened to estrange him from his right-wing colleagues – and has had innumerable meetings with Liberal and Reform rabbis to see if a concordat could be arranged. It soon became plain that it could not.

This is not the place to delve into Liberal and Reform doctrines. The two are generally lumped together as 'progressives' in Orthodox minds, though there are important differences between them. The latter is more conservative and has a greater hankering for tradition than the former, but both draw their clergy from the same seminary – the Leo Baeck College – and both look alike to the Orthodox in that neither are bound by the *halacha*, and every Liberal and Reform rabbi feels free to do 'that which is right in his own eyes'.

As a result, some of Jakobovits's colleagues refuse to recognize them as rabbis at all and Jakobovits himself, while avoiding outright hostility, has laid down a series of guidelines which suggest that his attitude towards them is less than cordial:

A. We cannot accept 'Progressive Judaism' as an authentic expression or branch of authentic Judaism.

B. We cannot recognize its religious leaders as authentic spokesmen of our faith, or do anything which implies such recognition.

C. We are appalled by the havoc and personal tragedies created as a result of marriage and conversions carried out in disregard of *halachic* requirements.

D. We grieve over the defection of our brethren from our common Torah heritage.

Though the guidelines were drafted for the benefit of rabbis, he expects the lay leaders of synagogues under his jurisdiction to approach progressive Jewry with the same circumspection.

Thus, when the honorary officers of the United Synagogue, including Alfred Woolf, the president, George Gee, the vice-president, and F. M. Landau, the treasurer, attended the centenary service of the West London Reform Synagogue in October 1970, he was deeply upset by what he regarded as a serious transgression and sent them a stern letter of rebuke: 'In my anguish and my inability to undo what has been done, all I can do is to urge you conscientiously to include your sincere contrition in your prayers for divine forgiveness and atonement on Yom Kippur.'

When Dr Brodie was Chief Rabbi he kept his Liberal and Reform colleagues at arm's length, while Hertz attacked Liberal Judaism with a vehemence which threatened to tear the community apart. There, at least, Jakobovits has followed a more temperate line, as he made clear in a series of further guidelines:

Vituperation and scurrilous language are not only unbecoming and unJewish but inexpedient. Nothing alienates our own members and swells the ranks of the dissidents more than intemperate outbursts by Orthodox spokesmen. All such diatribes are counter-productive. Friends can only be won by love and sympathetic understanding. . . .

While we cannot co-operate with progressives in any area in which they have chosen to dissent from our religious traditions, we should make it clear that we regard those who are Jewish-born or *halachically* converted as fellow Jews, as brothers in the House of Israel, however misguided they are, and however grievously they err in their interpretation of Judaism, leaving us free to work together in those fields which do not impinge on our religious differences.

And he offered a quotation from the Talmud as a sort of guiding principle: 'Let the left hand repel them, whilst the right hand draws them near.'

There have been occasions when his left hand did not seem to know what his right hand was doing, and if he was co-operative and conciliatory one year, he could be cold and distant the next.

In December 1984, he told colleagues 'not to allow their presence or their names be used for promoting or sanctioning any activities which could be construed as according legitimacy to non-traditional Judaism'. Although he did not mention anyone by name, the statement was aimed principally at Dr Alan Unterman, Rabbi of the Gatley Synagogue in Manchester, who was on the editorial board of, and contributor to, *Manna*, an excellent quarterly magazine produced by the Sternberg Centre, headquarters of the Reform Synagogue. The magazine is not, however, the house journal of the Reform movement but is designed as a forum for the airing of Jewish issues, which is, indeed, why Unterman was invited to join the editorial board.

Nothing he wrote in the magazine could have been construed as non-kosher, and his sin, if any, lay not in what he said but where he said it, and in keeping non-kosher company.

It was an unfortunate episode, for Unterman's transgression – if it may be called that – was noticed by a colleague, who, instead of remonstrating on the matter with Unterman himself, went behind his back and brought it to the attention of the Chief Rabbi.

God's self-appointed secret police are the bane of religious life. Jakobovits does not care much for them himself and he might reasonably have shown the man the door. Instead he acted on his information and, although he never applied any direct pressure, Unterman got the message and eventually resigned from the magazine.

The most extraordinary thing about the episode, however, was that Jakobovits himself has, as we have observed, often taken part in the adult education programmes of the Reform movement in America and – to the distress of his more right-wing colleagues – has often shared platforms with Reform rabbis in Britain, but he explained that while it was legitimate to find common ground on common issues, it was important not to blur the differences between them.

His statement did, in fact, suggest a hardening of attitudes and what may have caused it was the emergence of a new star in the Liberal firmament in the person of Rabbi Julia Neuberger.

Ms Neuberger, who was born in 1950, is a graduate of both Cambridge University and the Leo Baeck College. The first woman rabbi in England, as we have seen, was Dame Lilly Montagu, one of the founders of the Liberal Synagogue, but Ms Neuberger was the first of a new wave of woman rabbis and the very fact gave her a certain amount of prominence. Her personality and views did the rest. Blonde, resourceful, effervescent and energetic, with a strong sense of compassion, her theology is entirely of this world and might have been custom-made by the women's pages of the *Guardian*. There is hardly a good, or at least fashionable, cause with which she is not associated and she not only has radical views on a host of subjects, but a robust way of expressing them, all of which have made her the darling of the media.

Nor is she a respecter of Chief Rabbis and on more than one occasion when Jakobovits has made a public pronouncement on sexual morality or some similar issue, she has taken pains to point out that 'the Chief Rabbi does not represent us'.

Her views were the negation of almost everything he stood for and thus, when he was invited by the *Jewish Chronicle* in February 1985 to explain his stern attitude to progressive Judaism, his animus largely descended on her.

While he enlarged on the joys of family life and pointed to the dangers of artificial insemination and surrogate motherhood, she, he said, 'regarded pregnancy as a loathsome burden and loathes every minute of being pregnant, that she had had herself sterilized and if she wanted more children would be perfectly willing to have any further children through womb-hire ....' She also, he added, condoned promiscuity and supported the right of children to flout the wishes of their parents in such matters.

He might also have quoted her view that the Bible was the work of humans, 'who felt themselves to be, and no doubt sometimes were, inspired', and that while sodomy may have been unacceptable about the time the Bible was written, we 'now know that it is a wholly natural practice for a small section of the community'.

She became his *bête blanche*. 'Jewish-born' though she is, he finds it difficult to approach her with the 'love and sympathetic understanding' he commends to others. He has always regarded the very idea of a woman rabbi as offensive, and she not only confirms his worst fears of what such a phenomenon might entail, but colours his attitude to progressive Judaism as a whole.

He likes to be liked and never tires of quoting his father's dictum that a hundred friends are too few and one enemy is too many, for essentially he is a man of peace, but then, perhaps, he can afford to be. In Hertz's time, left-wing Judaism was growing apace and he felt compelled to confront it. Today it is in comparative decline while the Right is advancing on every front. Here, as elsewhere, Jakobovits has been fortunate in his time, though one might reasonably ask if he has not helped to make the times what they are.

For all his reservations about progressive doctrines, he is on the best of terms with several Reform and Liberal rabbis. He has often held meetings with them in his own home and enjoys a friendly relationship with Hugo Gryn, senior rabbi of the West London Reform Synagogue, and Rabbi Sidney Brichto, the executive director of the Union of Liberal and Progressive Synagogues. He tends to regard them and their colleagues (though he would make an exception for Rabbi Neuberger) as well-meaning Jews who have strayed so far from the fold that they are no longer even aware that they are lost.

The Torah camp, he once declared, 'is now secure, counting hundreds of thousands of adherents in the world. They must begin to shed their self-imposed isolation; to share their spiritual wealth, faith and idealism *with other less fortunate brothers....*'

And there we have it. His failures as a bridge-builder, in the last resort, arise not so much from his abhorrence of progressive doctrines as his conviction that the Orthodox have everything to teach and nothing to learn.

He has never, for example, paused to ask himself whether 'the havoc and personal tragedies' caused by the readiness of progressive rabbis to carry out marriages and conversions 'in disregard of *halachic* requirements' may not have arisen out of those requirements – or, indeed, whether the requirements are always *halachic*.

The laws of conversion, for example, are not particularly demanding, but the London Beth Din has, as a matter of policy, adopted the most rigorous interpretation of those laws. As a result, many couples who might have been content to remain within the Orthodox fold have joined a Reform synagogue.

And yet in spite of the Chief Rabbi's misgivings about progressive Jews, the rancour with which he has sometimes attacked them and the patronage with which he has always approached them, they have, on the whole, shown a readiness to turn the other cheek, which is almost Christian. They appreciate the dignity he has brought to his office, the courage with which he has challenged the excesses of Jewish nationalism, and the standing which he enjoys in the country at large, and they have, in spite of occasional grumbles, always accepted his role as titular head of British Jewry.

Towards the end of 1989, with the retirement of the Chief Rabbi in sight, and the search for a successor almost complete, Harold Sanderson, the chairman of the Union of Liberal and Progressive Synagogues, and Rosita Rosenberg, the director, issued a statement: 'It is appropriate for us to say on behalf of the Union of Liberal and Progressive Synagogues that the Chief Rabbi to be elected has no authority over our own rabbis or lay people, nor does he represent us or speak on our behalf.'

The Chief Rabbi, of course, never has had, nor has ever claimed to have, authority over Liberal rabbis and what they were saying was that they would not regard his successor as titular head of the community.

They did not say what prompted the statement, but Clifford Longley, religious affairs correspondent of *The Times*, suggested a probable cause: 'Leading members were saying privately that Lord Jakobovits had caused tension between progressive and Orthodox Jews because of his claim that "Thatcherism" was in line with Jewish principles, and because he had taken an over-rigid view on sexual morality.'

What had happened was that the Chief Rabbi had broken a tacit under-standing. Progressive Jews do not expect to be embraced by the Orthodox establishment and would probably be embarrassed if they were, but they do expect Chief Rabbis to train their thoughts on the next world, while they busied themselves with the amelioration of this one, or, to adapt the words of Psalm 115: The heavens, even the heavens are to the Orthodox, while the earth has he given to the progressives. Jakobovits had descended out of the skies to invade their domain.

But it was not just that. Progressive Jews are perfectly aware that all Orthodox rabbis have rigid views on sexual morality – they would not be Orthodox if they did not. However, in the past they had uttered them privately; even where they made them public, they were generally ignored, whereas the media pounce on almost anything Jakobovits says. This was also true of his pronouncements on social issues. They are, in other words, less troubled by his views than by the prominence they receive. A reticent Chief Rabbi, however bigoted, would have been tolerable; an outspoken one is not.

The Liberal Synagogue, which is about eighty years old and has some 12,000 adherents, has always had close affinities with the liberal wing of the Church of England. Its ideologue and founding father, Claude Montefiore (Lilly Montagu, though spoken of as a co-founder, was really his acolyte), came under the influence of Benjamin Jowett, the Master of Balliol, a leading liberal Christian thinker, while still in Oxford and sailed so close to Christianity as almost to land on its shore (some believe he did). A scholar and saint, wealthy, questing and restless, he admired much in the Jewish creed but found Christian ethics more admirable than Jewish ones. His followers busied themselves with philanthropy, social welfare, East End settlements and boys' clubs along the lines pioneered by Arnold Toynbee, Canon Samuel Barnett and other Victorian social reformers.

The Liberal movement has since become less Christian, but then so has the Church of England, so that the affinity remains. When the Chief Rabbi made his pronouncement on *Faith in the Cities*, they found themselves on the side of the Church rather than the synagogue. This was true also of his pronouncements on sexual morality.

All this happened in 1986 and the fact that it took them over three years to make their feelings known shows that timelessness comes as naturally to the Liberal Jew as to the Orthodox one.

It is significant that the Reform Synagogue, which dates back to 1842 and which represents the much larger wing of progressive Jewry, has not associated itself with the ULPS in this matter because, in the words of Marcus Bower, chairman of the Reform Synagogues of Great Britain, 'a public statement of this nature would sharpen divisions in the community'. He did not gloss over the differences between the Orthodox and Reform, but felt that there were 'many areas of common interest and concern to all Jews in which the Chief Rabbi, by virtue of his office and his own personal standing, is seen as holding a unique position within British Jewry'. The Chief Rabbi, he added, 'has never claimed to speak for all Jews.... On this basis our movement has endeavoured to work closely and harmoniously with Lord Jakobovits and we hope to be able to do so with his successor as Chief Rabbi.'

Reform Jews are much more pragmatic in outlook than their Liberal counterparts and they have never had ideologues like Claude Montefiore to inspire them. Basically they regard themselves as good, traditionally minded Jews who have come to their senses, and if they do not share the Chief Rabbi's extreme views on sexual morality, they are not totally out of sympathy with his so-called Thatcherism.

They have also moved steadily to the right. Where in earlier years they scorned the dietary laws, some of their synagogues now have kosher kitchens, and where they were anti-Zionist, they are now among the most vehement supporters of Israel. They have also set up their own Jewish day school and have refurbished many a usage which had previously lapsed.

This does not, of course, mean that they are happy with everything Jakobovits says or does, but unlike the Liberals they are less concerned with his public pronouncements on national issues than with his attitude to their movement as a whole and his passing bouts of what they regard as obscurantism and intolerance.

Several Reform rabbis have served notice that the continued acceptance of the Chief Rabbi as titular head of the community should not be taken for granted, but they are aware of the pressures he faces from the extreme Right and, indeed, from his own Beth Din. They are also aware of the many benefits he has brought to the community and they are prepared to 'keep hold of nurse, for fear of finding something worse'.

Though the Chief Rabbi has failed as a bridge-builder, it is, in some ways, surprising that his failure has not been more complete, for he is far more Orthodox than his predecessors. Yet they nearly all suffered major schisms during their years in office. Nathan Marcus Adler could not prevent the growth of the Reform Synagogue on the left, or the creation of the Federation of Synagogues on the right. Hermann Adler, though by far the most liberal-minded Chief Rabbi British Jewry has known, witnessed the emergence of the Liberal Synagogue on the left, and the Machzike Hadath on the right; and if Hertz was able to avoid schisms it was partly because of the external dangers posed by the rise of Hitler.

The last years of Dr Brodie's reign were shaken by the Jacobs Affair and, given the intelligence and appeal which Jacobs undoubtedly has and the sort of loyalty which he inspires, it was thought that once Jakobovits took office, Jacobism, or the Masoreti movement as it has come to be known, would quickly grow to become an alternative form of Orthodoxy.

It has grown and now consists of four synagogues and over five hundred families, most of them young, but its growth is due in good part to defections from the Reform movement. And many of those who have defected from Orthodox synagogues have done so out of disenchantment less with Jakobovits than with their own local rabbis.

There have, however, been large-scale defections to the right, from synagogues under the Chief Rabbi's jurisdiction to those which are not, but while he might regard any defections to the left as a measure of his failure, he is inclined to look on those to the right as a measure of his success, for if they no longer accept his authority, they still accept the authority of the Torah. In that sense, if in no other, he accepts that there are many pathways to heaven.

The United Synagogue itself used to include congregations which were thought of, or at least thought of themselves, as more Orthodox than the rest, and others – like Hampstead and the New West End – which were certainly more liberal. It is now much of a muchness. Not everyone thinks of this as an advantage, but the Chief Rabbi sees it as a mark of cohesion, and if he has failed to create the *Gross Gemeinde* of his dreams, he will leave a community which, with all its divisions, will be a good deal more united than he found it.

16

And Thou Shalt Teach

THE Chief Rabbi has always been a man with a clear sense of priorities, who has gone through life ticking off lists of things completed and things to complete. At the top of that list was the new Jewish High School at Bushey in Hertfordshire, which is due to open its doors in September 1990 and which, it is hoped, will eventually have over six hundred pupils. It is to be called Immanuel College in his honour and, if it should materialize as planned, it will be his crowning achievement.

There is a certain symbolism in the very site of the school, for Bushey also happens to be the site of a large Jewish cemetery and the opening of a school in the same area almost embodies the Jewish belief in education as a form of rebirth, of resurrection.

Numerous Jewish day schools were established in London and the provinces in the course of the last century, but they had sought to convert the rough progeny of the ghettos into English gentlemen. The Chief Rabbi's aim was to keep the grandchildren and the great-grandchildren of the ghettos, Jewish, which is a rather more formidable undertaking. He lost no time in applying himself to it. In his inaugural sermon he asked:

Wherein lies the glory of beautiful synagogues if tomorrow they will be empty monuments to our neglect? In this emergency of appalling defections among our youth, our expenditure in money and energy in Jewish education represents our defence budget in the communal economy, and it must be given the highest priority over every other Jewish effort.

He launched himself into his efforts with the usual energy, but his start was not too auspicious.

He had been impressed during his years in New York by the local Jewish school network and brought over a couple of Jewish administrators from New York to report on the Jewish schools in England and to advise on a plan of action. The circumstances of the two places however — to say nothing of the resources available – were so different that their visits, in the eyes of some observers, were a waste of public money. This is not, one must add, a view which Jakobovits shares for he believes that they laid the groundwork for his later achievements.

He then began to look round for a director of education. This time he turned to Jerusalem and eventually obtained the services of Jack Lehman, a government school inspector. Lehman was English and, although it was some years since he had left the country, was familiar with the scene. He and the Chief Rabbi made a thorough study both of the educational needs of the community and of the resources which would have to be mobilized to satisfy them.

A number of new ultra-Orthodox schools had been established in north London and Manchester in the post-war years, and others had been opened under the auspices of the Zionist Federation, but they found that even with the new establishments, only about twelve per cent of Jewish children of school age attended Jewish day schools. The rest were content with the smattering of education available in synagogue classes on Sunday mornings and one or two weekday evenings, while thousands of others received no Jewish education at all. They were, however, encouraged by the long waiting lists at some of the schools and were convinced by then that if they could only make the places available they could more than double the number of children at Jewish schools.

To that end the Chief Rabbi established the Jewish Educational Development Trust, and in November 1971 he unveiled a fifteen-year plan for Jewish education under the heading 'Let My People Know'. It was a striking title and he summed up his aims in two equally striking paragraphs:

Education lies at the heart of Jewish purpose and without it we perish. Today this is more acutely true than ever before. We have ample experience to prove that no Jewish loyalties can survive in our modern society without a thorough knowledge of Judaism.

Next to Israel, Jewish education must become our principal concern and top priority in our communal budgeting. Thoroughly modernizing our thinking and planning, congregations and individuals will have to accept the new facts of Jewish life already accepted elsewhere – whereby more money is spent on our schools than our shools. Shools preserve Jews; schools create them.

The first phase of the scheme envisaged the creation of two new secondary schools and three new primary schools, as well as several Jewish sixth-form colleges in London, and the provision of bursaries and various training programmes to encourage an adequate supply of teachers.

The second phase, which was more sketchily outlined, was concerned mainly with the needs of the provinces and the creation of further schools in the London area. In all it hoped to provide 2,250 new school places in the first phase, and a further 5,750 in the second, and the two together would cost nearly £7 million.

The Chief Rabbi was anxious to harness the resources of all sections of the community and cater to the needs of all sections. He therefore brought together what might be called a wall-to-wall board of trustees, which included not only pillars of the Orthodox establishment like Sir Isaac Wolfson, Leo Graham and Harry Landy, but Roland Franklin, a banker who belonged to Dr Louis Jacobs's New London Synagogue, and Trevor Chinn, a prominent member of the Reform movement.

The publication of the scheme caused some excitement and not a little controversy. The provinces, with good reason, felt that their needs were not sufficiently recognized, especially as they were excluded from phase one. Existing schools feared that they would be starved of funds and robbed of teachers, and there were murmurings on the far Right about the presence of Reform Jews on the board of trustees.

The Chief Rabbi was a little too impatient to get things done and the entire plan was too hastily prepared, too sketchily defined, looked too far into the future, had an extravagant idea of Jewish wealth, or at least generosity, and was too ambitious. Sir Isaac Wolfson came forward with a donation of £350,000 and other donors promised to bring up the total to about £1 million, but the money was slow in coming in and in some instances never arrived.

The Chief Rabbi had many skills, but as his wife said, 'he's a bad *schnorrer*', which is to say that he was a poor fund-raiser. He had failed to raise the funds for an adult education centre he had planned for New York, and at first he had no more success in London.

It was, he discovered, rather easier to raise money for synagogues than for education because people felt that in endowing a House of God they were, so to speak, mollifying their Maker and assuring a place for their loved ones, and perhaps themselves, in the hereafter. Synagogues also provided a more stately and conspicuous setting for the display of plaques. Schools did not hold out quite the same promise, or the same opportunities. His scheme did not get off the ground until he brought Moshe Davis in as director of his Trust and as executive director of his office.

Davis himself was also not a natural fund-raiser, but he worked on the principle that the best people to raise money were people who had money. He therefore introduced the Chief Rabbi to a number of eminent businessmen, including Gerald Ronson, owner of the Heron group, and Stanley Kalms, head of Dixons. He also engaged the energies of Fred Worms.

Worms has much in common with the Chief Rabbi. They are roughly contemporaries; both were born in Germany and both had a rigorously Orthodox education, but Worms had money behind him. When he came to London shortly before the war, he went to St Paul's School and was eventually trained as an accountant. He built up a group of successful engineering firms, sold out before the 1974 crash, built up another, sold out again, and found himself with ample time and resources to devote to communal affairs. Orthodox in practice, but a free thinker, an establishment figure who is yet something of a maverick, a leading Zionist, with strong reservations about Zionist policies, he is, like the Chief Rabbi himself, difficult to classify. He, however, shared the Chief Rabbi's priorities and had a clear idea of how to put them into practice.

Since 1948, most of the money raised in Britain for Jewish causes – which amounts annually to tens of millions of pounds – has gone to Israel through the agency of the Joint Israel Appeal. In 1976, Worms, working together with the Chief Rabbi and Davis, prepared a memorandum suggesting that the JIA should also take Jewish education under its wing, if only because 'improving the standard of Jewish education here is one of the best things we can do for Israel since the country depends on the commitment of Jews in the Diaspora'. It was less than two years since the Yom Kippur War, and Michael Sacher, vice-chairman of Marks & Spencer who was also joint president of the JIA, retorted that this was not the time to divert money from Israel.

Worms had no such plan in mind, but he thought that the machinery and expertise of the JIA could also be used to help Jewish education. Eventually a compromise was reached whereby JIA leaders – who included some of the most prominent figures in the Jewish business community – would lend their weight to the Jewish Educational Development Trust. It was almost as good as money in the bank and, in 1977, the Trust was reorganized and given a more practical foundation.

Every phase was carefully costed, every proposal carefully weighed, and nothing was allowed to proceed without an assured budget and the recruitment of necessary personnel. Existing schools were enlarged, or transferred from old and declining areas of Jewish life to new and expanding ones, so that, for example, the old Solomon Wolfson School in Notting Hill was reborn in much enlarged form and at a cost of over £2 million – the largest single commitment ever made by the community – as the Michael Sobell Sinai School in Kenton.

The new places provided were quickly snapped up and the proportion of Jewish children attending Jewish day schools moved steadily upwards. By 1982, it had grown to twenty-five per cent. Once the Bushey school has its full intake of 600 pupils, and other projects in the pipeline are complete, the proportion will have grown to over forty per cent, which, in some respects, will be the best measure of the Chief Rabbi's achievement.

He would not, of course, claim that he was the first man to discover that education was a good thing. The ultra-Orthodox have always attached the greatest importance to their schools, and he has often paid tribute to the work of Rabbi Solomon Schonfeld who, almost single-handedly, pioneered and sustained a whole system of schools, one of which was his own alma mater.

In 1955, the Jews' Free School, which had existed before the war in the East End (it was originally a Rothschild charity), was re-established in Camden Town under the aegis of the London Board of Jewish Religious Education (an arm of the United Synagogue) and quickly acquired a reputation as one of the best comprehensive schools in London. Several of the schools his Trust was helping had been thriving establishments long before he came on the scene. The Zionist Federation had established an Education Trust in 1953 and had not only spent millions on Jewish day schools, but had arranged a constant flow of qualified Hebrew teachers – without which some of the schools would have foundered – from Israel.

The Chief Rabbi, however, gave the matter a new urgency. He travelled the length and breadth of the country to preach education. He produced a torrent of articles and pamphlets, and pressed the issue to the point almost of becoming a bore, and eventually broke through. Schools became the major talking-point in every community, the focal point of local endeavour.

He also used the very considerable influence of his office to harness resources which might not otherwise have become available, but, more than that, he was able to reach people whose own way of life would not normally have induced them to send their children to Jewish schools, or even to think about them. In this, as in so much else, he has been fortunate in his time.

There are a growing number of parents with a new interest in Jewish culture and the Jewish past who are anxious that their children should share it, but there are a great many others whose interest – where it exists at all – is marginal but who are so appalled at the level of education available in the state schools that in their desperation they are prepared to expose their children to a Jewish education. The Chief Rabbi had already noticed this phenomenon in New York and it was being repeated in London.

Also with the growth of the coloured population, white children found themselves in a minority in some schools. That too encouraged many parents to opt for a Jewish school, if only because it did not lay them open to the charge of racism.

The Chief Rabbi, for his part, is unconcerned about the motivation of the parents, for if the children come for the wrong reasons they stay for the right ones, and the network of Jewish schools enabled him to reach families who would normally have been well outside his sphere of influence.

The Chief Rabbi, as founder of the JETD, is more than an eminence on high giving his blessings and vague guidelines and leaving others to cope with the details. He attends the frequent sessions of the executive committee, visits sites of proposed schools, examines plans, cross-examines architects, interviews actual and prospective senior staff, and goes through proposed allocations with a fine-tooth comb, if only because he is anxious that no money should go to anything unworthy or unkosher.

This last point can sometimes involve him in a fine balancing act, for while he is prepared to help Reform schools with their infrastructure and the teaching of secular subjects, or the Hebrew language, he will not allow any of his funds to be used directly for the inculcation of Reformist doctrines, which does show that he is capable of compromise on some issues.

He is also on call for any problems which might arise, which – as we shall see – they do with extraordinary frequency, though for all his dedication, he would be the first to admit that very few of the projects would have got off the ground without his executive director Moshe Davis (and his successor Simon Caplan), the chairman of the education committee, Fred Worms, and, above all, the chairman of the executive committee, Stanley Kalms.

Kalms was born in London in 1931 and within a few years built up a small family business into a major conglomerate, which now has over a thousand retail outlets, a UK workforce of 6,000 and an annual turnover of over £1.5 billion, though given the time he devotes to Jewish affairs one might think that Dixons was something he runs on the side.

A brisk, purposeful, testy figure, he does not hold any major office in the community. He is not president of the United Synagogue, nor of the London Board of Education, nor even a member of the Chief Rabbinate Council. Organizations mean committees, constitutions, consultations and the search for precedents, and he has no time for any of them. In the JETD, being a new body, he could make his own rules as he went along or, if necessary, dispense with them.

He approaches his tasks with a grim resolve and once he takes a matter in hand it is as good as done. Generous himself, he can excite generosity in others, and whenever money is mentioned he will retort, 'That's my problem.'

He and the Chief Rabbi are fairly close friends – he has entertained him for a cruising holiday on his yacht and when Jakobovits was sixty he gave him a surprise birthday party (organized by Moshe Davis) – but their working relationship has not always been easy. The Chief Rabbi finds him brusque, stubborn and peremptory; he finds the Chief Rabbi too cautious, or, as he put it, 'I see all the advantages, and he sees all the drawbacks', and he sometimes wonders how he gets anything done at all.

They also have occasional demarcation disputes of the sort which used to arise between Chief Rabbi Hertz and Sir Robert Waley-Cohen. Jakobovits, as head of the Trust, has a veto on all religious issues, and Kalms has assumed a veto on all temporal ones. However, he complains that the Chief Rabbi 'could make the colour of wallpaper into a religious issue, and he'll quote the Talmud to prove his point'.

When the idea for a new high school was first mooted, the Chief Rabbi would have preferred different buildings on adjoining sites for boys and girls, but he was eventually persuaded, on purely practical grounds, that they would have to share the same buildings, which was something of an advance at a time when some rabbis were insisting that even play-groups for toddlers should be segregated. Kalms, however, would have preferred a co-educational school in the full meaning of the term, but on the Chief Rabbi's insistence the boys and girls will have separate class-rooms, though they will use the same playgrounds, dining-rooms and assembly hall. In specialized subjects, where there are unlikely to be enough pupils for two sets of classes, boys and girls will share one.

All such points involved prolonged deliberations, and where friction arose between Jakobovits and Kalms, Davis was the ideal man to resolve it, for he was not only an able administrator, but tactful and diplomatic, the perfect go-between. They formed an effective trio, but then in May 1984, at a crucial point in the work of the Trust, Davis suddenly resigned because of ill-health.

Davis, who was suffering from cancer, had had two major operations in the previous year, which had largely alleviated his condition and was making a good recovery, but the malign symptoms returned. He had watched his condition develop with almost detached curiosity and had even written a poem about it:

> Unwilling to face physical and psychological consequences.
> Medical terms disguise realities.
> Am I being fooled?
> Am I still me?
> I carefully watch faces and check reactions.
> Odd how little others notice.
> But how much it means to me.
> Simple Proposition:
> Manhood removed, Cancer reduced. . .
> If it works!
> A year later, just under,
> I learn that it doesn't.

Sorry, says the surgeon.
Not your fault, I say politely.
What now?

He died in May 1987, aged sixty.

Davis had the disposition of a soldier and the vocation of a priest, and he was able to combine them in a way when he served as chaplain to the forces. He was a convivial man, at ease in any company, with a ready fund of barrack-room humour, yet he was also a pensive man who could be broody and introspective, who found much solace in religious contemplation. The mix somehow appealed to the Chief Rabbi. Although there was only a few years between them, each, in a curious way, tended to look on the other as a son, the Chief because he felt close to him and regarded him as a member of his own family, Davis because he regarded the Chief as a complete innocent who had to be led by the hand along the tortuous paths of a hazardous and corrupt world. He did not, perhaps, understand the Chief Rabbi as well as he thought, but he could read his mind and could anticipate orders before they were given. He was close enough to him to suggest that this course of action, or that, would be inadvisable. On occasion he could possibly show too much initiative and there were people who felt that he was assuming excessive authority. That was not the Chief Rabbi's view. He missed him deeply, as he still does.

When he stood down Shimon Cohen, a young man from Cardiff who had worked under him in the Chief Rabbi's office, took over as executive director, while Simon Caplan, a former director of the Glasgow Board of Jewish Education, took over the Educational Development Trust.

A major phase of the Chief Rabbi's scheme was completed with the opening of the Michael Sobell Sinai School in north-west London in 1981, and his Trust has helped over two dozen other Jewish schools in different parts of the country to enlarge their intake and improve their facilities. It has also provided grants for the training of teachers and has supported institutions as diverse as the Centre for Jewish Education, run by the Reform Synagogues of Great Britain, to Tzivos Hashem 'Bracha Bee' Competition, run by the youth wing of the Lubavitch Hassidim. In all it has disbursed several million pounds in the past twelve years, but its most ambitious endeavour was represented by the acquisition of Bushey.

An acting headmaster was found in the person of Denis Felsenstein, a former schools inspector for the Inner London Education Authority, who, in turn, found highly qualified staff for the first year's intake. Advertisements were being prepared inviting pupils to apply for places, but then in September 1989, exactly a year before the school was due to open, Kalms, without warning, suddenly resigned and the whole scheme threatened to come apart.

The project, initially costed at £7 million, in itself a vast sum for a small community with many calls on its resources, grew to £9 million, then £10 million and finally £12 million. Kalms, not finding the support he had hoped for, gave up. His resignation came on the eve of the High Holy Days, the busiest time of the year for a rabbi, but Jakobovits quickly flew into action and found other magnates to shore up the scheme.

Gerald Ronson, a robust, dynamic figure, who is one of the magnates involved in the salvage operation, shares something of his optimism. He is in some ways like Kalms. He too inherited a small family business, which he rapidly built up into a huge conglomerate and which is now one of the largest private companies in the country. He too is rather brusque and impatient. He has strong views on many issues and forceful ways of putting them, so that conversations with him take the form of a monologue, and he punctuates every point he makes by stabbing the air with a large cigar.

Unlike Kalms he is not religious but, as he put it, 'I can always find time for the Chief. He doesn't go in for anything airy fairy. He may not look like a practical man, he doesn't talk like a practical man, but he is practical and persuasive and if he comes to me with an idea, I find it difficult to say no. He can dither a bit and if you ask him a question he sometimes replies with a sermon, but he'll get there. People like him always do.'

When he examined the figures, however, he became rather less sanguine and for a time it was touch and go. On Sunday, 7 January 1990, exactly nine months before the school was due to open, a crucial meeting was held to determine its future. The trustees were still £3 million short of their target, which, in British terms, is not small change. Some of them thought that the whole project should be abandoned; others thought that it should be delayed. Ronson argued that it was too ambitious, while others feared it would conflict with the claims of other schools on communal resources; but whatever their differences, they agreed on one point: the project could not proceed as planned.

However, they reckoned without the persuasive power of the Chief Rabbi. Some eight hundred parents had turned up at a previous meeting to express their interest in the school, and he was not prepared to abandon them, or to write off the time, effort and hope he and so many others had invested in it. The need for the school had been established, not only because so many parents wanted it, but because without schools there was no hope of checking the erosions in Jewish belief and commitment. To abandon, or even delay, the scheme now would be an act of betrayal.

Jakobovits can seem weak and vacillating at times, but he is at his most powerful and effective in a crisis, and this was a crisis of the first magnitude. He had placed education at the forefront of his priorities, and the school in the forefront of his education scheme. If it had been abandoned or even seriously curtailed, he would have regarded his entire career as a failure, and everyone was carried along both by the force of his argument and the strength of his feeling. A new board of governors was formed under the chairmanship of Henry Knobil and the school will open as planned.

Immanuel College is to be run substantially on public-school lines. Fees will be about £3,000 a year, entry will be selective and it is unashamedly designed as a centre of excellence. Some people have argued that public money should not be used to subsidize the schooling of the well-to-do, and they include Sidney Frosh, the president of the United Synagogue.

Frosh yields to no one in his admiration of the Chief Rabbi and believes he has transformed the community, but he admits that when it comes to education his ways sometimes surpass all understanding.

The United Synagogue has under its aegis the Board of Jewish Religious Education, which is ultimately responsible for several London schools, including the Jews' Free School. Although the JFS, with some 1,600 pupils, is the biggest Jewish day school in Europe, it is bursting at the seams and the United Synagogue has plans to open another comprehensive school in the east London suburb of Redbridge. The school, once open, will, like the JFS, be run by the local education authority, but the capital costs of the building, amounting to some £4.5 million, will have to be met by the community.

The new school, like all the others controlled by the United Synagogue, will ultimately be under the aegis of the Chief Rabbinate, and Frosh does not see why £12 million should be lavished on Bushey before they are even within sight of the £4.5 million necessary for Redbridge. It is almost as if the Chief Rabbi was acting on the principle that unto him that hath shall be given.

The money is, however, a minor issue. Frosh, a mild-mannered, soft-spoken man, but with a steely determination, comes from an impoverished immigrant family. He himself went to the JFS, joined a large company of hardware merchants as an office boy and, after five years in the army, returned to become managing director. He now owns his own furniture company. He is a self-made man and prefers the comprehensive principles followed by the JFS to the selective entry to be adopted in Bushey.

The Chief Rabbi's answer to that is that there is room for both, and that no child who would otherwise qualify for entry to Immanuel College will be barred for lack of money.

Twenty or even ten years ago the whole ethos of the College might have been regarded as irredeemably elitist, but elitism is no longer the bad word it was. Jakobovits himself has never thought of it as a pejorative expression and it has never enjoyed much currency among Jews, if only because no one has defined its true meaning.

The very idea of being chosen inculcates a determination to be that much more chosen than others. Among the very Orthodox it was thus taken for granted that a boy with any academic ability at all would go on to a yeshiva, and such institutions, though in theory open to all, were necessarily exclusive. Most Jews, whether Orthodox or not, have always made great sacrifices in order to give their children the best possible education. And they still do, only they tend to send them to schools like the City of London, Haberdashers and University College. Jakobovits hopes that in future they will send them to Immanuel College instead.

The College prospectus states forthrightly that it 'would seek to gain entry for its students to the best universities, including Oxford and Cambridge'. Jakobovits preferred and eventually obtained equal stress on the yeshiva as the ultimate goal. He would also have liked a yeshiva stream in which boys would devote themselves to talmudic studies, but several members of the Trust pointed out that there were already schools in London and Manchester which provided such a stream, though they agreed that the College should assure a level of Jewish education which would enable boys to go on to a yeshiva.

As we have seen, Jakobovits has tried to transcend communal divisions in his allocation of funds, but some sections of the community have complained that he has not given them nearly enough, while others argue that as an Orthodox rabbi he had no right to give anything to Reform institutions at all, which has not prevented them from demanding their share, and more than their share, of any funds he has.

On a more serious level he has been criticized for excluding higher Jewish education from his scheme at a time when budgetary difficulties have compelled several universities to cut down or close their departments of Jewish studies. This is undoubtedly true, but he has always made it clear that he was not interested in funding Jewish studies under secular or non-Jewish auspices.

Though a graduate himself, he has always been slightly apprehensive about higher education, or at least the sort of higher education offered in university departments of Jewish studies. They leave nothing unquestioned. They dabble in biblical criticism and are, so to speak, disposed to look God in the teeth. He suspects that far from drawing students closer to traditional Jewish life, they alienate them from it. At best they are religiously neutral and are not geared to generate Jewish commitment.

One sometimes suspects that he may even have passing reservations about

Jews' College. We have seen that as an undergraduate at the College he also attended courses at a yeshiva and obtained his rabbinical diploma through the latter and not the former. When he became Chief Rabbi, he sought a principal who would improve what one might call the yeshiva quotient in the College and found him in the person of Dr Nahum Rabinovitch, a gifted mathematician and a profound talmudic scholar, who was rabbi of a Toronto synagogue.

Dr Rabinovitch is now head of Malei Adumin Yeshiva near Jerusalem which he has built up into an institution of the first rank, but he was rather less successful in London. He did not know Anglo-Jewry and did not understand it. For example, instead of becoming a member of the United Synagogue, whose prospective rabbis he had been hired to train, he attended the Hendon Adath Yisroel, which was outside the Chief Rabbi's jurisdiction.

The College, under his leadership, lost pupils, lost public support, lost money and lost heart, and was sliding towards extinction when it was saved, largely through the efforts of Stanley Kalms.

Kalms sold off the ornate College premises near Marble Arch and, with the help of Morris Serlin (who is also a governor of Immanuel College), converted a less ornate building in Hendon and set up a fund (out of his own pocket) to enable yeshiva graduates to study at Jews' College and Jews' College graduates to study at yeshiva. He thus brought about the confluence between the two worlds which the Chief Rabbi always wanted. But more important, the Chief Rabbi found a new principal, who, if not in Rabinovitch's class as a talmudist, is in a class of his own as a thinker, preacher and pedagogue: Dr Jonathan Sacks.

Sacks, a slight, donnish figure, gives an impression of cold aloofness, but he is never completely at ease in company and is much happier in his study than in the drawing-room. He has some of the Chief Rabbi's natural courtliness, but is more cerebral and less emotional – some find him a little too cerebral. He was born in 1948, took a first in philosophy at Cambridge and was rabbi of the Golders Green Synagogue before being appointed to Jews' College. He is also editor of L'Eylah. In the past few years, he has built up a considerable reputation as a broadcaster. He is to give the BBC Reith Lectures in 1990 and it was recently announced that he will be the next Chief Rabbi.

The College moved into its new premises in 1984 and is enjoying a new lease of life, with an intake that is not only larger than ever before, but of sounder quality. It is also involved in numerous extra-mural activities and has moved beyond the role of rabbinical seminary to become an important centre of adult education.

Jews' College is not a direct beneficiary of the Jewish Educational Trust and the Chief Rabbi has not been as closely involved in its work as in that of the

Trust, but it has enjoyed a fairly high place in his priorities.

As with the Trust, he was a little too impatient to get things going and thus made a false start. He was also rather slow to acknowledge that the start was, indeed, false, and there are people who claim that the College has made progress in spite of him and not because of him if only because he has never been quite certain what he wanted of it.

In fact, he has always known what he wanted, which was a sort of modern yeshiva which would also teach the vocational skills necessary in the rabbinate, but has reconciled himself to the thought that he is never likely to get it.

It is, however, acknowledged that the renaissance now enjoyed by the College would have been impossible without him, not only because of the energy and ideas he has applied to the work of the College directly, but because of the priority he has given to Jewish education, and his successful efforts to raise the status of the rabbinate.

He may have played a secondary role in shaping the College itself, but he has played a primary role in shaping the environment which is enabling it to flourish.

17

'Lucky Jack'

LORD Jakobovits is the most improbable of figures, the rabbi as a man of action. It is not that rabbis as a race are inert but, like many true believers, they tend to leave a little too much to God, as if a sense of urgent activity suggested a want of faith. Jakobovits has never been like that. Few men have set out in life with a clearer view of what they want, and fewer still have come nearer to achieving it, but he would never have been able to apply himself with such energy and devotion if he had not believed in God, and if he had not harboured at least a passing suspicion that God believes in him. Certainly his whole history suggests that Someone, somewhere, is striving strenuously on his behalf.

He arrived in London at fifteen, alone, penniless, knowing no one and unknown, and hardly speaking a word of English. By the time he was twenty, he had a London University degree and a pulpit; before he was thirty, he was Chief Rabbi of Ireland; by the time he was forty, he was in New York; and before he was fifty, he returned to London as Chief Rabbi of the United Hebrew Congregations of the British Commonwealth.

Now, at nearly threescore years and ten, a patriarch, fortunate in his wife, his six children and thirty-four grandchildren, admired as a scholar, celebrated as a preacher, sought after as a counsellor, revered as a rabbi, honoured among gentiles and Jews, a peer of the realm who is widely regarded as the Prime Minister's spiritual mentor, his whole career suggests that virtue is sometimes rewarded not only in heaven but right here on earth.

He has prospered like Jacob in the house of Laban, and he likes to quote Jacob to describe his fortunes: 'With but a staff have I passed over the Jordan and now I have become as two camps.'

He has never sought, nor expected, temporal honours, but glories in them now that he has them and his patent of nobility as Lord Jakobovits of Regent's Park is framed in the vestibule of his St John's Wood home. He often contemplates it with disbelief.

He has succeeded on two levels, both as Chief Rabbi and as a sort of prelate-at-large filling the vacuum left by the church. Where others voice doubts, he expresses certainties. Where bishops are disposed to condone or even sanctify, he is prepared to condemn. He has given new currency to words like right and wrong, goodness and virtue, obligation and duty, modesty and chastity, which have almost fallen into disuse, and has reintroduced censure to the language of debate. He has become the defender of faith and a spokesman for Victorian values.

The role comes naturally for him, for he is Victorian in his upbringing, his attitudes, his sense of duty, his courtliness, the size of his family and his thinking. As we have already observed, Victorian values were in fact German and were introduced into England by the Prince Consort. Jakobovits derives his philosophy from a German rabbi, Samson Raphael Hirsch, a contemporary of Prince Albert who was a candidate for the Chief Rabbinate in 1844 and who, but for the grace of God, might have been elected. If he had been, he might possibly have enjoyed the sort of relationship with the Prince that Lord Jakobovits has with the Prime Minister.

Hirsch was ultra-Orthodox and an extreme puritan, who formed his own breakaway community with its own synagogues and schools because he felt that the rest of German Jewry made too many concessions to modernity. And yet he was a German patriot, deeply versed in German culture, and published a translation of and a commentary on the Five Books of Moses in a German so elegant that it can almost be enjoyed as literature. (The English translation of his work is rather less elegant.) Where others tried to adapt their Jewishness to German life, he sought a synthesis of all that was best in Jewish and German culture and argued that one was a better German for being a good Jew. His schools, which were to be found in every major Jewish centre in Germany, continued to flourish until the outbreak of the Second World War and anyone who, like Jakobovits, was subjected to their influence, tended to emerge in a sort of Victorian cocoon.

If one sticks to one body of thought, and sticks to it consistently among a constant welter of changes, the chances are that one will sooner or later find oneself in fashion, which is precisely what has happened to Lord Jakobovits. He may have developed in style, in manner, in presentation and in approach, but there has been no basic change in his thinking. Which does not mean he has retired into complacent certitude, but the more he re-examines his ideas in the light of changing circumstances, the more he is convinced of their truth. He came to London as a disciple of Hirsch and remains one to this day, and if Hirsch failed to make it, Hirschism eventually did.

Jakobovits, for all his polish and sophistication, is a man of simple faith, and although he is sometimes beset by uncertainties and doubts, they only touch on the by-ways of life. The highway is defined by his creed, which is one of the secrets of his success, for he moves with all the certainty and confidence of someone who knows exactly where he is going.

Like many Jews – and not a few Christians – he believes quite literally that every word of Scripture is the word of God as handed down to Moses on Sinai. He, however, goes further and is convinced that the rabbis in interpreting the word of God were themselves divinely inspired, so that when faced with a problem he will search the ancient texts first and his own mind afterwards – if at all. He will try to discover what the rabbis would have said had they been faced with his problems in their times, but not what they would have said had they been alive today, and although he also draws on the interpretation of contemporary sages, they too rely on the guidance of their predecessors. He is, in fact, a little like the legatee of a vast entailed estate, which he can enjoy in his own lifetime but which he must pass on to his heirs untouched, so that he finds it difficult, if not impossible, to approach contemporary issues with an open mind.

He is capable of introducing an original idea, but only on virgin soil. If the rabbis have been there before him, he feels constrained to follow in their footsteps.

One can see this, for example, in his attitude to the Holocaust. 'The Holocaust and its victims, together with their historic legacy,' he writes, 'must of course be remembered for ever with supreme reverence. I also recognize that the Holocaust will remain a major factor both haunting and galvanizing Jewish life for a long time to come.' At the same time, he is worried about 'breeding a Holocaust mentality of morose despondency among our people, especially our youth', and commends the attitude of the Orthodox who, while suffering enormous losses, seem to be less concerned 'to commemorate the catastrophe or to give tangible expression to grief and mourning, not even by some special prayer or annual fast days to honour and preserve the memory of the martyrs'.

There is, for perfectly understandable reasons, a Jewish obsession with the Holocaust, and he was the first, and perhaps the only, rabbi of eminence to express his misgivings about it. His reference to 'morose despondency' won him few friends, but it was a typically courageous utterance. It may suggest the words of a forward-looking, hopeful and progressive man, but in fact the very people he commends for not dwelling excessively on the Holocaust still set aside three fast days every year and designate three weeks of mourning for the destruction of the Temple, which took place nearly two thousand years ago.

He speaks of the Temple as a manifestation of the divine presence and what is being mourned, therefore, is not the destruction of a material object but a spiritual calamity of the greatest magnitude. Yet, if the Temple was destroyed, it was rebuilt again, and if destroyed again it could be rebuilt once more. The same cannot be said of the six million lives lost in the Holocaust and it might be thought that the cataclysms of the distant past seem to weigh more heavily on him than the emotions excited by the events of yesterday, but that is not the case.

The rabbis have laid down elaborate rules on commemorating the destruction of the Temple, which he feels obliged to uphold, whereas they have been comparatively silent – perhaps with good reason – on the Holocaust, so that he feels free to develop his own attitude, and his attitude, in this instance at least, is indeed that of a forward-looking, hopeful and progressive man. Where he has no such freedom, however, he speaks with a different voice, as one can see, for example, in his attitude to women.

He presides over a community which includes female judges, female writers and artists, female professors, female politicians, female peers, female presidents of Jewish community councils, all of some distinction. He also has a natural chivalry and approaches women with the greatest deference – except where they happen to be rabbis, or 'rabbis' as he would call them – and has often paid tribute to their sagacity, their tenacity and their central role in maintaining the continuity of Jewish life. Yet he feels unable to ease their disabilities, or even to accord them a full role in the management of their local synagogues.

He welcomes them in every other capacity – on welfare boards, on charity committees, on social and educational committees, and on representative councils – and when the executive director of his office, Shimon Cohen, resigned recently, he appointed a woman, Mrs Jennifer Wagner, to take his place. This was a startling innovation which surprised his own colleagues and caused some murmuring in right-wing circles. It was an affirmation of his belief that women should be given the widest scope for their abilities, but she in fact resigned because the job did not offer the scope she had anticipated. Women are at liberty to manage this world, but not the next one.

He argues that he does allow them to serve on synagogue boards, but although they may have consultative status the fact remains that they cannot vote on anything which may affect the conduct of synagogue services.

The selection of rabbis, for example, an important matter in the life of a congregation, is in the hands of men and so, above all, is the selection of a Chief Rabbi.

Many Jewish laws affecting women evolved when most Jews were living in the Orient and reflect the attitudes prevailing in Oriental societies. It might therefore seem reasonable to adapt them to contemporary conditions, but while adaptations are possible they are uncommon, certainly where women are concerned. Most Orthodox rabbis take their cue from a volume by the medieval philosopher Maimonides on the laws of kingship, in which he ruled that a woman cannot be a queen in Israel in her own right, from which he inferred, and Jakobovits and others infer, that a woman cannot hold public office.

This may seem a strange belief in a man who has enormous admiration for Mrs Thatcher. It may, of course, be argued that Mrs Thatcher is not, and is unlikely to become, a queen of Israel, so that the rules do not apply, but in fact he also enjoyed a close rapport with Golda Meir, who was a queen of sorts. He was critical of her secularism and her inflexible policies, but never suggested that she was holding office in defiance of Jewish law. When she died, he described her as 'the personification of "a mother of Israel", whose leadership as a woman recalled that of Deborah'.

The rabbis, in fact, made allowances for unique individuals and unique circumstances, and so does Jakobovits, but he finds no fault in their general attitude and argues that, if anything, contemporary conditions justify the limitations they have put on the emancipation of women, except that he does not think of them as limitations.

He believes that a woman cannot aspire to a nobler role than that of wife and mother and he tends to ascribe many of the social evils of our age – infidelity, promiscuity, juvenile delinquency, drugs and AIDS, as well as broken marriages and broken homes – to the abdication of women from their traditional roles. He is hostile to feminism – even in the mild forms it has assumed among some Orthodox women – as a threat to the family, and he thinks of the family as the very foundation not only of Jewish life, but of all civilized life.

He denies that he is at all reactionary on this matter. His attitude to the role of women in synagogue may derive from Jewish law, but his attitude to the role of women in society, though derived from Jewish tradition, is, he claims, reinforced by common observation and, indeed, common sense. He has nothing against women assuming wider burdens in society once they have fulfilled their duties to their own families, but the family and home must always come first. He finds that those women who make a fetish out of women's rights' issues usually suffer from an inferiority complex.

He believes that no man is born with a God-given right to a job, or a home, or even his daily bread, but only with a God-given motivation to acquire them. That motivation is sustained by his feelings as a family man, for there is nothing like hungry children and a demanding wife to induce the most sluggish individual to greater effort.

He also tends to ascribe the speed with which Jews have transcended their many handicaps to the mutual support system offered by the family, especially the extended family, with fathers assuming the heaviest burdens to advance the prospects of their sons and sons, in turn, assuming the care of their aged parents, and at the centre of it all the ever-active, ever-watchful, ever-caring wife and mother.

To him the family is the main source of joy and its breakdown the main source of grief, but in stressing its importance he does not give sufficient weight to the fact that not all people can marry, that not all marriages are fruitful, and that not all fruitful marriages are happy, and the Jewish stress on marriage is, in fact, not untouched by scepticism. 'Bury one person', goes an old Yiddish saying, 'and they cry; bury two, and they dance.'

Yet one cannot spend a lifetime addressing young couples on the joys of marriage without either believing it or becoming a hardened cynic, and Jakobovits is no cynic. On the contrary, he is an incurable romantic and in the matter of the family he is too prone to draw general conclusions from his own particular, and particularly happy, experience.

He takes great pride in Jewish attainment and the extent to which Jews have been able to transcend their economic problems. He suffered hardships himself when he first came to England and had some passing contact with the poor as a rabbi in south London and the East End, but that was forty years ago. In Dublin, he moved among the moderately prosperous; in New York, among the very rich; while his London associates are hardly impoverished. He may have visited every Orthodox congregation in the British Isles, but Orthodox congregants are nearly all middle class; they have to be if only to afford the burdens of Orthodox life. (It is, for example, accepted that Jewish schools which hope to attract Orthodox teachers have to pay them special subventions to enable them to live in Jewish areas.)

There are, in fact, any number of poor Jews who may seem non-Jewish through their very poverty, scattered among the housing estates and crumbling terraces of the capital and other major cities. One rarely sees them in synagogue or at the social and cultural events organized by the synagogues, so that the Chief Rabbi is not fully aware of their existence or familiar with their problems.

He has visited Jews in the slum areas of London and other big cities and in prison, and his wife has been active in welfare work for many years, but the atmosphere which surrounds a visiting dignitary often insulates him – or her – from reality.

Nor can he draw on the experience of his colleagues. The United Synagogue may support young but unviable congregations on the way up, but is less generous to old and unviable congregations on the way down. Synagogues, in the long term, are meant to be self-supporting. If they show a chronic deficit they are closed down, so that rabbis, in the main, minister to the moderately prosperous. Unlike their Catholic or Protestant colleagues, they thus have virtually no working-class constituency and are divorced from the problems of working-class life.

And he is not all that informed about what is happening in the country at large. He may have entertained people from all walks of life, but his social contacts among non-Jews is confined largely to prelates and to lay leaders of the various ethnic minorities. He describes how Jews have transcended their handicaps, but has slight inkling of the handicaps of colour in a colour-conscious society so that his pronouncements on social issues are sometimes ill-informed and one-sided.

He is not uncritical of Tory policy and is particularly unhappy about the decline of the national health service and educational facilities. He also likes to point out that many of the principles of the welfare state were already enshrined in Scripture, which is perfectly true, yet his constant stress on self-reliance and self-help does leave the impression that God is a Thatcherite.

On the other hand, self-help obviously does help, in the way that reliance on others does not, and 'cheap labour', as he put it, *is* 'more dignified than a free dole'. Truisms are not the less true for being uttered by a clergyman and his words would not have had the same impact had they not struck a strong chord of public sympathy.

He is often accused of religious bigotry, but he believes there is such a thing as secular bigotry which prevents people from looking the truth in the face, and in pointing to the deficiencies of modern life he sometimes feels like the little child in the story of the emperor's clothes.

If Samson Raphael Hirsch was a German patriot, Jakobovits is an English one, and yet while admiring English liberalism, English tolerance and the English sense of fair play, he is rather troubled by what he calls the tendency to blur 'all human differences and distinctions'.

How, he asks, can Jewry 'maintain its identity as a tiny minority swimming against a mighty tide'? And how can one 'advocate religious particularism and so risk popular antagonism if not hostility'? Such advocacy, he believes, calls for 'sacrifice and courage of a high order', and 'a defiance of conformity, and nothing is harder in this age of conformity than to defy it'.

Coloured people may feel that the process of blurring has not gone far enough, but English society is a good deal more hospitable to the distinctive and different than it used to be, to the point almost of blurring its own identity.

211

Where there was pressure on the newcomer to assimilate – as there was during the years of mass Jewish immigration – he is now encouraged to maintain his own culture and the only conformity around is the sort Jakobovits demands, and increasingly obtains, from his own followers. Indeed, Orthodoxy is another word for conformity and he does not deny it, but argues that Orthodoxy is, in fact, a revolt against the dominant mores of the age and is thus a type of non-conformity.

As we have seen, he does not believe in a multi-cultural society and keeps himself slightly distant from those who do. Minorities, he feels, have every right to tolerance for their traditions and culture, but they should not expect their host society to abnegate its own traditions in the process. He believes that England, while making allowances for the needs of minorities, should be unmistakably and unapologetically English and Christian, and that if only Englishmen were more conscious of their own identity it would be easier for Jews to maintain theirs.

Which is true, but in the past Jewish disabilities were almost directly related to Christian and nationalistic fervour. In the pre-war years, anti-Semitism was most virulent in the most Christian and nationalistic country of all, Poland; and in our times one can see it re-emerging with the growth of Christian and nationalistic fervour in Russia. Pamyat, a right-wing, conservative organization, is in many ways a protest against the blurring of all human differences and distinctions.

The enviable situation of British Jewry is due in no small part to the fact that 'human differences and distinctions' have indeed become blurred, and it is unlikely that British Jewry would have been so happily placed, or that a Chief Rabbi would have been elevated to the House of Lords, had they not. Jakobovits, arguably, is a beneficiary of the very tendencies he deplores.

He is also, in a way, a victim of the very tendencies he admires. He has made Jewish education his first priority and to that end he has secured large sums from various Jewish philanthropists – some of whom are far removed from the sort of Judaism he preaches – and has in the course of his incumbency helped Jewish schools to about double their intake. He is, however, only concerned with Jewish education in its narrowest, most kosher sense, and, as we have seen, institutions involved in secular subjects like Jewish philosophy, history or sociology have never received a penny from him, nor has any department of Hebrew or Jewish studies in any university.

To which he answers, neither have yeshivoth. He has reservations about secular Jewish studies but points out that the Jewish Educational Development Trust was founded to deal with the needs of children of school age and tertiary education was outside its scope.

He applauds the tendency of many Jewish high-school graduates to go on to a yeshiva, but those who do are often disinclined to go on to university, for they are nervous of exposure to alien ideas. Moreover, when they marry and settle down, few of them join the synagogues over which the Chief Rabbi presides, for Orthodox as the synagogues are, they are not Orthodox enough for them.

This is true even of his own family. All his four sons-in-law are university graduates, but of his own six children, only one went on to medical school; none of the others have set foot in a university. And, of those still in this country, all belong to synagogues outside his jurisdiction.

He believes that where university attendance is concerned the tide has turned and that a growing number of yeshiva graduates now take a professional degree. This may be the case, but a sizable proportion do not.

He has tried to make the United Synagogue more receptive to the tastes of the very Orthodox, to the point almost of making it less receptive to the tastes of the not-so-Orthodox, but by and large it has not worked.

Most of his colleagues on the Beth Din, which is still formally known as the Court of the Chief Rabbi, though employees of the United Synagogue, do not normally attend its houses of worship and one suspects that if he were not Chief Rabbi he might have followed their example.

The Chief Rabbi, on the whole, enjoys fairly amicable relations with both Left and Right, though they are rather more amicable with the latter than the former, and there have, as we have seen, been occasions when some of his progressive colleagues have distanced themselves publicly from his views.

He has rarely suffered such criticism from the far Right, partly because ultra-Orthodox rabbis are not used to airing their views in the general press, and largely because he has rarely uttered a thought to which they could take exception, for as he once said: 'Their Torah is my Torah, their beliefs are my beliefs, their customs are mine, they do not question the authority of the written and oral law and neither do I.'

What he has done, however, is to question their detachment not only from the world at large, but from the less Orthodox Jewish world, and he has tried, with some success, to involve them more in the affairs of the community.

There is a talmudic saying: 'A name made great is a name lost.' Some suspicion always attaches to the Jew who is too warmly embraced by gentiles, and his elevation to the peerage was not greeted with the same enthusiasm among ultra-Orthodox rabbis as it was in the rest of the community, and there have been murmurings every time he has stepped over the threshold of a church. There is also the fact that no matter how rigid one's stance it will never be rigid enough for some people, and his very readiness to mix in the outside world has in itself incurred criticism. But as Jakobovits puts it: 'They know these things have to be done, and they're glad that I'm around to do them. They think of me as a sort of Shabbos *goy*.'

This is perhaps an unduly modest way of defining their attitude to him for with all their mutterings they have never seriously questioned his piety, sincerity, Orthodoxy or scholarship, and they tend to think of him as a good man fallen among *goyim*.

At the same time, they do not hesitate to make use of his good offices where the need should arise (as it does fairly frequently), to resort to his Educational Trust to help finance their schools. He finds this a little galling for the ultra-Orthodox community includes some extremely wealthy men who can be generous to those immediately around them, but who rarely give a penny to the wider community.

Which brings us to the greatest paradox of all. Where the Chief Rabbi sought a modern Orthodoxy, he has helped to spread a modern ultra-Orthodoxy which does not recognize his authority and which regards his very office as too English to be quite Jewish. Thus in widening the degree of observance he has narrowed the base of his own following, and the Hirschian belief in the synthesis of culture has been not so much discredited as discarded. The new ultra-Orthodox only differ from the old in that they have the outer trappings of modernity. To them synthesis means dilution and they want the heady wine of Judaism neat.

It must be added that the growth of ultra-Orthodoxy is part of a worldwide trend, and that Jakobovits enjoys a greater standing among the ultra-Orthodox than any of his predecessors, but so he should, for he has helped to pull the entire community in their direction.

He himself denies that he has done so and claims that the United Synagogue has not declined in size during his twenty-three years in office, but that members have grown in knowledge and, being more knowledgeable, are more observant. The moderate Orthodoxy which had characterized the United Synagogue in earlier years was not something which his predecessors had sought, but something they had come to live with.

For all his Orthodoxy Jakobovits is, in one important respect, a worldly man. He is no wild-eyed, cobwebbed mystic pointing with a quivering finger to signs and portents. He has never probed the darker recesses of the Kabbalah, and the *Zohar*, the kabbalists' Bible, has never coloured his utterances. Nor does he have much patience with neo-Messianism whether as preached by Zionist zealots or Hassidic sects. He has enough to keep him busy in this world without worrying unduly about the next and, as we have suggested

214

before, he feels that if one looks after the former, the latter will look after itself.

He is convinced that the teachings of Judaism have universal relevance, not only because they are holy but because they work, and can be seen to work, and certainly there is, as a rule, a stability, amity and contentment in Orthodox homes which are rarely to be seen in other societies. But his idyllic picture is jarred by two factors.

One, as we have seen, is Israel. The Jewish state is not the Jewish family writ large, for it is characterized by anything but stability, amity and contentment. Nor can he advance the argument that it is, after all, not an Orthodox state for, as he has himself observed, the Orthodox form the most chauvinistic elements in Israeli society and it is the so-called secularists who have had 'to articulate the Jewish conscience and to salvage Jewish honour'. It is as if his particular brand of Judaism can flourish only in exile, except that Orthodox rabbis in the Diaspora — and especially in America — are, if anything, even more chauvinistic than their Israeli colleagues.

The second factor is local. He is a constant figure in an inconstant world, and a particularly inconstant Jewish world, and if those on his left tend to fade into secularism, those on his right tend to darken into ultra-Orthodoxy.

As we have seen, he abhors all extremes, and if he is opposed to the former for obvious reasons he is troubled by the latter because of their exclusiveness, their narrowness, their rejection of the outside world and their abdication from the Jewish mission. Yet while he has constantly battled against secularism, his challenge to religious extremism has been muted and equivocal and in some ways he has helped to sanctify it. He is fighting on one front, while his world is being eroded on two.

We come finally to what many people regard as his greatest achievement, his role as ambassador to the gentiles.

No one questions the dignity, goodwill and tact he has brought to his work. No Jewish leader has been regarded more warmly by the non-Jew and perhaps the most telling tribute he has received came from Norman St John Stevas (as he then was), a leading Catholic layman and a former Arts Minister, in a letter to *The Times*:

... the writings and speeches of the Chief Rabbi Sir Immanuel Jakobovits, by their upholding of the intrinsic connection between the moral and social orders, one resting on the other, are a major contribution to the continuance of civilized life in Britain.

He is the first Chief Rabbi to have been knighted in office, the first to be raised to the peerage, the first to have attained national prominence. All his predecessors were comparatively anonymous, and many Jews wish he had

215

remained the same. 'He hogs the headlines,' complained one major businessman whose own takeover battles have covered acres of newsprint. 'He should never have accepted the peerage,' said another; 'we excite enough envy as it is.'

There are also Jews who like to think that they have blended completely into the society around them, and the very fact that the Chief Rabbi is singled out so frequently as their spiritual head gives them an uneasy feeling that they are being singled out as a distinct entity. Still others have argued that if the Chief Rabbi cannot help exciting national attention then the community would be better off without one, for they feel that the Jewish community should, for its own sake, stay invisible. And there are finally those who deplore his eminence because they deplore his views.

Jakobovits treats such objections with equanimity. He is not only proud of Jewish achievements, Jewish history and Jewish teachings, but, as he has often declared, Jews have a duty to make their teachings known. This cannot be done if they stay invisible, which is one of the reasons why the media have, on the whole, found him fairly approachable, or, as his critics aver, too approachable.

He also has sufficient faith in the goodwill of the general public to believe that they do not resent Jewish success and may even admire it, which may have been true of America. It may be rather less true of Britain, at least where monetary success is concerned, but he himself, certainly, is the focus of considerable admiration.

He has certain failings as a man, some of which are minor and in a way endearing – at least to those who do not have to work with him. For all his confidence in the fundamentals of his faith, and the belief that he has a destiny to fulfil, he often wonders if he is capable of fulfilling it, and he is not always sure whether he has done the right thing or said the right word. His actions involve him in agonies of doubt and he frequently needs reassurance to sustain his confidence. Yet at other times he thrusts ahead with a self-assurance verging on the reckless.

More serious, and less endearing, is an inability to accept that he can make mistakes, or at least he has never confessed to them, has never apologized and has never withdrawn anything he has said, though he sometimes allows that some of his utterances could have been more felicitously put.

Nor does he confess readily to failure. One suspects that this is due less to *amour propre* than to the feeling that such confessions would reflect not so much on himself as on everything he stands for, though it is always difficult in such cases to know where the love of God ends and self-esteem begins. He can also, in unguarded moments, be fairly petty, not on personal issues but on matters of policy.

216

His errors, given his restless energy, the length of his service, the range of his interests and his readiness to speak out in emphatic terms on controversial issues have, in fact, been remarkably few, and his failures are insignificant compared to his achievements.

When the Chief Rabbinate fell vacant in 1965, three American rabbis were considered for the job before a fourth was found who was prepared to take it, and the attitude of American rabbis to British Jewry and the Chief Rabbinate may be gauged from the fact that one of them – Emmanuel Rackman – who turned down the job which Jakobovits accepted, was happy to accept the post he vacated.

For the better part of a century the authority of the Chief Rabbi was shored up by that of the Cousinhood. Their influence, however, gradually waned and by the time Jakobovits became Chief Rabbi it was virtually extinct and he has had to rely on his own resources. And yet he has not only maintained the authority of his office, but has enhanced it. At the same time, he has raised the standing of British Jewry in the outside world, so that the question of his succession posed fewer problems. Several eminently suitable candidates were in line, and the king-makers had the pick of some of the finest talents in the rabbinic world. No one was surprised, and Jakobovits was delighted, when Jonathan Sacks was named as his successor.

Jakobovits has applied himself to his duties with almost frantic dedication and where his predecessors presided over unbroken periods of religious decline, he has witnessed a religious revival. He does not, of course, claim that this was largely due to his efforts. As we have observed before, and as he has frequently confessed himself, he is fortunate in his age. If he should ever acquire a nickname, it would have to be 'Lucky Jack', but then luck is in itself a major quality in anyone aspiring to public office.

Jakobovits has not only broadened the appeal of Judaism to the Jew, but has made it seem relevant to the life of the nation. All Chief Rabbis, to a greater or lesser extent, leave their mark on British Jewry; Jakobovits has also left his mark on the British people. It is perhaps too early to say whether he is the greatest Chief Rabbi Britain has had, but he is certainly the most memorable and among Jews to be remembered is to be immortal.

Dr Sacks is to spend a year in talmudic studies in Israel and will not be assuming office until September 1991, and so Lord Jakobovits has been persuaded to delay his retirement by six months. In the meantime, he and Lady Jakobovits are preparing to move out of their St John's Wood mansion into a modest home in Hendon, where they will be within easy reach of their four daughters and grandchildren, but they will be spending as much time in Israel as in London. A Centre in Jewish Medical Ethics has been endowed in his name at Beersheba University and he looks forward both to teaching the subject and to furthering his researches in it.

In London, he hopes to attend the House of Lords with fair regularity. He has come to love the place, admires the sagacity and eloquence which colour the debates, and looks forward to making the occasional contribution himself.

He will no doubt be deluged with invitations to speak both at home and abroad, as, indeed, he always has been, but he will now have the time to consider them more favourably. He will have to be careful about local engagements if only because he will have no wish to upstage his successor, but foreign engagements pose no such problems. As he loves both teaching and travel, he expects to cross the Atlantic and Pacific at least once a year.

And finally there are the books: books he has started, books he hopes to complete, books he hopes to revise, books he has been asked to consider, and books which he has played with in his mind and now hopes to commit to paper.

His energies are undiminished, his mind is alert, his strength of feeling unimpaired and his sense of mission intact. If he was fairly outspoken in office, he will be more so in retirement. We have not heard the last of him yet. Or of her ...

Index

219

INDEX

INDEX

Jakobovits, Immanuel, Lord, 1–8, 205–18; takes advice, 100; apolitical, 5; appearance, 3, 46; approachable, 99, 109; and ancient authorities, 101, 163, 207; birth and upbringing, 4, 11, 13, 15–16; as Chief Rabbi, *see under* Chief Rabbi; compassionate, 6, 65; his chief concerns, 162–3; conscientious, industrious, 25, 31; conservative, and liberal, 5, 6, 41, 75, 76; consistent, 4, 5, 162–3, 206; at his best in a crisis, 201–2; decision-making, 122, 129; degree and rabbinical diploma, 23, 29–30; early posts in London, 23–8, 30–1; failings and failures, 216–17; his faith, 206–7; and his father, 28–9; not a fund-raiser, 194; leaves Germany for England (1936), 17–18; a 'harmonizer', 183; health, 7; on Hertz and Brodie, 83; and higher education, 202, 213; holidays, love of nature, 57, 94–5; sense of humour, 45; becomes Chief Rabbi of Ireland (*q.v.*), 31, 32; leaves Ireland for Fifth Avenue Synagogue, New York (*qq.v.*), 44–7; and major and minor issues, 98, 160; marriage, 34; and medicine (*q.v.*), 41; his Orthodoxy, 26, 38–9, 43, 46, 60–5, 75, 87, 90–1, 95, 105, 107, 156, 160, 213–15; pastoral tours, 110–11, 112; pay, 112; peerage, 1–2, 7, 205, 215–16; personality, 13, 25, 31, 33, 43, 55, 65, 97, 121; a practical man, a pragmatist, 156, 200; and the press, 35, 40, 151–2, 153, see also under *Jewish Chronicle*; as public figure, 100; puritanism, 41, 175; retirement impending, 7, 217–18; never retracts or apologizes, 40, 216; schooling in Germany, 15, 20; in Second World War, 27–8; sermons, 25, 31, 58, 111; and social issues, 210–12; as speaker, 28–9, 31, 44–6, 58, 111, 113, 163–4; studies in London, 19–23, 25, 26; and theology, 56; values, 3–7, 206
Jakobovits, Joseph (brother), 13, 27, 41
Jakobovits, Dr Julius (father), 10–11, 12–18, 20, 27–9, 30

Jakobovits, Lotti (sister), 13, 25, 44, 56, 120
Jakobovits, Manfred (brother), 13
Jakobovits, Paula (formerly Wreschner; mother), 13, 30, 33, 34–5, 86
Jakobovits, Shulamith (sister), 13
Jakobovits, Solomon (brother), 13, 56
Jakobovits family: parents, brothers and sisters, 25, 27, 30, 86, 134; children and grandchildren, 86, 118, 127, 129, 130–1, 134, 213
Janner, Sir Barnett, 26, 87
Janner, Greville, 178
Jerusalem, 36–7, 40–1, 148–9
Jerusalem Post, 149
Jewish Care, 128
Jewish Chronicle, 90; editors, 71, 90, 96; and Israel, 147, 151; and Jacobs Affair, 70, 71, 90; and J.'s appointment to Brondesbury, 24; and J.'s rabbinical diploma, 29; suggests J. as possible Chief Rabbi, 66; relations with J., 76, 88, 90–1, 92, 96, 107, 125, 147, 187; and microphones in synagogues, 62; mentioned, 40, 106–7
Jewish Educational Development Trust, 96, 193, 195, 212
Jewish Herald, 152
Jewish Hospital Compendium, 58
Jewish Law Faces Modern Problems, 167
Jewish Marriage (Guidance) Council, 31, 33, 128
Jewish Medical Ethics, 41, 162
Jewish Theological Seminary, New York, 82
Jews: and Christians, 54, 93, 170–8, 181–3, 212; 'vanishing', 55, 139–41; world mission, 5, 42, 157, 159
Jews' College, 20–1, 22–3, 29, 68–70, 202–4
Jews' Free School, 196, 201
John xxiii, Pope, 172
John Paul ii, Pope, 172–3, 181
Joint Israel Appeal, 128, 195
Jordan, 37
Joseph, Rev. Morris, 80–1
Joseph, N.S., 79
Journal of a Rabbi, 52, 54, 161–2

INDEX

INDEX

INDEX